GEORGE ENESCU

HIS LIFE AND MUSIC

T0204448

GEORGE ENESCU

HIS LIFE AND MUSIC

NOEL MALCOLM

With a Preface by
SIR YEHUDI MENUHIN

TOCCATA
PRESS

First published in 1990 by Toccata Press.

© Noel Malcolm and Sir Yehudi Menuhin, 1990.

Music examples drawn by Harry Dinsdale.

British Library Cataloguing in Publication Data
Malcolm, Noel
   George Enescu: his life and music.
   1. Romanian music. Enescu, George 1881–1955
   I. Title
   780.92

ISBN 0–907689–32–9
ISBN 0–907689–33–7 pbk

Typeset in 11/12 pt Baskerville
by Alan Sutton Publishing Ltd., Stroud
Printed by SRP Ltd., Exeter

Contents

List of Illustrations

PREFACE

Sir Yehudi Menuhin

If it is possible for the reader to imagine a man with an encyclopaedic mind which never forgot anything he heard, or read, or saw in the course of his lifetime and could recall instantaneously and play in the most incandescent way any work from Bach, Wagner to Bartók; if the reader could imagine that mind allied to the most generous and selfless of hearts in a human being with a nobility and beauty of build, of presence, romantic in the lineaments of his face, and always propelled by a creative genius whether in speaking, teaching, conducting, playing the violin, the piano, and, very particularly, in composing, the image would still not be complete; a man full of humour (and a most amusing caricaturist) as well as deep philosophy, conversant with the languages and literatures of Europe and England, a man imbued with the highest forms of chivalry and fundamental earth-loving patriotism – this would be the teacher I had since I was eleven, continuously for two years, then again for five years and then intermittently over the years that were left to us together. No book can do justice to a man of this breadth and nobility.

Although I am older now than Enescu was when he died, and although I have not seen this great man in over thirty years, he remains for me the most extraordinary human being, the greatest musician and the most formative influence I have ever experienced.

Yehudi Menuhin

For Geoffrey,
in memory

Introduction

The fall of the Ceauşescu regime in December 1989 came just in time. It was already clear that Romania had embarked on a new, hard-line policy of cultural and political isolation, which before long would have closed the country's borders to all but a trickle of closely monitored official delegations. Now it will be possible, I hope, for Romania's cultural life to flourish once again, and for the rest of the world to discover what riches it contains. And among those riches the music of George Enescu must count as one of the most valuable, extraordinary and unjustly neglected of all the treasures in the inheritance not only of Romania, but of Europe too.

Here is someone whose mature compositions – above all, the late chamber works – stand comparison with the finest music of Bartók or Ravel. And yet these works remain virtually unplayed in the West. Some of the reasons for this neglect are all too easy to understand. The inefficiency of the Romanian Communist regime in producing scores and recordings, for example, was gross even by the standards of other Communist states. The record shops of Western Europe are full of Czech, Hungarian and Polish recordings; this has helped enormously to establish the reputations of composers such as Martinů and Szymanowski in recent years. But no Western importer has ever been able to obtain a regular supply of records from Romania. As for scores, my experience on attending the Enescu Centenary Conference in Romania in 1981 may serve as an illustration. At the main music shop in Bucharest the only available scores of music by Enescu were of one early song and Enescu's cadenza to the Brahms Violin Concerto. All other scores tantalisingly ranged in the shop window were for 'display' only.

Of course there is no lack of enthusiasm for Enescu's music in his native land. But even there the coarse chauvinism which was the stock-in-trade of Ceauşescu's cultural policy had the effect of narrowing Enescu's reputation and diminishing his stature in the eyes of the world. By presenting him as a nationalistic, 'folkloric' composer, this policy strengthened the impression that his music must be of rather provincial significance in European terms. Enescu was in truth one of the most universal composers and musicians of this century, and it is frustrating to find that he is still best known in the West for his two early and untypical *Romanian Rhapsodies*. Judging Enescu by these works alone is like trying to form one's opinion of Ravel when one has heard only *Bolero*.

Some people find it easy to assume that if any past composer's works are good enough they will somehow have found their own way into concert programmes by now. Anyone professionally involved in the musical world will know how misguided this assumption is. Quite apart from the vagaries of publishing (from which Enescu has suffered badly), much can depend on the composer's own powers of self-advertisement or the efforts of his sponsors and supporters. A few pieces by Enescu have been played and recorded by some of the most distinguished musicians of our time (Silvestri, Lipatti and Menuhin, for example), but outside Romania there has never been any thorough-going campaign on his behalf, of the sort which, for example, helped to save Delius from obscurity in England.

And Enescu himself was the last person to engage in self-advertisement of any sort. He was a man of immense and genuine modesty and selflessness, and the whole business of self-promotion was utterly foreign to him.

Enescu's own nature offers another reason for his obscurity as a composer: the sheer multiplicity of his musical gifts, which meant that he was best known to the public either as a violinist or as a conductor. The public's reluctance to accept that someone they know as a famous performer may also turn out to be a fine composer is not a recent phenomenon. In 1919 George Bernard Shaw wrote to Busoni: 'But you should compose under an assumed name.

It is incredible that one man could do more than one thing well; and when I heard you play, I said, "It is impossible that he should compose: there is not room enough in a single life for more than one supreme excellence" '.[1] I still sometimes find that my enthusiasm for Enescu's compositions is met with the sort of polite indulgence that might be extended towards similar claims on behalf of a string quartet by Thibaud or a symphony by Beecham. In Enescu's case there was not one but three or four supreme excellences to contend with: violinist, conductor, pianist and teacher. But what matters most about all these talents is that they were simply the partial expressions of a single, extraordinary, total musicality of mind. Music was transparent to his understanding. His prodigious memory absorbed virtually the entire classical canon, from Bach to Stravinsky. He could sit down at a piano and begin at any point in *The Ring*, or a Beethoven quartet, or *The Rite of Spring*, or any one of at least 150 Bach cantatas, and play from memory, bringing out every nuance of the writing. Yet his memory was not automatic or photographic: the music spoke to him, and he remembered what it said. (Of some serialist compositions he could remember nothing, because they meant nothing to him.)

The nature of these gifts did, I believe, influence at a deep level the character of Enescu's own compositions. Of course, having such mental powers does not in itself ensure that a composer will write works of great beauty or originality; someone with these gifts may write the music of a Mozart, or he may equally produce nothing but brilliant trivia. But given that Enescu did possess creative powers of a high order, his gifts of comprehension and memory must have helped to mould his compositional style into the complex inner organicism of construction which became more and more essential to it as his writing developed. With all the material of a work completely present to his mind at any moment, it is not surprising that Enescu became fascinated by the task of creating a complicated and delicate

[1] Busoni, *Letters to his Wife* (trans. Rosamund Ley), Edward Arnold, London, 1938, p. 289.

web of thematic interconnections in each piece, and using cyclical form to bring all those related elements into a final temporal conjunction at the climax of the work. Every note is there for a reason; Enescu's mature music is never dull in the sense of routine, and if the listener's interest ever fades it is only because the music sometimes passes into what seems like a realm of private fascination, in which the significance of each note was luminously clear to Enescu, but remains obscure to the listener until repeated hearings have gradually enabled the music to illuminate itself from within.

With the increasing concentration of this organicist style, as Enescu's generative motifs became more germinal and cellular, his music began to sound less like that of a late Romantic and more like that of a fully-fledged modernist. But however modern Enescu's music sounded, there remained a profound difference in spirit between him and most of his modernist contemporaries. If Enescu crossed the threshold of modernism, it was not out of any dissatisfaction with Romantic ideals of expressiveness, but simply out of a search for more powerful means of expression. Enescu remained angelically untouched by any sense of the 'crisis' of modern music; his works are free of all the devices of irony, pastiche and alienation by which other composers proclaimed their view that direct, unselfconscious expression in music was no longer possible. 'Music', Enescu said on his deathbed, 'should go from heart to heart.'[2]

This last remark also suggests the connection between Enescu's character and his greatness as an interpreter of music. His playing was both deeply expressive and completely self-effacing, reflecting both his warmth of feeling and his humility in the face of the music he loved. I have often found, in talking to instrumentalists who played in English orchestras in the late 1940s or early 1950s, that I have only to mention Enescu for a different look to come into their faces – his devotion to the music he performed

[2] Sergiu Comissiona, 'The God-given', *Adam*, Year 43 (1981), Nos. 434–36, pp. 31–2 (here p. 32). Enescu was paraphrasing a remark made by Beethoven about the *Missa Solemnis*.

was different from that of any other conductor they played under, and it inspired their playing in a way which they have never been able to forget. Why this depth of feeling should produce better and more revealing interpretations of the music remains hard to explain, but a passage in Bernard van Dieren's recollections of Busoni may provide a way of explaining Enescu's own greatness as a performer. Busoni told his friend that intellect and feeling are indivisible in a great musician, but *not* because intellectual comprehension penetrates all the mysteries of feeling: 'I believe on the contrary that the fullest understanding born from the heart reveals every mystery of technical structure, all the intricacies of organic build'. When van Dieren protested at this, Busoni replied: 'I said "the fullest understanding". The emotion of a moment does not suffice'.[3]

I have, I fear, written too little about Enescu's emotional and moral character – but this is something which only those who knew him personally can properly describe. He was, clearly, a man of extraordinary integrity and warmth: kind, patient, generous, unfailingly courteous, but also capable of mischievous and uproarious humour. Everyone who knew him loved him. And yet even those who knew him well felt that there was an inner life of burning emotion in him to which no one else had access, save through his music. His devotion to composition was the form in which this emotion was expressed; to some extent it insulated him from the world around him, and helped him to bear a life of such repeated frustrations and disappointments as would have crushed any lesser man. But at the same time the disappointments of his life, because they consisted of those obstacles and reversals which prevented him from devoting all his time to writing music, must have weighed on him all the more unbearably.

Nadia Boulanger, who knew Enescu well and loved him, once spoke these words about him: 'Deep down, only composing mattered to him. I think no-one met Enesco without revering him; he was a very great person, totally

[3] Bernard van Dieren, *Down among the Dead Men*, Oxford University Press, Oxford and London, 1935, p. 94.

disinterested [. . .] Enesco was a person of such great stature, such great significance. For all of us he remained an emblem of generosity, of profound musical knowledge, in his inner-most soul'.[4]

[4] Bruno Monsaingeon, *Mademoiselle: Conversations with Nadia Boulanger* (trans. R. Marsack), Carcanet Press, London, 1985, p. 104.

A Note on Sources

The most important biographical source is Enescu's own account of his life. This was recorded for French radio in a series of conversations with Bernard Gavoty which were broadcast in 1952. Gavoty later moulded Enescu's replies into a single continuous monologue, which was published as Enescu's autobiography in 1955 under the title *Les Souvenirs de Georges Enesco* (Flammarion, Paris). I have used the reprinting of this work which is currently available from Editrice Nagard (Paris and Rome, 1982) under the title *Contrepoint dans le miroir*. However, I have also used the original tapes which are preserved in the Institut National de l'Audiovisuel, Maison de la Radio, Paris; Gavoty per-formed a miracle of editing in transforming the interviews into a single narrative, but inevitably some insertions, omissions or alterations were made in the process. (Gavoty did also publish one short section of the conversations in an unaltered transcription, in a book edited by him and Daniel Lesur, *Pour ou contre la musique moderne?*, Flammarion, Paris, 1957, pp. 131–34). I have quoted from the tapes (referring to them under the title '*Entretiens*') where they differ sig-nificantly from the published version. The copyright in this material rests with the Institut National de l'Audiovisuel; I am grateful to them for permission to consult these record-ings, and I have confined myself to brief quotations from them within the 'droit de citation'.

I have normally translated all foreign quotations in the text; for reasons of space I have not given the original version in the notes except where it is a matter of words written or spoken by Enescu which would be difficult for the ordinary reader to check. Thus when the source can be found in major libraries I have not supplied the quotation in the original, but when it can be found only in the Maison de la Radio or the microfilm room of the Library of the Romanian Academy I have always given the original, even at the risk of clogging a few pages with footnotes in Romanian. In these cases it is usually a matter of newspaper interviews with Enescu, and here a word of caution is necessary. It would be rash to assume that every music critic or features writer on every Romanian local paper in the 1920s or '30s was proficient in shorthand; what we have is probably the gist of what Enescu said, rather than his exact words. But from reading a large number of such interviews one finds that some common themes and arguments recur; I have tried to quote from passages of this sort, and to avoid basing arguments on untypical reported remarks.

Everyone who studies Enescu's life and music owes an enormous debt to the Romanian scholars who have already produced some monumental works of scholarship on Enescu: above all, the collaborative *George Enescu. Monografie* (two volumes, Editura Academiei Republicii Socialîste România, Bucharest, 1971), edited by Mircea Voicana, the two-volume edition of Enescu's letters (*Scrisori*, Editura Muzicală, Bucharest, 1974–81) prepared by Viorel Cosma and the reference work simply entitled *George Enescu* (Editura Muzicală, Bucharest, 1964), co-ordinated by Voicana and issued under the general editorship of George Oprescu and Mihail Jora. (This last book may be listed under any of these names in library catalogues, or under the names of its contributors: Fernanda Foni, Nicolae Missir, Mircea Voicana and Elena Zottoviceanu. I have listed it under Oprescu and Jora.) I have, inevitably, relied heavily on these works, but I have tried whenever possible to check their findings and supplement them with further evidence.

Some readers may tire of my instructions to 'see' works written in Romanian, but those in search of exhaustive musical analyses, of the sort which show the relationships between the different thematic elements in each of Enescu's works, would do well to pursue these references: many of these books are densely illustrated with musical examples, and musical analysis in Romanian can probably be guess-read by anyone with a good grasp of one or two other Romance languages. However, in most of Enescu's late compositions the inter-relationships which are at work within the music are so complex that even an analysis illustrated with numerous examples will make little sense to the reader unless he also has a copy of the score in front of him. It is for this reason that I have confined myself mainly to an 'adjectival' account of what happens in the music.

Acknowledgements

My first debt is to those devoted friends of Enescu who generously gave their time to talk to me about him: Helen Dowling, Romeo Drăghici and Sir Yehudi Menuhin. I must take the full blame if I have in any way misrepresented what they said. I am also especially grateful to Constantin Stihi-Boos of the music department of the Library of the Romanian Academy, and to Eugen Pricope, Director of the Enescu Museum, for their assistance during my visits to Bucharest in 1981 and 1982, when much of the research for this book was done. I was, I believe, the first Westerner to be allowed to study Enescu's manuscripts in the Enescu Museum since the Museum was closed in 1977. No adequate reason was ever given by the Romanian authorities for the closure of this museum from 1977 to 1989, though rumour had it that Mrs Ceauşescu wanted the house for her private use. I sincerely hope that the future of the Museum is now secure.

I should like to thank the following publishers for permission to quote from their publications: Flammarion (for *Les Souvenirs de Georges Enesco*); Gollancz (for Ida Haendel, *Woman with Violin, an Autobiography*); Weidenfeld and Nicolson (for Diana Menuhin, *Fiddler's Moll. Life with Yehudi*); Macdonald and Jane's (for Yehudi Menuhin, *Unfinished Journey*). The holders of copyright in the music examples are: the Romanian Union of Composers (Exx. 1, 2, 8 and 22); the Romanian Academy (Ex. 3); Salabert (Exx. 7, 9–15, 20–1 and 23–5); Enoch (Exx. 4–6, 17 and 18–19); *La Revue musicale* (Ex. 16).

I am grateful to the staff of the Library of the Romanian Academy, the Ciprian Porumbescu Conservatoire and the Central University Library in Bucharest; the Institut National de l'Audiovisuel, and the Bibliothèque Nationale in Paris (excluding the surly and vengefully unhelpful staff of the Periodicals Room); the Stiftelse Musikkulturens Främjande, Stockholm; the Bodleian Library, Oxford; the National Library of Scotland, Edinburgh; the British Library and the National Sound Archive, London; and the Pendlebury Library and University Library, Cambridge.

I am grateful to many individuals who have helped my work in various ways, especially Lady Alexandra Dacre; Mr and Mrs John Goelet; Dr Robert Simpson; Malcolm Mac-Donald; Mr and Mrs Roger Fletcher; Richard Fairclough; Bruce Nightingale; John Harniman and Teresa Kassell. I should also like to thank the Union of Composers for their generous gift of scores, and Constantin Stihi-Boos, Horia Şurianu and Professor Romeo Ghircoiaşu for their gifts of indispensable reference works on Enescu. And finally, a word of thanks to Robin Holloway for his advice and his encouragement.

This book is dedicated to the memory of Geoffrey Vere. He too was made of music. I had just begun to learn Enescu's Third Violin Sonata with him when he died.

I

MOLDAVIA

It might be expected that a book on George Enescu would begin with a discussion of Romanian folk music. Enescu is still widely thought of in the West (when he is thought of at all) as a 'folklorist'. One of the main aims of this book will be to show that he was much, much more than that. But it is true that some of his first experiences of music came from the local fiddlers and players of Moldavia (in the north-east of Romania), where he spent his early childhood. In 1951 he recalled, among his earliest memories, listening at the age of three to a gypsy band (composed of panpipes, a few violins, a cymbalom and a double bass), and hiding away in an orchard in order to hear an old gardener playing the flute.[1]

The musical traditions which Enescu absorbed from such sources were extremely rich and varied. Romanian folk music embraces widely different genres and styles: ballads, carols ('colinde'), pastoral music, dances, wedding-songs, funeral laments and so on. It uses a large number of pentatonic scales and a wide variety of modes, both diatonic and chromatic. And the Romanians have assimilated techniques and materials from all the various peoples who have lived among them, ruled them or inhabited their borderlands. Interviewed in 1921, before the major researches of Béla Bartók and Constantin Brăiloiu had shown how much of the heritage of Romanian music was native and original, Enescu emphasised the richness and diversity of these

---

[1] Enescu, *Contrepoint dans le miroir* (ed. Bernard Gavoty), Editrice Nagard, Paris and Rome, 1982 (henceforth cited as *Contrepoint*), p. 17; *Entretiens*, tape 2.

foreign influences: 'Romanian music is [. . .] a composite of Arabic, Slav and Hungarian music, possessing nevertheless its own peculiar character, which you won't find in the music of other peoples. [. . .] In Muntenia the music is more Turkish, and in Moldavia more Hungarian. Don't be upset by these facts; as I said, from all these musical dialects Romanian music draws an individual character which is peculiar to it'.[2] Previously, when asked to describe this special character, Enescu had replied: 'the general characteristic which stands out in the music of our country [. . .] is: sadness even in the midst of happiness. [. . .] This yearning ('dor'), indistinct but profoundly moving, is, I think, a definite feature of Romanian melodies'.[3] The word 'dor' cannot be neatly translated: it describes a state of mind which may be nostalgic, longing or grieving, and which may be accompanied, like nostalgia, by a type of pleasure which is not anchored in any immediate object of feeling. Asked again by Gavoty to describe the essential character of Romanian music, Enescu answered: 'Dreaming. And a tendency, even in fast sections, towards melancholy, towards minor keys'.[4]

The genre of Romanian music which expresses these qualities of melancholy and dreaming to the utmost is the 'doina'. For the Western concert-goer folk elements in Enescu's music may be represented mainly by the rapid, rhythmical dances of the *First Romanian Rhapsody* (1901); but it was in fact the doina that exerted the strongest influence on his writing, an influence which can be heard most clearly

[2] Enescu, 'Despre muzica românească', *Muzica. Revista pentru cultura muzicală*, Vol. 3, Nos. 5–6, May–June 1921, p. 115. The Romanian musicologist Constantin Brăiloiu (1893–1958) founded the Archive of Folklore in Bucharest in 1928 and the World Collection of Recorded Folk Music in Geneva in 1951.

[3] A. Şerban, interview with Enescu, 8 September 1912, quoted in Mircea Voicana (ed.), *George Enescu. Monografie*, two vols., Editura Academiei Republicii Socialiste România, Bucharest, 1971 (henceforth cited as *Monografie*), p. 400. Enescu also describes 'dor' in 'De la musique roumaine', *La Revue musicale*, July–August 1931, p. 158.

[4] *Entretiens*, tape 2: 'Le rêve, et, même dans les mouvements rapides, un retour vers la mélancolie, le mineur'.

in the First and Third Piano Sonatas (1924 and 1935) and the Third Violin Sonata (1926) – besides, of course, his *Doina* (1905) for baritone, viola and cello. This term has been popularly used to describe any song of a slow and melancholy nature; the researches of Bartók and Brăiloiu showed that the doina properly so called was a special, and in some ways peculiarly Romanian, genre of song or instrumental music, consisting of an improvisatory recitative based on some more or less invariable melodic elements. Bartók first found this genre in Maramureş, in northern Transylvania, and listed it under the local name of 'hora lungă', 'long song'. Brăiloiu found it throughout the rest of Romania, and pointed out that its local name in Maramureş was in fact 'hora frunzii', 'leaf song'. This is significant because it alludes to the use of an oak-leaf by shepherds as a sort of primitive hand-held reed instrument, and thus helps to confirm Bartók's own judgement that 'the entire Hora lungă melody is of an instrumental character'.[5] Bartók's comparative studies in Muslim musical cultures suggested a distant Arabic-Persian origin for this type of melody. He found similar features in Ukrainian 'dumy' (the result, probably, of Romanian influence), but nothing resembling the doina in the southern Slav cultures of Croatia, Serbia, Macedonia or Bulgaria. So it is striking that when a journalist in 1916 (before Bartók's research appeared) asked Enescu to explain the nature of the doina, 'instead of listing its elements he began, in a voice charged with sadness and emotion, to sing Muslim, Arab, Sicilian, Spanish, Greek and Ukrainian folk songs'.[6] Enescu's technical knowledge of folk music has not generally been appreciated. In later years he

---

[5] See Bartók, *Rumanian Folk Music* (ed. Benjamin Suchoff), five vols., Nijhoff, The Hague, 1967–75, Vol. 2, pp. 24–5 and Vol. 5, pp. 9–11; Constantin Brăiloiu, *Opere* (ed. E. Comişel), five vols., Editura Muzicală, Bucharest, 1967–81, Vol. 3, p. 364 and 'La Musique populaire roumaine', *La Revue musicale*, special no., February–March 1940, pp. 146–53, p. 152; and Tiberiu Alexandru, *Romanian Folk Music* (tr. Constantin Stihi-Boos and A. L. Lloyd), Musical Publishing House, Bucharest, 1980, pp. 49–55.

[6] 'Cleante', 'Psihologia creaţiunei artistice. Cum o defineşte Maestrul George Enescu', *Rampa nouă ilustrată*, Vol. 1, No. 279, 19 June 1916, pp. 1–2, here p. 2.

took a close interest in current research, and influenced the thinking of Brăiloiu. But the appeal of folk music for Enescu was not one of anthropological or historical interest: it appealed to him because of its expressive qualities, and it was for that reason that the doina appealed most of all. It was for the doina that Bartók had introduced the phrase 'parlando rubato', 'in a free, speaking rhythm'. The doina is characterised by constant inflections of feeling; it is essentially melodic, establishing tonal bases through the extended use of melodic devices of repetition and accentuation. And it is richly ornamented, especially in its instrumental versions, to a point where it becomes impossible to separate the ornaments from the nature of the melody itself.

The masters of improvisation and ornamentation in instrumental music were the 'lăutari', a term which means 'fiddlers', but is also applied generally to professional folk musicians, whatever instrument they play. Most of these professional musicians in Romania were gypsies. Because of this fact they have often been unfairly dismissed by folk musicologists in the Bartókian tradition. This tradition has inherited not only Bartók's historical purism but also the peculiar prejudice against gypsy music which was an inevitable feature of his writings on Hungarian music, given that he was trying to overturn Liszt's claim that the music of the Magyars was derived from the music of the gypsies. The impression has somehow arisen that gypsy music consisted of the most degenerate sort of urban café-chantant repertoire; this was scarcely true in Hungary, and it was even less true in Romania, where they played such an integral part in the musical life of the countryside.[7]

---

[7] This impression gives rise to absurdities such as T. Sofronia's claim that Enescu had little knowledge of Romanian folk music because he only knew the music of the lăutari, 'which consisted of popular "town" music' ('George Enescu a dieci anni dalla morte, la vita e l'opera il suo capolavoro: l' "Edipo"', off-print from *Iniziative*, Vol. 14 (1965), Nos. 3–4, p. 7). For an instance of Bartók's hostility to gypsies in a discussion of Romanian music see Tiberiu Alexandru, *Béla Bartók despre folclorul romînesc*, Editura Muzicală, Bucharest, 1958, p. 65, where Bartók speaks impatiently of the 'unstable psychology' of the gypsy.

The gypsies did bring certain stylistic elements of their own, such as a more lavish use of ornamentation and a predilection for chromatic modes of oriental origin. But the boundaries between these and native Romanian practices cannot be drawn with any clarity. Nor should it be forgotten that they were professional musicians: they played what they were asked to play, they could adopt a variety of local styles and materials, and they were more the servants of popular taste than the masters of it. Enescu often spoke dismissively of the 'gypsy' music of the salon or the café, but he took care to distinguish this from the true role of the gypsies in Romanian music, remarking to Gavoty that 'these people, who are so musical, do not deserve the sort of contempt which the "connoisseurs" affect towards them'.[8] In 1928 he said: 'I have derived a great deal from the music of the lăutari'; and in 1921 he wrote, with pardonable exaggeration, that 'we should be thankful to the gypsies for having preserved our music, this treasure which we are only now appreciating; they alone have brought it to light, passed it on and handed it down from father to son, with that reverential care which they feel for what is the most precious thing in the world: melody'.[9]

George Enescu was born in 1881, on 19 August (7 August according to the Julian calendar then in force in Romania). His birth certificate gives his name as 'Gheorghe', and he seems to have used both forms of the name in his youth; in

[8] *Contrepoint*, p. 16. There follows a denial that gypsy music and true Romanian music had anything in common; this was added by Gavoty. Enescu merely said, after describing the music of the gypsies, 'Mais il y a une musique populaire autochthone, d'une richesse incroyable' (*Entretiens*, tape 2).

[9] Enescu, 'Ce ne-a spus Maestrul Enescu', *Revista muzicală*, Vol. 1, No. 1, pp. 9–10, p. 9: 'Eu m'am luat mult după muzica lăutarilor'; Enescu, 'Despre muzica româneasca', p. 115. The late Helen Dowling told me that Enescu firmly denied that the folk influence on his music came from gypsy music. I have to assume that he was referring to gypsy music of the urban café variety. No doubt he also wanted to insist that some areas of the native Romanian tradition were untouched by gypsy influence (e.g., the 'colinde'). But the areas on which he drew *were* influenced by the style of the lăutari, as he had often previously said.

later life he preferred 'George', influenced no doubt by the frequent use in print of the French form 'Georges Enesco'. (The final 'o' here is simply the conventional French transcription of this Romanian ending, since the French pronunciation of 'u' produces too acute a sound to represent the Romanian unaccented vowel.) Enescu's father, Costache, was an estate administrator for a local land-owner. He owned some land himself and rented two estates at Liveni and Cracalia in the north of Moldavia, an area of rich arable farming in a landscape of gently rolling plains. He was thus the overseer, and for most practical purposes the employer, of most of the peasants in those villages. Enescu later liked to call himself a 'campagnard' and 'son of the soil', particularly when contrasting himself with his aristocratic wife; but he did not come from a peasant family. In addition to the small house at Liveni where Enescu was born, his father also owned a handsome villa at the nearby town of Dorohoi; a surviving photograph of his parents, uncles and aunts shows an imposing array of ladies in crinolines and men with stiff collars and ties.[10] Yet Enescu's family did not come from the old land-owning classes. Both his grandfathers, and some of his uncles, were Orthodox priests. His father was an autodidact who had taught himself French from the *Grand Larousse* and had learned Latin in order to read the sources of early Romanian history. He had also travelled widely abroad, and was clearly a man of extraordinary energy and ability; King Carol, a dour Prussian not in the habit of making frivolous remarks, once told him: 'In England you would soon have become an MP, and then a minister'.[11]

[10] *Monografie*, p. 14. For details of Enescu's childhood and family see *ibid.*, pp. 7–57; Romeo Drăghici, *George Enescu, biografie documentară. Copilărie şi anii de studii (1881–1900)*, Muzeul de istorie şi artă al judeţului Bacău, Bacău, 1973, pp. 1–55, and Viorel Cosma, *Enescu azi. Premise la ridimensionarea personalităţii şi operei*, Facla, Timişoara, 1981, pp. 26–39.

[11] Romulus Dianu, 'Cu d. George Enescu despre el şi despre alţii', *Rampa*, Vol. 13, No. 3148, 23 July 1928. Prince Karl von Hohenzollern-Sigmaringen, who belonged to the Catholic branch of the Prussian royal family, was appointed King of the newly united Romanian state in 1866, and took the Romanian name of Carol.

The house at Liveni where Enescu was born

There was some music-making in Enescu's childhood home: his father sang, conducted a choir and played the violin, and his mother played the guitar and the piano. On both sides of the family there were also connections with the music of the church. Romanian liturgical music is broadly similar to that of the Russian church, but more closely affected by Byzantine and Greek influences. The choir is usually lighter in timbre and register than in the Russian or Bulgarian traditions, and the vocal lines are often delicately embroidered with ornamental *fioriture*. The choral singing alternates between polyphony and monody; often the choir develops melodic variations over a single sustained bass note. (It may not be fanciful to feel the influence of this technique in Enescu's liking for gradual musical climaxes built over a long pedal point, as in the last movement of his Octet of 1900.) Enescu showed an interest in Romanian liturgical music throughout his life. Asked about the future of Romanian music in 1928, he replied: 'I think that the most difficult, necessary and urgently useful work that needs to be done in Romanian music is that which is required by church music'.[12] As a child he frequently heard his uncle, the priest Ioan Enescu, who was famous for his singing as cantor at the nearby church of Zvoriştea. A compilation of biographical materials on Enescu, published (by a local priest) in 1928, includes a story about the young Enescu returning from a service there in a speechless daze, having been overwhelmed by the music, the incense and the sunlight streaming through the windows.[13]

Emotion and the church were closely linked in the person of Enescu's mother, a hyper-emotional woman who was fervently devout and lavished affection on her son to an almost suffocating degree. He was her twelfth and only surviving child: four had been still-born and seven had died of meningitis or diphtheria. During his infancy she took him on frequent pilgrimages to the monastery at Suceava to pray for his health.[14] In later years he was to say that he had acquired from her an emotionally hypersensitive character, which he had tried to counteract partly by following the example set by his more robust and outward-going father, and partly by retreating defensively into an interior world.[15] Those who knew him well as an adult would often feel that there was a hidden, highly-charged emotional life lurking beneath the courteous, patient, practical and energetic self which he presented to the world around him. And Enescu

[12] Dianu, *ibid.*: 'Cred însa că activitatea cea mai grea, cea mai necesară şi mai urgent utilă în domeniul muzicei româneşti este reclamată de muzica bisericească'. Viorel Cosma discusses Enescu's interest in church music, quaintly including as evidence the fact that he attended the Romanian church in Paris (*Enescu azi*, p. 16).

[13] N. Hodoroabă, *George Enescu. Contribuţiuni la cunoaşterea vieţii sale*, Iaşi, 1928, pp. 32–3. Enescu's grandfather had also been a famous singer at the same church: see Ţiţeica's 'Reply to Enescu', printed in Enescu, *Despre Iacob Negruzzi şi despre intrarea muzicei la Academia Română*, Discursuri de recepţiune, No. 64, Academia Română, Bucharest, 1933, p. 12.

[14] A. M. Ginisty-Brisson, 'Floraison musicale roumaine', *La Revue musicale*, special no., February–March 1940, pp. 154–60, p. 156; N. Hodoroabă, *George Enescu. Contribuţiuni*, p. 17.

[15] *Contrepoint*, p. 14. Enescu describes a 'nervous angina' from which he suffered as a child in Ioan Massoff, 'George Enescu – omul', *Adevĕrul*, Vol. 50, No. 15995, 13 March 1936.

Enescu with his parents

also acquired his mother's religious faith; interviewed in his fiftieth year, he said: 'I am not superstitious, but I believe fervently in God. I am a mystic'.[16]

Enescu led a strange, isolated childhood, prevented by his

[16] Ioan Massoff, 'George Enescu intim', *Rampa*, Vol. 14, No. 4131, 26 October 1931: 'Nu sunt superstiţios, dar cred cu ardoare în Dumnezeu. Sunt un mistic'. See also M. Bocu, 'De vorbă cu George Enescu', *Vestul*, Vol. 7, No. 1828, 25 December 1936, where Enescu describes himself as 'un profund religios'.

over-protective mother from mixing with other children. From an early age he showed a strong talent for painting; in later life he was a skilful caricaturist, and some of his drawings survive of musicians such as Nikisch and Strauss.[17] At the age of four he was given a violin, and his first lessons in how to play it came from a gipsy 'lăutar' called Lae Chioru ('Squinting Nick': his real name was Nicolae Filip).[18] Chioru could not read music, and taught by getting his pupils to imitate him by ear. Another pupil recalls that the tunes Chioru taught included 'Am un leu' and 'Pe o stîncă neagră'.[19] Enescu later used both melodies in his *Romanian Rhapsodies*; Romeo Drăghici, a close friend of Enescu, told me that the composer had heard the latter tune when he was five, so it seems quite likely that Chioru was its source.

The young Enescu quickly showed such promise that he was taken to see Eduard Caudella, the violin professor and Director of the Conservatoire at Iaşi (the capital of Moldavia). 'Would you like to play me something?' asked the professor. Enescu replied with all the shrewd truculence of a five-year-old: 'You play something first, so that I can see whether you know how to'. Caudella was, fortunately, a patient and kindly man; he recommended that Enescu be taught how to read music, and then brought back to him. The parents complied, and at the same time started their son at the piano. Immediately, the flood-gates were opened. Enescu began to compose. As he later remarked to Gavoty, there is something strange about the passion with which this small child, who had heard only a very limited range of

---

[17] V. Cosma, *Enescu azi*, pp. 150–60; four caricatures, including that of Strauss, are reproduced in *Adam*, Year 43 (1981), Nos. 434–6, p. 63.

[18] Doubts are cast on the existence of this lăutar in *Monografie*, pp. 40–48; but Viorel Cosma presents a mass of evidence (*Enescu azi*, pp. 49–57; 'Date noi cu privire la familia lui George Enescu', *Studii muzicologice*, Vol. 5, 1957, pp. 19–48). N. Hodoroabă, a writer with local knowledge who also interviewed Enescu in 1927, asserts that Enescu had lessons from Chioru and later gave money to the lăutar's widow: *George Enescu. Contribuţiuni*, pp. 20, 35.

[19] G. Ananiescu in V. Cosma, *Enescu azi*, p. 43.

Eduard Caudella

the parlour repertoire, began to devote himself to writing in
those classical forms which he knew or imagined. Enescu
kept his childhood manuscripts up to the end of his life, and
in his radio interviews he played three works written at the
age of five: a *Pièce d'Église* (a hymn-tune with a solemn
arpeggio-chordal accompaniment), a waltz and an 'opera'
for violin and piano, lasting 24 bars. Learning notation and
playing the piano also enabled him to satisfy what was to
remain one of the most powerful demands of his musical
personality, his craving for polyphony.

At the age of seven he was taken again to Caudella.
Clearly he had made rapid progress with his battered copy
of Bériot's *Méthode de violon*. Caudella was impressed, and
immediately recommended sending him to the Vienna
Conservatoire. This was a peculiarly selfless decision;
although Romania could not compete with the capital of

Enescu aged around five

Central European music, nevertheless it was not a musical desert. Bucharest had a Philharmonic Society (founded in 1834), a Conservatoire (1864) and an orchestra (the 'Concerts Symphoniques de Bucarest', later to become the Philharmonia under George Georgescu). Iaşi had a particularly strong tradition, and its Conservatoire even predated that of Bucharest. Caudella was devoted to the idea of developing a national musical tradition: at the time of his second interview with Enescu he was already writing his major Romanian historical opera, *Petru Rareş*, and it was Caudella who was later to comment, when he heard of Enescu's projected opera *Oedipe*, 'what a pity that it isn't on a Romanian subject'.[20] But the violin professor, who had

[20] Hodoarabă, *George Enescu. Contribuţiuni*, p. 20. Details on Caudella and Romanian music are given in Alfred Alessandrescu, *Scrieri alesi* (ed. I. Raţiu), Editura Muzicală, Bucharest, 1977, p. 190; Viorel Cosma, *Compozitori şi muzicologi români. Mic lexicon*, Editura Muzicală a Uniunii Compo-

studied with Ries in Berlin and Vieuxtemps in Paris, decided that Enescu should get the best international training possible. Enescu was always grateful for this decision, and remained a friend of Caudella up till the latter's death in 1924. In 1915 he gave the first performance of Caudella's First Violin Concerto, which was dedicated to him. It is a lovely, tuneful but immensely old-fashioned work: contemporary with Bartók's Second Quartet and Stravinsky's *Song of the Nightingale*, it sounds exactly like a lost – very lost – concerto by Spohr.

zitorilor din R. P. R., Bucharest, 1965; and Octavian Cosma, *Hronicul muzicii româneşti*, Vol. 4, Editura Muzicala a Uniunii Compozitorilor din R. P. R., Bucharest, 1976, pp. 483–92 and 519–37. On their later friendship see George Pascu, 'Enescu and Caudella', in Mircea Voicana (ed.), *Enesciana*, Vols. 2–3, Bucharest, 1981, pp. 17–22.

II

VIENNA

In the autumn of 1888, armed with Caudella's recommendations, Enescu travelled to Vienna with his parents.
Help with the arrangements came from a friend of the
Enescus, Joseph Hommer, a music teacher who had lived at
Dorohoi and was now at Vienna.[1] The original plan was for
the parents to stay there with their child; but Maria Enescu
became ill and they had to return to Romania. George's
relations with her fell into the pattern which they would
have for the rest of her life: long visits in the summer
holidays, and through the rest of the year a constant stream
of letters and postcards to keep her happy, some of them
consisting only of a few words (which sometimes connected
up to form sentences or jokes serialised on up to thirty
successive postcards). She later separated from her husband, and after a brief attempt to retire to a convent she
lived with her relations at Mihaileni until her death in 1909.

Freed in Vienna from the stifling cocoon of her affection,
the seven-year-old Enescu was placed in a pension under
the care of a governess, Lydia Cèdre, who taught him
German and French. In 1891 she left Vienna to become the
governess of two princesses in Montenegro; in a letter of
that year she thanked Enescu for a Wagnerian 'Fantaisie' he
had sent to Princess Milena, but the manuscript of this work
seems not to have survived.[2]

[1] On Hommer, who later gave concerts with Enescu, see B. Lazarovici,
'Una din primele cronici apărute la noi despre George Enescu', *Studii
muzicologice*, Vol. 3 (1957), No. 5, pp. 57–63.

[2] Romeo Drăghici, *George Enescu, biografie*, pp. 72–4. The chronology later
given by Enescu, and relied on by Mircea Voicana (*Monografie*, p. 62) is
wrong.

Enescu joined the Conservatoire on 5 October 1888. He was only the second entrant ever accepted below the age of ten: the first had been Fritz Kreisler, also aged seven, in 1882. The Conservatoire belonged to the Gesellschaft der Musikfreunde (usually known as the Musikverein), which also organised one of the main series of orchestral concerts in Vienna. Supported by the Musikverein and housed in a grandiose new building on the Ringstrasse, the Conservatoire still charged high fees; Mahler had had to plead for a reduction in his second year, and Enescu was supported by the piecemeal sale of an estate which his father owned.[3] The Conservatoire was run by a Director with a committee of twelve official teaching staff, not all of whom have gained any place in musical history for achievements outside the classroom. The greatest of them all, Anton Bruckner, could still be seen there when Enescu arrived, but he ceased teaching in 1890. Robert Fuchs was the professor of harmony, and also gave classes in counterpoint. He was a thoughtful and kindly man, of whom former pupils often speak warmly in their memoirs; and his pupils included Mahler, Wolf, Sibelius, Zemlinsky, Schmidt and Schreker. He was known as 'Serenaden Fuchs' because of his five popular orchestral serenades, but his finest compositions were in the field of chamber music, where he shows a strong affinity with the late chamber works of Schumann. His friend Brahms spoke highly of him: 'Fuchs is a splendid musician; everything is so fine and skilful, so charmingly invented, that one is always pleased' – words which were probably not intended to sound as belittling as they do.[4]

The Director of the Conservatoire, who conducted the

---

[3] Henry-Louis de La Grange, *Mahler*, Vol. 1, Gollancz, London, 1974, p. 30; Dianu, 'Cu d. George Enescu', p. 3: Enescu later paid out of his concert earnings for the gradual re-purchase of the estate at Sendriceni. On the significance of the Ringstrasse, see Carl Schorske, *Fin-de-Siècle Vienna. Politics and Culture*, Weidenfeld and Nicolson, London, 1980, pp. 24–115.

[4] The quotation is from Robert Pascall, 'Robert Fuchs', *The New Grove Dictionary of Music and Musicians*, twenty vols., Macmillan, London, 1980, Vol. 7, pp. 4–5, (referring to Richard Heuberger, *Erinnerungen an Johannes Brahms* (ed. Kurt Hofmann), Schneider, Tutzing, 1971).

students' orchestra and gave a class in chamber music, was
Joseph Hellmesberger senior, a member of an extraordinary
Viennese musical dynasty. Like his father (Georg senior) he
was a violinist; he edited the Peters edition of unaccompanied Bach, and is famous for engagingly pragmatic
remarks such as 'You should always play octaves slightly
impurely, otherwise the audience won't realise that you're
playing octaves'. He was, by all accounts, a vain, irritable
and pompous man, dandified in old age; Carl Flesch
suffered from his prejudices against Jews and myopics, and
Wolf had been expelled from the Conservatoire for threat-
ening (in a less than entirely frivolous spirit) to assassinate
him.[5] His most important contribution to music (apart from
being the violin teacher of Leopold Auer) came through his
string quartet, which, predating the Joachim Quartet by
twenty years, had raised the standards of chamber playing
and introduced the quartet repertoire to a wider public than
ever before. The Beethoven quartets were one of their
specialities; Joseph senior had studied them under his
father, who had, it seems, received advice on how to play
them from Beethoven himself. Nearly sixty years after he
left the Conservatoire, Enescu imparted to Olive Zorian the
tempi which had been handed down in this way, having
learned them from Joseph junior (son of Joseph senior), who
played second violin in the Hellmesberger Quartet for many
years before replacing his father as leader of it.[6]

Joseph Hellmesberger junior also taught the violin at the
Conservatoire. A more attractive character than his father,

---

[5] Walter Kolneder, *Das Buch der Violine*, Atlantis, Zurich, 1972, p. 424 (for
the advice on octaves); Carl Flesch, *Memoirs* (trans. and ed. Hans Keller),
Rockliff, London, 1957, pp. 22–4; de La Grange, *Mahler*, p. 31.

[6] John Amis (husband of Olive Zorian) tells this story in 'Master Classes
at Bryanston', *Adam*, Year 43 (1981), Nos. 434–6, pp. 39–42; p. 40. Georg
senior would have known Beethoven only during the latter's extreme
deafness, so the claim that he learned the tempi by playing the quartets
in the composer's presence seems doubtful. Enescu told Gavoty: 'I was
present, in his [i.e., Joseph junior's] house, at chamber music sessions
which utterly fascinated me. I gathered from them some priceless – and
precise – instructions on how Beethoven and Schubert wanted their works
to be played' (*Contrepoint*, p. 25).

he was amusing and gregarious: his pupil Kreisler described him as 'a fine young fellow, but very gay, with a weakness for ballet dancers'.[7] He got on particularly well with Brahms. They were close neighbours: Joseph junior's apartment was in the Nibelungengasse, and Brahms lived just on the other side of the Karlsplatz. From 1891 Enescu stayed in Joseph junior's apartment as a lodger. Maria Fotino, a pupil of Enescu, relates that on several occasions Brahms visited Hellmesberger, heard the young Enescu playing in an adjoining room, and went in to give him advice on the cadenzas he was practising. Enescu was no doubt the source of this story, but it seems slightly garbled in this form.[8] Giving advice on how to play to a young violinist in the house of his violin teacher seems an impertinence, even from Brahms – unless of course it was Brahms's own concerto that Enescu was studying. However, Fotino specifies 'the cadenzas'; there is only one in the Brahms Concerto, for which the composer simply left a pause in the score. It would be nice to think that what Brahms heard was different versions of the cadenza composed by Enescu. He did write a cadenza for this concerto, but it was published in 1903, and its assured and sometimes elliptical harmonic treatment seems to place it firmly at that later date. (It is sad that it is never played today outside Romania; it does not have the technical bravura of Joachim's cadenza, but it uses more thematic material from the first movement with greater economy, and conveys a fine and meditative sense of inwardness with Brahms's own processes of theme-development.)

[7] Louis Lochner, *Fritz Kreisler*, Rockliff, London, 1951, p. 8.

[8] Maria Fotino, 'The Mentor', *Romanian Review*, Vol. 35 (1981), No. 8, pp. 141–3 (p. 143). The best explanation of this story may lie in a conversation between Helen Dowling and Enescu after the latter had given a master class on Brahms in New York (to, among others, Leon Fleischer). When asked about his account of how Brahms said he wanted the music played, Enescu roared with mischievous laughter and said that this was the best thing to tell one's pupils to make them really attend to what one was saying. But it remains very likely that Enescu *did* meet Brahms in Hellmesberger's apartment; and I do not think this story explains away Enescu's remarks to Gavoty, quoted above in note 6, p. 36.

Throughout his life Enescu remained devoted to the
music of Brahms. Whether or not he may have had this sort
of tuition from him, it is known that he attended the private
first performance of the Clarinet Quintet; he also played in
the first violins of the Conservatoire orchestra when it
performed the First Symphony and the First Piano Concerto
in the presence of the composer, who often sat through their
rehearsals of other composers' works, following the music in
the score and muttering under his breath.[9] And Enescu
once heard Brahms perform at the piano, later recalling that
'he played with a real virtuoso's technique, but hammered
at the keys as if he were deaf'.[10]

Brahms was, of course, the household god of the Conservatoire. It is true that the battle-lines between the
Brahmsians and the Wagnerians were, despite Hanslick's
trumpetings, never strictly drawn – witness Bruckner's
employment as professor of composition. But it is also true
that the academic staff of the Conservatoire, with their
distrust of innovation and their many personal links with
Brahms, were generally suspicious of the new Wagnerian
vogue. The leading Wagnerians were the opera conductors
Hans Richter and Felix Mottl; their supporters had also
formed a 'Wiener Akademische Wagnerverein', which acted
as a counterpart to the Tonkünstlerverein (of which Brahms
was the honorary president). Enescu belonged to both
camps; he was as profoundly influenced by Wagner as he
was by Brahms. In later life he tried to explain why he felt
no difficulty in this conjunction of allegiances: 'Wagner and
Brahms were not at all as antithetical as people have made
them out to be. They were opposed to each other much
more by reason of policy than musically'. He added, riding a
favourite hobby-horse, 'You can even find in Brahms
themes strongly suggestive of Wagner. In the Horn Trio you
can hear the *Walküre*; in the Third Symphony, *Tannhäuser*'.[11]

[9] Amis, 'Master Classes', p. 40; *Contrepoint*, p. 24.

[10] *Entretiens*, tape 4: 'en grand virtuose, mais il tapait comme un sourd'.

[11] Enescu, programme note for a Chicago Symphony Orchestra concert,
1931–2 season, quoted in Ioana Ştefănescu, 'Brahms-Enescu', in Sper-

Enescu at Vienna

Wagner did not appeal simply for his thematic material. 'I love Wagner's music, and I have always loved it [. . .]. Wagner is the most overwhelming of all composers [. . .]. Certain Wagnerian chromaticisms have been in my blood-stream since I was nine: to renounce them would be like amputating a limb'.[12] It was in Vienna that Enescu began

anţa Radulescu (ed.), *Centenarul George Enescu 1881-1981*, Editura Muzicală, Bucharest, 1981, pp. 347–65 (p. 352).

[12] *Contrepoint*, pp. 52, 25.

the process of assimilation which enabled him, in later years, to sit down at a piano and play from memory any passage he wished from almost all Wagner's operas, including the entire *Ring*. He had quickly fallen under the spell of Hans Richter's conducting at the Hofoper, where he heard *The Ring, Tannhäuser, Die Meistersinger, Lohengrin* and *The Flying Dutchman*.[13]

The Opera was not confined to performances of Wagner, of course. The enthusiasms of Richter and Mottl were balanced by those of the Director of the Hofoper, Wilhelm Jahn, who specialised in recent Italian and French works: Mascagni conducted *Cavalleria Rusticana* in 1891, and Massenet's operas, which enjoyed a particularly strong reputation in Vienna, were often performed: *Werther* received its world premiere there in 1892. Artur Schnabel, who was studying with Leschetitzky in Vienna in the 1890s, later recalled that the Viennese public (which flocked to the operettas of Zeller and Millöcker) considered many of Verdi's operas trivial; but a fair number were put on, and in the 1892–93 season alone Enescu went to hear *Otello, Il Trovatore* and *Aida*.[14] Schnabel describes spending the whole afternoon queueing up at the Opera until the gates opened at seven, passing the time arguing about music with other music students in the queue, and then dashing up the stairs in a wild rush to get one of the best seats in the gallery. 'There were, of course, many, mostly young, musicians. Among them often Arnold Schoenberg, he too racing up the stairs.'[15] Perhaps the studious Viennese bank clerk was sometimes overtaken, in the race to get the best vantage-

---

[13] *Ibid.*, p. 24. Despite his comment on chromaticism, *Tristan* is not included in this list; and in a sentence excluded from Gavoty's text he said: 'à cet époque, j'avais du Wagner plein à la tête, plein le cœur, notamment *Tannhäuser* et *Les Maîtres-chanteurs*' (*Entretiens*, tape 5).

[14] Artur Schnabel, *My Life and Music*, Longmans, London, 1961, p. 27 (commenting also, astonishingly, that up till 1899 in Vienna he had never heard or even *heard of* any piano concerto by Mozart); details of Enescu's attendance from Viorel Cosma, *Enescu azi*, p. 75 (from a list of 14 operas attended, recorded by the young Enescu).

[15] Schnabel, *My Life and Music*, p. 29.

point for an evening of Donizetti, Meyerbeer or Mascagni, by a small and energetic eleven-year-old Romanian boy.

It is difficult to tell what contacts Enescu may have had with other future composers in his Vienna years. His studies at the Conservatoire overlapped with those of Franz Schmidt, Franz Schreker and Alexander von Zemlinsky; Sibelius also spent the winter of 1890–91 in Vienna studying under Robert Fuchs. In his interviews with Gavoty Enescu reserved special praise for Zemlinsky, regretting the obscurity into which his music had fallen. He recalled performing one of Zemlinsky's early symphonies in the Conservatoire orchestra – and, being Enescu, not only recalled performing it but went over to the piano and began to play it from memory.[16] In 1963 a bundle of manuscripts by Zemlinsky was found among Enescu's papers in the Library of the Romanian Academy; it contained a four-movement piano sonata, three short piano pieces and a trio for two violins and viola. The works are dated 1890, 1891 and 1892 respectively: precisely the period when both composers were at the Conservatoire. But it seems most likely that Enescu had obtained the manuscripts from his pianist friend Theodor Fuchs, who had been a fellow-student at the Conservatoire; one of the manuscripts is inscribed to Fuchs by Zemlinsky. Enescu's later ownership of these scores does not necessarily indicate, as Mircea Voicana has tried to argue, any special personal contact between the two young composers, who were separated by an age-gap of ten years. This is, after all, a large gap when the younger of the two is only ten or eleven years old.[17]

[16] *Entretiens*, tape 5. The symphony was the one in D minor of which the first movement was played at a Conservatoire concert in 1892; another symphony, No. 2, in B flat major, was later played at a concert of the Tonkünstlerverein. See Horst Weber, *Alexander Zemlinsky* (Österreichischer Komponisten des XX. Jahrhunderts, Vol. 23), Verlag Elizabeth Lafite, Vienna, 1977, pp. 11–12, and W. Pass, 'Zemlinskys Wiener Presse bis zum Jahre 1911', in Otto Kolleritsch (ed.), *Alexander Zemlinsky. Tradition im Umkreis der Wiener Schule*, Institut für Wertungsforschung/Universal Edition, Graz, 1976, pp. 80–92 (pp. 83–4).

[17] Mircea Voicana, 'Un coleg vienez al lui Enescu – Zemlinsky', *Studii şi cercetari de istoria artei*, Vol. 15, 1968, pp. 214–20; and *Monografie*, pp. 113–19

Enescu was satisfying his prodigious thirst for music. He
attended services at the Imperial chapel to listen to the
choir, and when Hellmesberger senior conducted the choral
society of the Musikverein in 'all the great Masses' he sat
among the singers studying the scores.[18] His progress at the
Conservatoire was rapid. On arrival he was placed under
the violin teacher Sigmund Bachrich for the three-year
preparatory course; in 1889 his studies were interrupted by
whooping-cough, but when he took the postponed exam in
the autumn he got the maximum marks possible and was
allowed to pass straight into the third year. At the age of
nine he was playing Paganini's D major Concerto.[19] In 1890
he joined the full secondary course, and during the next
three years he studied harmony with Robert Fuchs,
counterpoint with Hans Fuchs, history of music with Adolf
Prosnitz, chamber music with the elder Hellmesberger and
the violin with the younger, and the piano with Ernst
Ludwig.[20] He also had lessons on the organ and, in his spare
time it seems, became a first-rate cellist. (In later life he very
occasionally performed as an organist; he never played the
cello in public, but Romeo Drăghici told me that he once
heard Enescu playing through the Lalo Concerto with an
accompanist. Once in America, at the home of the musico-

(giving Zemlinsky's date of birth incorrectly). Fuchs first accompanied
Enescu at a concert in Bucharest in March 1896: Enescu, *Scrisori* (ed.
Viorel Cosma), two vols., Editura Muzicală, Bucharest, 1974–81, (henceforth cited as *Scrisori*), Vol. 2, p. 154. Enescu wrote, or at least joked that
he would write, a work for Fuchs of which only the theme and dedication
survive: 12 variations for piano on the popular song 'Fuchs, du hast die
Ganz gestohlen' (Drăghici, *George Enescu, biografie*, p. 194).

[18] *Entretiens*, tape 5; Herbert Peyser, 'Enesco, Composer and Violinist,
Analyses Himself', *The Musical Standard*, illustrated series, Vol. 38, 28
September 1912, pp. 194–5 (p. 194). See also V. Cosma, *Enescu azi*, p. 76.

[19] Drăghici, *George Enescu biografie*, p. 49.

[20] Details in *Monografie*, pp. 79–85 (referring mistakenly to 'Emil
Ludwig'); John Waterhouse and Viorel Cosma, 'Enescu', *The New Grove
Dictionary of Music and Musicians*, Vol. 6, pp. 163–6 (p. 163) (referring
mistakenly to 'Ludwig Ernst'); Drăghici, *George Enescu, biografie*, pp. 111–7;
Erich Schenk, 'Zu Enescus Wiener Lehrjahren', *Studii de muzicologie*,
Vol. 4, 1968, pp. 61–6 (pp. 61–2).

logist Helen Kaufmann, he took part in a string quartet and played each instrument in turn.)[21] In the summer of 1893 Enescu took his final exam, gaining Grade I in all subjects (including history of music, which he had been allowed to forgo for one year because of language difficulties), and a distinction in all subjects except choir; he was also awarded the prize medal of the Musikverein.[22] He then stayed on for a year of supplementary study in Robert Fuchs' composition class. He was already, quite clearly, a fully-fledged musician. Joseph Hellmesberger junior was immensely proud of him, and was keen to further his career as a violinist. In 1894 he even travelled to Romania with his young pupil in order to accompany him in a concert in Bucharest.[23]

Enescu's concert career had begun in his first summer holiday from Vienna, when he took part in a charity concert in the small Moldavian spa town of Slănic. From October 1891 onwards he gave nine public performances in Vienna, playing a succession of dazzling showpieces by composers such as Vieuxtemps, Wieniawski and Sarasate. (The only musically substantial work in the list is the Mendelssohn E minor Concerto.[24]) According to Antoine Goléa, who was in later years his pupil, Enescu also gave a private concert at Court in Vienna at the age of ten, in the presence of the Emperor.[25] In September 1894, after his

[21] Enescu told Herbert Peyser that he 'took up piano, organ, 'cello' at Vienna (Peyser, 'Enesco Analyses Himself', p. 194). For Enescu's organ playing in a Bach Tercentenary concert in Siena in 1950 see Roman Vlad, 'Enescu şi Italia', in M. Roşu (ed.), *Simpozion George Enescu*, Bucharest, 1984, 313–20 (p. 315). For the chamber music at Helen Kaufmann's house, and for other details of Enescu's organ and cello (and piccolo) playing, see V. Cosma, *Enescu azi*, pp. 124–34.

[22] For slightly differing accounts see *Monografie*, pp. 83–4, and Drăghici, *George Enescu, biografie*, p. 111.

[23] *Monografie*, pp. 121–25.

[24] Schenk, 'Zu Enescus Wiener Lehrjahren', p. 62; V. Cosma, *Enescu azi*, pp. 70–74; *Monografie*, pp. 85–91 and 120. For his second concert appearance (April 1892) his father bought him his first full-size violin, a San Serafino, which he used till the end of his student years (Drăghici, *George Enescu, biografie*, p. 86).

[25] V. Cosma, *Enescu azi*, pp. 70–71.

successful début in Bucharest, Enescu gave an informal concert at his father's house in Cracalia, accompanied by the Enescus' old friend Joseph Hommer. As well as performing as a violinist Enescu played a 'Fragment' from *Tannhäuser* at the piano and joined Hommer in a four-handed version of Beethoven's Fifth Symphony. Then a significant thing happened. Enescu played two works of his own: a Piano Sonata and a fragment of an orchestral piece. For the first time, he appeared before the world (or at least that part of the world which was present in his father's drawing-room) as a composer.[26]

Enescu's urge to compose had continued unabated at Vienna. When describing to Gavoty the compositions of those years he mentioned in particular 'some overtures inspired by Wagner', and played an example from one of them. He is known to have completed two such works at the age of ten or eleven, and to have embarked on another in his final year at Vienna.[27] His other most ambitious work was a *Fantaisie für Klavier und Orchester* which was eventually performed by Theodor Fuchs in Bucharest in 1900; Voicana sums up its character as 'in the spirit of a *Konzertstück* by Weber, though by a Weber who had heard Brahms'.[28] Brahms is certainly a more obvious influence than Wagner in the rest of the surviving manuscripts of this period, which consist predominantly of piano pieces, either completed or sketched. Often one finds a few Brahmsian elements grafted onto a much more traditional Viennese classical style, in which the usual fault is an excessive repetition of rhythmical patterns. One persistent feature, a sign of the young Enescu's delight in the sonority of the piano, is a grandiose pounding of melodic statements in right-hand octaves; a *Ballade* of 1894, dedicated to Hommer, suffers badly from this. But at times one is struck by the assurance and even the daring with which this young boy gave free rein to his

---

[26] The audience included a journalist, whose detailed review is given in Lazarovici, 'Una din primele cronici', pp. 60–63.

[27] *Entretiens*, tape 5; Drăghici, *George Enescu, biografie*, p. 141.

[28] *Monografie*, p. 106.

sense of the dramatic – as in these opening bars of an unfinished (six-page) sonata (Ex. 1):[29]

Ex. 1

[29] Enescu Museum, MS 2778. The *Ballade* is in MS 2786, which also contains an *Introduction and Allegro*, equally afflicted by right-hand octaves.

III

PARIS

One morning in 1895 the seventeen-year-old Alfred Cortot was standing with his fellow-pupils in the courtyard of the Paris Conservatoire. They were waiting for the arrival of their piano professor, Diémer, who was always late for his classes. A strange figure entered the courtyard, clutching a violin case. According to Cortot's description, his stocky build and strange gait made him look from a distance like some small, sturdy peasant farmer, until one realised from the cut of his clothes, which he was obviously outgrowing, that he was a young boy. 'A large head, curly-haired, extraordinarily pensive, the expression in his eyes distant and dream-like [. . .] strange, reticent, almost sombre – he didn't seem like a child at all [. . .].' The new boy was subjected to a ritual fusillade of questions. Asked if he could play anything, he took out his fiddle and started to play the Brahms Concerto. Taken to a piano, he sat down and launched into the first movement of the 'Waldstein' Sonata. (Throughout the long years of their subsequent friendship, Cortot always reserved special praise for Enescu's piano playing; 'Why is it', he once complained, 'that you, a violinist, have a better technique at the piano than I do?[1]) But, the young stranger explained, what he most wanted to study was composition, now that he was starting to write symphonies. . . . [2]

[1] Story related to me by Romeo Drăghici, about a meeting between Cortot and Enescu on the day after the premiere of *Oedipe*.

[2] I have used the account given by Cortot in Bernard Gavoty, *Alfred Cortot*, Buchet/Chastel, Paris, 1977, pp. 47–8; Enescu's version is in *Entretiens*, tape 6.

This desire to study composition was the most important reason for Enescu's move to Paris. It is true that in previous years something of a tradition had grown up of violinists passing from Vienna to Paris in order to complete their technical studies; both Fritz Kreisler and Carl Flesch had done this. But in Enescu's case it was Massenet, professor of composition at the Conservatoire, who was the strongest attraction. It was to him that Enescu and his father went at the beginning of January 1895, soon after their arrival in Paris, to present Hellmesberger's recommendations and the young composer's portfolio of manuscripts. Massenet looked indulgently through the sketches and said: 'you'll do'.[3] Enescu joined his composition class. He was already at work on his first full-scale symphony; but according to the regulations he was too young to be admitted to the class and had to attend merely as an 'auditeur' until the beginning of the new academic year in September.[4] Massenet seems to have treated him from the start as a full member of his class, taking in his exercises and discussing them just as he did those of his other pupils.[5]

This was typical of the way things were done at the Conservatoire: either a flexible and easy-going approach to teaching, or adherence to a set of narrow and restrictive regulations – or both. The restrictions often worked to the disadvantage of foreign students: they were not allowed, for example, to compete in the instrumental competition until their second year, and they were excluded altogether from the most sought after composition prize, the Prix de Rome. The reason for these exclusions was that the Conservatoire was funded by the French state; this also meant that the tuition, given by nearly 70 staff to roughly 700 pupils, was free. In some ways the courses there were peculiarly un-fettered by regulations. There was no obligatory curriculum

[3] *Contrepoint*, p. 28.

[4] *Entretiens*, tape 6.

[5] Charles Koechlin, 'Souvenirs de la classe Massenet (1894–5)', in: (i) *Le Ménestrel*, Vol. 97, No. 10, 8 March 1935, pp. 81–2; (ii) *ibid*. Vol. 97, No. 11, 15 March 1935, pp. 89–90; (iii) *ibid*. Vol. 97, No. 12, 22 March 1935, pp. 97–8; here (ii).

and no diploma examinations for pupils to sit when they
had finished a course or reached a certain standard of
playing. The only examination was the public competition
at the end of each year, in which prizes were awarded in
strict order (by juries which were often accused of bias in
favour of French citizens).

The Conservatoire still enjoyed a high public reputation,
but among musicians there was increasing dissatisfaction.
Many complained of its narrowly academic attitudes to
theory and counterpoint, which rejected examples taken
from Bach when they did not conform to the 'style de la
maison'. The founding of the rival Schola Cantorum in 1894
expressed, among other grounds for hostility, the feeling
that the Conservatoire gave inadequate attention to choral
music and the history of earlier polyphony; Maurice Emmanuel had left the Conservatoire in 1886 because his interest
in the revival of modes had met with strong disapproval.
Carl Flesch, who studied in Paris from 1890 to 1896,
remarks that instrumental training at the Conservatoire was
generally poor, orchestral training was non-existent, and
'the general education of the average student, too, was of a
very low standard'.[6] To this portrait Alfredo Casella (who
arrived there from Italy in 1896) adds the final touches in
his autobiography: 'The old Conservatoire was a large and
horrible edifice with a courtyard which was murderously
drafty. The rooms were small and inferior even to those in
our most dilapidated music schools'.[7]

Enescu's own judgement was summed up in a remark
which Gavoty tactfully omitted from the printed version of
his interviews: 'in spirit, I left the Conservatoire the day I
entered it'.[8] He felt little affinity with his harmony teachers,
Ambroise Thomas (who inspired Chabrier's comment that
'there are three kinds of music: good music, bad music, and
music by Ambroise Thomas'), and Théodore Dubois (who

[6] *Memoirs*, p. 68.

[7] Casella, *Music in my Time* (tr. Spencer Norton), Oklahoma University
Press, Norman, 1955, p. 39.

[8] *Entretiens*, tape 9: 'en esprit, j'ai quitté le Conservatoire le jour même où
j'y suis entré'.

succeeded Thomas as Director of the Conservatoire in 1896 and was eventually forced to resign by the public outcry over *l'affaire Ravel* in 1905, when Ravel was failed at the first stage of the Prix de Rome competition). Nor did Enescu warm to his principal violin teacher, Martin-Pierre-Joseph Marsick. (He did also have some tuition from the Cuban-born violinist José White, with whom he remained on terms of personal friendship.) Marsick was a pupil of Lambert-Joseph Massart and Joseph Joachim, and enjoyed a high reputation for his technical skill, especially his bowing. Carl Flesch, who believed rigorously in the importance of technique, later spoke warmly of his teaching. But when Gavoty asked Enescu if he had learned much from Marsick he replied: 'in terms of knowing music and loving it – no. In terms of playing the violin better – perhaps'.[9] Coming from someone as good-natured and compulsively polite as Enescu, this was perhaps the equivalent of saying that he found Marsick's teaching stupendously arid and dull.

The spirit of the Conservatoire was not, however, represented by all Enescu's teachers. Massenet, he declared, was 'the most approachable, talkative and enthusiastic person I've ever known [. . .] highly intelligent, a born musician and a great teacher'.[10] Charles Koechlin, who complained that the tuition at the Conservatoire was unfairly cried down by musical snobs and avant-gardists, spoke in similarly grateful terms of the stimulus of Massenet's conversation and advice.[11] Certainly Massenet's musical interests were wider than the stylistic range of his own works might suggest. And he by no means shared the narrowness of outlook which afflicted the Conservatoire juries. His comments (preserved by Koechlin) on his pupils' exercises include this one on a cantata by Florent Schmitt: 'Very interesting! I'm not saying that they would understand you at the competition; those gentlemen of the jury would

[9] *Ibid.*, tape 7: 'Il vous a beaucoup appris?' 'À connaître la musique, ou à l'aimer – non. A mieux jouer du violon, peut-être.' For Flesch's praise of Marsick, see his *Memoirs*, pp. 65–6.

[10] *Contrepoint*, p. 30.

[11] Koechlin, 'Souvenirs de la classe Massenet', (iii), p. 98.

probably think you were slightly mad! But you don't care! Nor do I!'[12]

Three of Massenet's comments on compositions by Enescu have survived. On 19 March 1895 the young pupil presented the first movement of his Symphony in D minor (the first of four 'school' symphonies, numbered 'Op. 1' in a series of opus numbers which he abandoned in 1897). This was a work for which Enescu always retained a special affection. He conducted it in Bucharest nearly forty years later, and in his interviews with Gavoty he played a passage from it and commented, aptly, 'it was very Brahmsian, but it didn't sound too bad'.[13] Massenet's judgement was: 'very remarkable, extraordinary for his instinct for development'. On 2 April he commented on a 'scène épique', the *Vision de Saül*: 'an instinct for symphonic writing, development, unity, and a very true conception from the dramatic point of view'. This was an ambitious work in five scenes; the manuscript (129 pages long) was completed in June. It uses different styles of vocal writing; Saul's part is in a declamatory style throughout, and the only traditional arias are those of his daughter Michol, telling the story of her love for David, and David's aria at the harp when he pacifies Saul. One striking feature is the use, in addition to the orchestra, of a wind band of about twenty instruments on stage, which in scene five leads a 'triumphal march into the distance'.[14] Finally, on 29 October 1895 Massenet commented on the first scene of another exercise in this genre, the cantata *Ahasvérus*: 'Astonishing in terms of *development*, and much more "modern" in its harmonies than his work of last year'.[15]

What seemed 'modern' to Massenet was probably the

[12] *ibid.*, (i), p. 82.

[13] *Entretiens*, tape 6: 'c'était très Brahmsien, mais ça sonnait [. . .]'; performance in Bucharest, 15 February 1934: see George Oprescu and Mihail Jora (eds.), *George Enescu*, Editura Muzicală, Bucharest, 1964, p. 224. The symphony was finished on 3 May 1895.

[14] Enescu Museum, Paquet No. 19.

[15] Massenet's comments are in Koechlin, 'Souvenirs de la classe Massenet', (ii), pp. 89, 90, and (iii), p. 97.

amalgam of Brahms and Wagner which still prevailed in Enescu's harmonic thinking. Brahms' music was not well known in Paris. Lamoureux's orchestra played some of the Symphonies, and the Requiem was quite well regarded, but the critic Pierre Lalo was expressing a common attitude when he wrote (of the Violin Concerto): 'he has no sense of timbre, he orchestrates like a pianist, and if one of our orchestral composers had produced this sort of mediocrity we would tell him: my dear fellow, you have some of the makings of a composer, but get back to the classroom [. . .]'[16] Casella was befriended by Enescu as soon as he arrived at the Conservatoire, and was introduced by him to the music of Schubert and Brahms. He later wrote that 'this was especially fortunate in the latter case, as the Hamburg master was completely misunderstood and under-valued in France [. . .].'[17] Some of the hostility to Brahms arose from musicians taking sides, as Saint-Saëns did, on the Brahms-Wagner debate. Wagner's music was becoming increasingly well known to French musicians: the list of French composers who went to Bayreuth is a roll-call of most of the major names.[18] But the cult of Wagner gained its original support in France from poets and writers; it was rendered controversial by the Franco-Prussian war and subsequent political or diplomatic issues (to the point where Lamoureux conducted rehearsals of *Lohengrin* armed with a revolver, while crowds outside hurled bricks through the windows); and many of the most fervent Wagnerians were simply unmusical culture-snobs.[19] Some of the ignorance

[16] Quoted in Claude Rostand, *Brahms*, two vols., Plon, Paris, 1954–5, Vol. 1, p. 14.

[17] Casella, *Music in my Time*, p. 51.

[18] From 1876 to 1889: Widor, Saint-Saëns, d'Indy, Chausson, Delibes, Duparc, Dukas, Magnard, Massenet, Messager, Debussy, Chabrier, Ropartz and Debussy again (see Gavoty, *Cortot*, pp. 56–7).

[19] Massenet remarked: 'It's like in politics: I like the Republic, but I don't like the Republicans. [. . .] the Wagnerians are exclusive admirers, society ladies who place on their pianos copies of *Tristan*, uncut [. . .]'. (Koechlin, 'Souvenirs de la classe Massenet', (ii), p. 90). On Lamoureux see Gavoty, *Cortot*, pp. 55–6 and Flesch, *Memoirs*, pp. 72–5.

was gradually dispelled by two devoted Wagnerian pianists, Cortot and Edouard Risler, who began in 1895 a famous series of performances of their own transcriptions of the operas; Cortot (who had quickly become a close friend of Enescu) also accompanied at the piano the first concert performance of *Tristan* in Paris.[20]

We have to wait until the slow movement of Enescu's first mature symphony (finished in 1905) in order to hear the full impact of *Tristan* on his writing. This extract gives a taste of the tamer and more Brahmsian mixture which is characteristic of his early student works: it is the climax of the orchestral introduction to the first movement of a violin concerto written in 1895. (The rather bathetic dominant seventh leads to a dramatic but traditional solo entry, a series of rising A minor arpeggios 'in modo di recitativo': Ex. 2.)[21]

Ex. 2

(Andante)

This first movement was finished at the end of the year, and Enescu performed it with a students' orchestra at the Salle Pleyel in March 1896. The second movement (a gentle *Andante* in $\frac{6}{4}$ with a vigorously Brahmsian middle section in dotted rhythms) was written in the summer of 1896; but Enescu never added a last movement. Thereafter, unlike almost every other composer who was also a great violinist, he never wrote a violin concerto. No doubt he dreaded the idea of producing a warhorse which he would be obliged to ride through all the concert-halls of Europe. But in addition, he seems to have grown to dislike the traditional devices of large-scale virtuosity used in violin concertos. His later writing for the violin cultivates the expressive intimacy of

---

[20] Gavoty, *Cortot*, p. 59.

[21] Enescu Museum, Paquet No. 16.

the instrument: although it often sounds, and is, very difficult and 'violinistic', it never seeks those effects simply for their own sake.

Enescu's early Paris compositions include several works for the violin, all of them written in 1895 and dedicated to Éva Rolland, a talented violinist who was the daughter of his landlady. Among them is a violin sonata; it is written in a rather four-square Viennese style but has some very characteristic Enescian features, such as its arresting opening statement with the piano in octaves below the violin.[22] It was performed by Éva Rolland and Enescu in a concert of chamber music in June 1897, which consisted entirely of pieces by the fifteen-year-old composer – including a piano quintet which has not survived.[23] This was the first public concert of works by Enescu; by now there could be no doubt that his chosen path was that of a composer, not a violinist. In the two-and-a-half years since his arrival in Paris he had accumulated an impressive list of compositions: as well as those already mentioned it includes a *Tragic Overture*, two more symphonies, a *Triumphal Overture*, a *Prelude and Scherzo* for piano, a *Fantaisie* for piano and orchestra, four orchestral *Divertissements* and a piano suite. The list is not exhaustive, and it excludes academic exercises such as the dramatic cantatas which formed one of the staples of the composition class; by the end of his studies he had written at least eleven of these, among them a 217-page manuscript of *La Fille de Jéphté* and 116 pages of *Antigone*.[24]

Massenet was in the audience at Enescu's concert in June 1897; but he had by then ceased to teach at the Conservatoire. In 1896 he resigned and was replaced by a composer who was even less representative of the *esprit de la Conser-*

[22] Enescu Museum, MS 2736. There also survive a *Tarantelle* for violin and piano, in a very Schumannesque style (MS 2737), and a *Ballade* for violin with orchestra or piano (filed with Paquet No. 19).

[23] See Drăghici, *George Enescu, biografie*, p. 210, and V. Cosma, *Enescu azi*, pp. 78–81.

[24] Drăghici, *George Enescu, biografie*, pp. 197, 217 and 244. Of the second symphony only one movement survives (June 1895); the third is complete in four movements (March–April 1896). See *Monografie*, p. 107n.

vatoire: Fauré. Casella attended his classes a few years later, and afterwards wrote: 'Fauré was an unusually likeable person. He was a small man, with a beautiful white head and the large, languid and sensual eyes of an impenitent Casanova. [. . .] The lessons were very pleasant, even if they often turned into conversations on artistic problems rather than professional analyses of student works'.[25] Enescu recognised that in some ways Fauré was the opposite of Massenet; he was not a born teacher, he was not very interested in technical matters and he could at times be quite uncommunicative (though Casella emphasises his ability to show a pupil something about his work with a single fleeting comment). But, Enescu said, 'He was inspiring – and we adored him'.[26] The class itself was of a peculiarly high standard. It included not only Florent Schmitt, Louis Aubert and Paul Ladmirault (who was later to dedicate a violin sonata to Enescu), but also two special favourites of Fauré: Roger-Ducasse and Maurice Ravel.[27] Fauré also thought highly of Enescu. His first report described him as 'very gifted, very hard-working, very entrenched in classical forms'. Later comments repeat the same phrases: 'hard-working, thoughtful and extraordinarily gifted'; 'very gifted, very hard-working', and so on.[28] A firm friendship developed between the two, and in later years they would often play chamber music together; Enescu described the elder composer as a fine pianist – though (surprisingly) careless of nuances, even in his own works.[29]

Throughout the time of his tuition by Massenet and Fauré Enescu was also studying counterpoint and fugue

[25] Casella, *Music in my Time*, p. 59.

[26] *Contrepoint*, p. 30.

[27] See *ibid.*, p. 31, for Enescu's account of Fauré's relations with his pupils. On Fauré's special esteem for Roger-Ducasse see Laurent Ceillier, *Roger-Ducasse. Le Musicien – l'œuvre*, Paris, 1920, pp. 7–11. In later years Roger-Ducasse bore such an uncanny resemblance to Fauré that he was rumoured (absurdly) to be his illegitimate son.

[28] *Monografie*, p. 151, quoting Conservatoire archives, 'Rapports des professeurs', 1896–7, 1897–8.

[29] *Contrepoint*, p. 31; *Entretiens*, tape 7 ('insoucieux des nuances').

André Gédalge

under another influential teacher, André Gédalge. In 1937, in a review of a performance of Enescu's Second Orchestral Suite, Florent Schmitt described the counter-balancing effect of Gédalge's teaching: 'A pupil of Fauré and Gédalge, he owes to the former his elegant melodic lines, subtle harmonies and unexpected modulations, and to the latter the solidity of his construction, the wonderful free-standing quality of his writing [. . .].'[30] Helen Dowling recalls that Enescu felt more deeply indebted to Gédalge than to any other teacher; he also told her that Gédalge made him write a different fugue on the same subject every week for a year. Gédalge was a passionate contrapuntist – Enescu described him, to Gavoty, correcting the mistakes in his pupils' exercises with tears in his eyes – but he was not narrowly

---

[30] Florent Schmitt, Concert Review in *Le Temps*, Vol. 77, No. 27678, 19 June 1937.

academic. His masterly *Treatise on Fugue*, published in 1900, contains some defiant remarks on the subject of the 'style de la maison': he points to examples from Bach which break the Conservatoire's rules, and he distinguishes ironically between 'le fugue d'École' and 'le fugue, composition musicale'. At the end of the treatise he sums up with a few axioms in bold print: 'A fugue – even a scholastic one – is a piece of music. [. . .] Writing fugues is useful only when it is a way of developing musical ideas'.[31] In an appendix to the book he included, in a collection of model fugues written by his pupils, a sonorous four-part fugue with three counter-subjects, composed (on an original subject) by Enescu. Underneath Enescu's name is the phrase 'classe de Massenet', implying that it was written in 1895–6. Gédalge was probably making a point in thus displaying the quality of his pupil's earlier work; one of Enescu's deep disappointments at the Conservatoire was his failure to win a prize in the fugue competitions in 1897 and 1899. He was ticked off by the jury for following Bach rather than the house style; in 1899 he was unplaced, and in 1897 he received only second honourable mention, after Koechlin.[32] The young Enescu still had enough of his childhood hypersensitivity to be deeply hurt by this rebuff. Gédalge, in a touching gesture, published a violin sonata a few months later with the dedication, 'À Georges Enesco'.

In his interviews with Gavoty Enescu summed up the true nature of his debt to Gédalge. 'I was, am and always shall be Gédalge's pupil: what he gave me was a doctrine to which I was already naturally attuned.' The doctrine was that music is in its essence a matter of musical *lines*, of expressive statements which can be developed, contrasted and super-

---

[31] *Traité de la fugue*, Part 1, Enoch, Paris, 1900, pp. 1–2, 233n and 278.

[32] *Monografie*, pp. 158, 216; this account casts doubt on whether the story of the jury's comments is authentic. But Brăiloiu, who knew Enescu well, gives it in his biographical article on him; and Alessandrescu gives a detailed version told to him by Enescu, in which Lenepveu informed the young candidate that one could not learn how to write fugues from Bach, and Dubois added: 'Ce n'est pas dans le style de la maison' (George Bălan, *George Enescu. Mesajul – estetica*, Editura Muzicală a Uniunii Compozitorilor din R.P.R., Bucharest, 1962, pp. 27–8).

imposed. 'Polyphony', Enescu declared, 'is the essential principle of my musical language; I'm not a person for pretty successions of chords. I have a horror of everything which stagnates. [. . .] Harmonic progressions only amount to a sort of elementary improvisation. However short it is, a piece deserves to be called a musical *composition* only if it has a line, a melody, or, even better, melodies superimposed on one another.'[33] Gédalge's influence encouraged Enescu to work in forms with a strong potential for polyphonic writing, such as the string quartet (which Gédalge called 'the touchstone of music'): his manuscripts include drafts of no fewer than ten string quartets from the period 1896–1904.[34] And it is fitting that his most massively contrapuntal chamber work, the Octet for Strings (1900), was dedicated to Gédalge. Finally, Enescu gave to his teacher the manuscript of one of the most impressive of all his pre-Opus 1 compositions, the fourth 'school' symphony (written in 1898).[35] It is an ambitious work in four movements, and more than any other early composition it displays a debt to Bruckner with its large-scale handling of strings and brass. The third movement pays tribute to Gédalge's tuition with a tautly constructed fughetta. The contrasting subjects of the first movement (Ex. 3) turn out to be related in a manner which Enescu may have learned from Brahms, but which may also reflect Gédalge's more Franckian view of thematic development.[36]

---

[33] *Contrepoint*, p. 36.

[34] Gédalge quoted in José Bruyr, *Honegger et son œuvre*, Corrêa, Paris, 1947, p. 36; Titus Moisescu, 'Cvartetul de coarde în creaţia lui George Enescu', in: (i) *Muzica*, Vol. 25, No. 6, June 1975, pp. 5–11; (ii) *ibid*, Vol. 25, No. 9, September 1975, pp. 7–14, here (i), p. 5.

[35] The MS passed from Gédalge's family to the Bibliothèque Nationale, Paris; I have used the copy of this MS in the Library of the Romanian Academy. The second movement is dated 11 April 1898.

[36] In a footnote criticising the Conservatoire doctrine that the episodes of a fugue should be based on themes completely different from the fugue's subject, Gédalge wrote that 'this contradicts not only the usual practice of the masters of the fugue, but also the procedures of *symphonic development*' (*Traité de la fugue*, p. 233n).

Ex. 3

Gédalge's other pupils included Ravel, Koechlin, Schmitt and Roger-Ducasse. (He later taught Nadia Boulanger, Honegger, Ibert and Milhaud.) In 1923 he wrote that of all his pupils Enescu was 'the only one to have real ideas and inspiration' – an exaggeration, no doubt, but a striking tribute nevertheless.[37] Among those contemporaries, Enescu developed a particularly close friendship with Roger-Ducasse, a reserved young man with a mordant wit who advised his friend to stop trying to write several symphonies at once and try instead to write one single thing which would show that it came from the heart.[38] Enescu also remained a friend and admirer of Schmitt. He had a natural sympathy for the densely lyrical style of works such as Schmitt's Piano Quintet; in 1912 he described Schmitt as 'one of the supremely great men of the present, one who is truly modern and original, one who has warmth and emotion'.[39] With Ravel Enescu enjoyed a lasting friendship – though perhaps Ravel was not a source of much warmth and emotion. There was a difference in temperament between them which involved a difference in musical taste. They went together to the *répétition générale* of *Pelléas et Mélisande* in 1902; Ravel was captivated by it, but Enescu, though fascinated, found the musical language too finely pared to

[37] Marc Pincherle, *The World of the Virtuoso*, Gollancz, London, 1964, p. 115.

[38] *Contrepoint*, p. 32.

[39] Peyser, 'Enesco Analyses Himself', p. 195.

satisfy his appetite. In their student days their tastes were
perhaps less divergent. Ravel's early Violin Sonata in A
minor (1897) was probably first performed by Enescu and
Ravel in the Conservatoire, and in the interviews with
Gavoty Enescu played from memory the early *Shéhérazade*
Overture (1898) which he had once played through with
Ravel in Fauré's class, but which had since remained
unpublished.[40] One of Enescu's closest personal friendships
was also developing during these years, with Alfred Cortot.
It was probably through Cortot that he got to know the
other Wagnerising pianist, Edouard Risler. And Cortot's
other companion, Jacques Thibaud, also became a close
friend. Years later Cortot commented on his own concert
career with Thibaud, and explained that it had worked, like
a successful marriage, precisely because of the difference
between their musical temperaments; the reason that he
had not performed so often with Enescu was that their
feelings and understanding of music were too closely in
sympathy.[41] Enescu heard Thibaud (who was the year
above him in Marsick's class) for the first time in 1896 and
was entranced by the passionate delicacy of his playing.
Three years later he captured something of that particular
musical quality in his Second Violin Sonata, which he
dedicated to Thibaud. The first performance was given by
the dedicatee, with Enescu at the piano.[42]

Enescu's own studies under Marsick had finally restored
the honour which had suffered so badly at the fugue
competitions. Marsick's reports had praised him in terms as
superlative as those he applied to Thibaud: 'this pupil
possesses *in the highest degree* all the qualities which belong to
a great virtuoso, in timbre, intonation, technique and

---

[40] On *Pelléas: Contrepoint*, p. 39; *Shéhérazade* Overture: *Entretiens*, tape 7 (it
has since been published by Salabert).

[41] Gavoty, *Cortot*, p. 46.

[42] *Contrepoint*, p. 42; Oprescu and Jora, *Enescu*, p. 273. When I asked
Romeo Drăghici who were Enescu's closest friends among all the
musicians he had known, he replied without hesitation: Cortot and
Thibaud.

*The Bernardel violin awarded to Enescu as first prize in the Paris
Conservatoire competition of 1899. This violin was later acquired
by the Romanian Union of Composers, and displayed at the villa of
Teţcani. It was illegally removed from there by Communist officials
in 1989, and its present whereabouts are unknown*

profundity of style'.[43] In 1896 Enescu was unable to take
part in the instrumental competition because of his foreign
nationality; in 1897 an accident which crushed a finger
prevented him from entering. In 1898 the jury awarded him
only a second prize; it was widely believed that they were
expressing disapproval of his precocious success outside the
Conservatoire as a composer. Only in 1899 was he finally
placed first, after a dazzling performance of the finale of
Saint-Saëns's Third Violin Concerto.[44] Enescu left the
Conservatoire, with the prospect of a glittering career as a
violinist ahead of him. But his thoughts were turned not to
the career which might earn his living, but to the life which
it would enable him to lead – a life of composition.

---

[43] *Monografie*, p. 216n; Marsick's italics.

[44] *Ibid.*, p. 220.

IV

EARLY COMPOSITIONS

Enescu's early success as a composer, which raised some
academic eyebrows at the Conservatoire, came with the
performance of his *Poème Roumain* in January 1898. This
work became Opus 1 in his mature series of opus numbers.
It is a symphonic suite with a Romanian programme,
employing some folk material in a thoroughly classical
harmonic language. Enescu described it as a distant evocation of the familiar images of his homeland.[1] When it was
first performed in Bucharest, in March 1898 (under the
baton of Enescu, conducting for the first time in public), it
met with such wild acclaim that one might almost imagine
that it was the first 'national' Romanian work of this sort;
but one would be wrong. Enescu was writing in a tradition
which had already been established by several leading
Romanian composers, in works such as Alexandru Flechtenmacher's *National Moldavian Overture*, Iacob Mureşianu's
overture *Stephen the Great* and a series of programmatic
symphonic poems by George Stephănescu with titles such
as *In the Mountains*. Caudella had written a *Romanian Fantasy*
(a piano piece which he subsequently orchestrated), and
was re-orchestrating a piece entitled *Longing for the Homeland*
during the summer of 1896.[2] Enescu may well have come
into contact with Caudella during his summer holiday in
Moldavia that year; and it is from 1896 that his first

---

[1] *Contrepoint*, p. 34.

[2] See Petre Brâncuşi, *Muzica românescă şi marile ei primeniri*, Vol. 2, Editura
Muzicală, Bucharest, 1980, pp. 425–7 and 438, and O. Cosma, *Hronicul*,
pp. 422 and 431–6.

The poster for the first Romanian performance of the Poème
Roumain, *at the 'Atheneum' concert-hall in Bucharest*

sketches of a *Suite Roumaine* are dated. The second draft of
this work (January 1897) also contains some of the material
later used in the *Romanian Rhapsodies*; in that genre too there
were precedents, not only from Liszt but also from Romanian composers such as Ciprian Porumbescu, who had
published a *Romanian Rhapsody* for piano in 1882.[3]

---

[3] O. Cosma, *ibid.*, p. 403. The sketches of the *Suite Roumaine* are in Enescu
Museum MS 2808/A1, A2, A5 and B1, B2.

The Atheneum, Bucharest

The *Poème Roumain* in its final form was completed in 1897. Of the earlier sketches only a flute doina was incorporated into the *Poème*'s programme. The programme is in two parts. The first evokes a summer evening, with the hypnotic repetition of a broad descending theme (strangely reminiscent of Mendelssohn's *Hebrides* Overture, at half the speed); church-bells are heard in the distance, and a wordless male choir conjures up the modal singing of the priests over a sustained note; night falls and the shepherd plays his doina. In the second part a storm breaks and then passes away, a cock crows, and a country festival begins with a succession of dances. As a grand finale Enescu included the Romanian national anthem. (The version played in Communist Romania simply cut this out and substituted a final chord over a drum roll.) The programme thus stated sounds flatly episodic, but the musical procedures are more complex. Throughout the piece, Enescu delights in tying together apparently disparate material through thematic connections and superimpositions. The cock-crow, for example, is a reversed and rhythmically altered version of the motif played by the church bells, which is itself a counterpart to a

section of the opening theme, and the crowing is transformed in turn into a tune which acts as a spruce and
slightly four-square overture to the dances. The dances
themselves receive a curiously mixed treatment. The
writing chops and changes more abruptly here, alternating
sections of the different tunes; but on the other hand Enescu
cannot resist a final energetic and imposing feat of superim-
posing.

One senses here the dilemma which Enescu resolved four
years later when he wrote his *Romanian Rhapsodies*. There the
music occasionally sets up clever thematic superimpositions; but they are accomplished with such ingenuity
and delicacy that the effect is of two streams flowing
smoothly in parallel, rather than of a turbulent confluence
of currents generating contrapuntal energy. The brightness
and freshness of the *Rhapsodies* lie in the spontaneity with
which different contrasting dance-tunes and songs succeed
one another, without any labouring of thematic connections. But his later dismissive remarks about these two
pieces, in which he claimed simply to have thrown a few
tunes together without thinking about it, should not be
taken very seriously. Preparatory sketches survive in which
one finds the tunes carefully numbered and ordered, with a
series of drafts of connecting passages and notes on the
instrumental timbre to be associated with each melody.[4]
Scholarly opinions are very divided on the question of how
Enescu had acquired those particular tunes. As we have
seen, two of them may have been learned from Chioru: the
opening theme of the *First Rhapsody* ('Am un leu şi vreau să-l
beau' – 'I want to spend my shilling on drink') and the main
theme which follows the introductory statement in the
Second Rhapsody ('Pe o stîncă neagră, într-un vechi castel' –
'On a dark rock, in an old castle'). The latter melody was
associated with a popular nineteenth-century ballad and
was available in several published versions stemming from
Flechtenmacher. A few of the other tunes can be found in a
printed collection by Gheorghe Dinicu; this need not mean
that Enescu used a copy of it, since he might only have

[4] *Monografie*, p. 281.

heard the tunes played by others who had.[5] In some cases (as with the wonderful lurching 'hora' dance in the *Poème Roumain*) there is no single likely source, and in other cases Enescu was adapting creatively a particular genre of melody, such as the 'ciocîrlie' or 'skylark' tune in the *First Rhapsody* (the tune built up with an accelerating pattern of trilled quavers in the violins).

These pieces are often touched with an exotic modal colouring. Of the most common scales some are simple chromatic modes but others have 'mobile' thirds, sixths or sevenths, creating a shifting major/minor atmosphere which Enescu described as one of the characteristics of Romanian music.[6] It was Enescu's sensitivity to the modal character of folk melodies that made him increasingly reluctant to apply the full weight of Western harmony and counterpoint to them. In a letter to the composer Sabin Drăgoi in 1942 he explained that at most a few contrapuntal ornaments could be added to a folk tune 'with extreme caution and discretion'; in an interview in 1928 he said that 'an essential feature of folk song is the way it distances itself from harmony: the lightest harmonising is the most authentic'.[7] In another interview he complained about the symphonic treatment of folk melodies, and compared one (unnamed) Romanian work of this sort to diamonds set in concrete. 'You can develop a folk tune in

[5] See Mircea Chiriac, 'Rapsodiile Romîne de George Enescu', *Muzica*, Vol. 8, 1958, No. 7, pp. 19–28, for the main derivations or affinities (arguing, tenuously, for a direct debt to Dinicu). On 'Pe o stîncă neagră' see O. Cosma, 'Istoricul unui cîntec patriotic: "Mama lui Stefan cel Mare"', *Studii de muzicologie*, Vol. 8, 1972, pp. 71–95. Enescu gave the name of one of his tunes in *Entretiens*, tape 3: to illustrate a doina he played the plangent minor episode in the *Second Rhapsody* with the words: 'Valeu, lupa mă manîncă' ('Alas, the wolf is going to eat me').

[6] Enescu, 'Ce ne-a spus', p. 9: 'Cântecul popular şovae între minor şi major'. There is a detailed discussion of the modes used by Enescu in Clemeansa Firca, *Direcţii în muzica românească 1900–1930*, Editura Academiei Republicii Socialiste România, Bucharest, 1974, pp. 13–27.

[7] *Scrisori*, Vol. 1, pp. 368–9; Enescu, 'Ce ne-a spus', p. 9: 'Dacă ar fi vorba de cântecul popular, caracterul important este îndepârtarea armoniei, o armonizare cît mai puţină e cea mai adevărată'.

only one way: dynamic progression and repetition.'[8] And in 1924 he remarked that the only thing one could properly do with folk music was 'to rhapsodise it, with repetitions and juxtapositions'.[9]

By the end of his life Enescu was heartily sick of the success enjoyed by his *Rhapsodies*, which had eclipsed all his other works.[10] But he did not extend the same hostility to the *Poème Roumain*. Although it does seem a rather ordinary work by comparison with his later compositions, it was after all the *Poème* that had launched him as a composer. Its performance, which had in the first place been partly the result of his contacts with Parisian aristocratic circles, brought him to the attention, and patronage, of the Queen of Romania.

Enescu's patroness in Paris was the Romanian princess Elena Bibescu, who is best known today for the friendship which she and her two brothers enjoyed with Proust. She was herself a brilliant pianist; when Paderewski visited Paris she and Enescu gave a performance of his Violin Sonata in his honour, and she sometimes played the Franck Sonata with Enescu at her salon.[11] In a letter to a friend Proust once listed the three main ingredients of his Vinteuil Sonata: a phrase from Saint-Saëns's Violin Sonata in D minor, a motif from the Good Friday music in *Parsifal*, and, for the passage where the violin and piano call softly to each

---

[8] Aurel Broşteanu, 'De vorbă cu Enescu despre muzica românească', *Propăsirea*, Vol. 2, No. 75, 17 December 1928: 'Se poate amplifica motivul popular într'o singură manieră: aceea a progresiuni dinamice, prin reluarea lui, prin repetarea lui . . . '.

[9] Ioan Massoff, 'George Enescu vorbeşte "Rampei"', *Rampa*, Vol. 8, No. 2111, 7 November 1924.

[10] See his letter of 1950 quoted in *Monografie*, p. 1051 ('des deux Rhapsodies j'en ai *plein le dos* [. . .]'). Louis Lochner suggests that the reason was that Enescu had signed away the royalties (*Fritz Kreisler*, p. 359). This must have added injury to insult; but the real reason was clearly the way they dominated his reputation as a composer.

[11] Drăghici, *George Enescu, biografie*, p. 269; Oprescu and Jora, *Enescu*, p. 142.

other, the Franck Sonata 'especially as played by Enescu'.[12] It seems that Enescu was never introduced to Proust (despite their mutual friendship with Reynaldo Hahn), and he claimed never to have read the description of the Vinteuil Sonata in *À la recherche du temps perdu*; but the truth is that he had read enough to be shocked by the thought that Proust's violinist, Morel, might be modelled on him in any way at all.[13] Enescu did meet many of the stars of Elena Bibescu's salon: the writers Colette and the Comtesse de Noailles, the painters Vuillard and Bonnard, and the politician Léon Blum.[14] He also met d'Indy and Saint-Saëns there, and, most importantly, Edouard Colonne, conductor of the famous Colonne orchestral concerts. And so it was that after a cursory but favourable judgement of the manuscript by Saint-Saëns, Colonne accepted the piece for one of his Sunday concerts.

Interviewed on his fiftieth birthday, Enescu said that the most emotive moment of his life had been when he first heard the Colonne Orchestra playing his *Poème*.[15] The concert itself was a success, attracting glowing reviews – among them two by Paul Dukas, who commented on the sureness of the writing, the skill of the instrumentation and 'the extraordinary grasp of rhythmical effects and contrasts of timbre'.[16] Its reception in Bucharest was even more enthusiastic, where the *Poème* brought Enescu sudden national fame. One consequence of this was that a committee was set up to buy him a fine violin for his concert career; 9,000 francs were raised by public collections and

[12] Letter to Jacques de Lecretelle in *Hommage à Proust*, special number of *La Nouvelle revue française*, Vol. 10, No. 112, 1 January 1923, p. 201. Proust heard Enescu play the work in 1910: see Georges Piroué, *Proust et la musique du devenir*, Denoël, Paris, 1960, p. 20.

[13] See Adrian Ranta, 'Sub vraja lui George Enescu', *Lupta*, Vol. 15, No. 4501, 18 October 1936, p. 5, and Gigi Tomaziu, '"Mosh" Georges', *Adam*, Year 43, 1981, Nos. 434–6, pp. 28–30 (p. 30).

[14] Ranta, 'Sub vraja'. The Romanian-born poetess the Comtesse de Noailles was a cousin of Elena Bibescu.

[15] Massoff, 'Enescu intim', p. 2.

[16] *Monografie*, p. 179n.

subscriptions, and with another 10,000 from his father
Enescu was enabled to buy a Stradivarius in Stuttgart in
1899. (In later years he found its tone too light and small,
and bought a Guarnerius instead, comparing the two to a
light soprano and a dramatic mezzo.)[17] Another consequence of his fame was that he was taken up by the Queen
of Romania. He may have had some help in this from
Princess Bibescu, but the Queen was always on the look-out
for promising young artists to play in the chamber concerts
which took place at Court three or four times a week. Some
of these were of a high standard; her private secretary,
Edgar dall'Orso, had himself been a pupil of Marsick (he
was to end his strange career teaching philosophy at the
Sorbonne), and Carl Flesch writes, in the course of a rather
jaundiced account of Romanian musical life, that the Queen
'loved music more than anything else, and her apartments
were the focus of all real and alleged musical interests'.[18]

The Queen was a strange creature. A total contrast to her
strict Prussian husband, she must often have embarrassed
him with her artistic yearnings, her bizarre attempts at
national costume and her little volumes of belles-lettres,
published under the pseudonym of 'Carmen Sylva'. There is
a thoughtful, if somewhat resentful, portrait of her in the
memoirs of Queen Marie, who came to Romania as the
young bride of Prince Ferdinand (nephew of Carmen Sylva
and King Carol), and gradually fell out with her domi-
neering in-law:

> She was ardent, warm-hearted, of impetuous temperament,
> but certainly not discerning [...]. She saw all things as
> tragedies and therefore dramatised even the simplest events
> of everyday life [...]. Aunty could not exist without the
> excitement of continually discovering rare beings and of

---

[17] *Ibid.*, p. 210 and n; Drăghici, *George Enescu, biografie*, pp. 246–7; Massoff,
'Enescu intim', p. 2.

[18] Flesch, *Memoirs*, p. 164. The statement that Enescu was funded at Paris
by the Queen (see Enescu, 'Ce ne-a spus', p. 9) appears to be wrong,
though he did get some assistance from the Romanian government.
Enescu himself dated his patronage by the Queen to after his successes in
Paris: Dianu, 'Cu d. George Enescu', p. 3.

promoting their talents [. . .]. Aunty wanted to share all
things with all men, even her faked geniuses, and we were
continually called upon to adore, admire, and go into rap-
tures over these very ordinary and sometimes absurd per-
sonages [. . .].[19]

One of Carmen Sylva's odder discoveries was the composer
August Bungert, who wrote an operatic tetralogy, *Die homer-
ische Welt*, and a symphony called *Zeppelins erste grosse Fahrt*.[20]
But with Enescu she struck gold. Formed as he was by the
hyper-emotional character of his own mother, he responded
readily to the Queen's emotional extravagance; he called
her his 'other' mother, and she dedicated a book to her 'dear
spiritual son'.[21] She gave him the permanent use of a study
in a quiet corner of Peleş castle, at the mountain resort of
Sinaia, fifty miles north of the capital.[22] On his seventeenth
birthday she gave him an almost complete copy of the
Bach-Gesellschaft edition of Bach's works – most of which,
during the course of his life, he memorised.[23] And her
patronage bore musical fruit in a series of songs by Enescu,
written mainly during 1898, on verses by the Queen. Some
of these songs are deliberate and delightful exercises in
archaism, such as the Bachian canon for baritone and
soprano, *Junge Schmerzen*, or the chocolate-box Mozartian
duet, *Die Kirschen*. But most of them are serious lieder,
dominated either by the darker, balladic and declamatory
style of Schubert (as in Enescu's *Reue* and *Schlaflos*) or by
Schumann at his most tenderly lyrical (*Zaghaft*, *Der
Schmetterlingskuss* and *Frauenberuf*).

Nowhere in these lieder is there any trace of Romanian

[19] Marie, Queen of Romania, *The Story of my Life*, three vols., London,
1934–5; Vol. 1, p. 268; Vol. 2, p. 87.

[20] Flesch, *Memoirs*, p. 167.

[21] Ranta, 'Sub vraja'.

[22] *Ibid.* and Dianu, 'Cu d. George Enescu', p. 3. V. Cosma, in the *New
Grove* article on Enescu, quaintly writes of the period 1900–4 that he 'had
a house at Sinaia'. Enescu began to build his own house at Sinaia in 1923:
see V. Cosma's account of this in *Enescu azi*, p. 157.

[23] *Contrepoint*, p. 50.

Peleş castle

folk song; nor should one be surprised by that. Despite the
early fame of the *Poème*, folk music gained its real importance in Enescu's work much later in his career, when his
finer understanding of its inner structures and procedures
engaged with the problems he had arrived at in developing
his own Western musical language. The multi-directional
early development of that language can be seen in several of
his other compositions of the late 1890s. The First Violin
Sonata, Op. 2 (written in 1897 and dedicated to Joseph
Hellmesberger junior), shows a debt to Beethoven,
Schumann and Saint-Saëns in its outer movements, and in
its slow movement the influence of the romanticised Bach of
the 'quasi una fantasia' slow movement in César Franck's
Violin Sonata. Although the Germanic half of Enescu's
musical background is predominant, the sonata is more
classically clear-textured than his most Brahmsian works; it
is strikingly less indebted to Brahms than, for example, the
comparable first violin sonatas by Schreker (1898) or Busoni
(1890). It is not a showpiece sonata for the violinist. The
violin often plays a secondary role to the piano, and there is
frequent use of tremolo bowing, which was normally associated much more with orchestral writing than with music in

the solo repertoire. This device is put to best use in the mysterious, slightly sinister opening of the slow movement (Ex. 4).

Ex. 4

When Enescu visited Joachim in Berlin in December 1899 he brought a copy of this sonata, which they played through together. It must have been this movement that prompted Joachim's horrified comment: 'Why, it's even more modern than César Franck!'[24]

As one might expect, a pattern of thematic links runs through this work; but it is not a simple matter of developing in different directions a single initial stock of thematic material. The alternating semitones of the violin in this passage are a motif developed in the final pages of the first movement, and the first half of the piano's *espressivo* recitative grows out of a phrase used as a counterpart to the first movement's second subject. The pattern is one of an overlapping sequence of thematic variation, in which it is the secondary, answering phrases of one section which become, in altered guise, the primary material of the next. This is how the slow movement in turn generates the subject of the finale.

The First Cello Sonata (Op. 26, No. 1 – sharing the later opus number of the Second Sonata) was completed in November 1898. It is in a similar language to the First Violin Sonata – closer perhaps to Brahms, but sharing the same primary debt to Schumann. However, unlike that sonata it draws almost every theme with fanatical ingenuity out of the same small stock, which is set out in the first movement. It is a large four-movement work, lasting at least 35 minutes in performance, and if the listener's interest sometimes flags it is because the generating motifs begin to seem too small a foundation on which to raise such a vast and roomy structure. The most attractive movement is the Scherzo, which begins with some Germanic jollity of the contrapuntal variety, but then evolves into a delicate and light-hearted Trio which has all the sophisticated insouciance of Saint-Saëns at his most playful. The movement ends, characteristically, by failing to end for several pages:

[24] Margaret Campbell, *The Great Violinists*, Granada Publishing, London, 1980, p. 134 (from an interview with Enescu). Campbell says Enescu was 15; this does not fit his visit to Joachim, but it is the age at which he wrote the sonata.

*Carmen Sylva (in white), with Enescu standing behind her,
at Peleş*

Enescu seems here, as often in his later works, to love returning to his material yet another time, handling it again and placing it in a more distant, meditative light with a sort of introverted fascination.

In another work of the same period (written in the summer of 1898) Enescu was more strictly confined by formal restraints. The *Variations for Two Pianos on an Original Theme*, Op. 5, seem at first sight an unambitious work for someone who was so stimulated by the challenge of thematic transformation. The melody, an ambulatory theme whose contours are rendered strangely elusive by its $\frac{5}{4}$ time, is retained in recognisable form (together with its underlying harmonic scheme) for much of the work, becoming the subject of a spacious fugue in the eleventh and final variation. There are no dramatic effects of contrast between variations, and the overall pattern is one of gentle amplification. The work is close in sprit to Brahms' two-piano version of the *Variations on the St Anthony Chorale*, though the impulse to write it came most probably from Fauré's *Theme and Variations*, Op. 73, completed in the previous year. A place might be found for Enescu's work in the rather neglected tradition of this genre in French piano music, stemming from Bizet's *Variations Chromatiques* and Saint-Saëns' two-piano *Variations on a Theme by Beethoven*, and leading to major works by Dukas, Pierné and d'Indy. Its first performance was given in Paris by the most famous of all French piano duos, Risler and Cortot.[25]

Later in 1898 Enescu wrote another, less ambitious work for two pianists: the *Suite for Piano* (four hands) in G major. This composition remained unpublished in Enescu's lifetime, and was not given an opus number. It is an uneven work, combining neo-classical canonic writing (in the opening 'Prélude') with a more modern French style (especially in the second movement, 'Valse triste') indebted to Fauré and Saint-Saëns. The other movements are a puzzlingly episodic 'Intermède', a 'Barcarolle courte' which has some kinship with the slow movement of the First Violin Sonata, Op. 2, and a 'Marche' which re-works elements from all the previous movements.

This *Suite* is technically undemanding, and was probably written not for the concert-hall but for private music-making with friends. The same can be said of another unpublished work, a *Pastorale, Menuet et Nocturne* for violin and piano (four hands) in G major (1900). Here only the *Pastorale* is of real interest, with its initial use of an archaic modal style (prefiguring the *Sept Chansons de Clément Marot*, Op. 15), which opens up gradually into a more romantic idiom. The *Menuet* and *Nocturne* are specimens of salon music, with little to distinguish them except for the turning of one or two unexpected chromatic corners in the harmony.

It is surprising how long it took for the various French musical idioms to surface in Enescu's writing after his arrival in Paris. The *Barcarolle* for piano of 1897 is inevitably influenced by Chopin, but it is a much more strongly stated,

---

[25] See Oprescu and Jora, *Enescu*, p. 271. *Monografie* (pp. 230–1) finds the theme 'authentically Romanian' in character, but this is far from obvious. It also finds similarities between melodic cells in this theme and the material of the First Orchestral Suite. There is clearly a similar pattern of thought at work, but the claim that the latter is derived from the former (Zeno Vancea, *Creaţia muzicală românească sec. XIX–XX*, Vol. 1, Bucharest, 1968, p. 245) would be hard to substantiate.

Enescu in 1900

less nuanced work than the available models of barcarolles by Fauré. As a dyed-in-the-wool Wagnerian, Enescu was a natural candidate for a place in the Franckian tradition; but although he admired Franck and Chausson, and became famous as a violinist for his interpretations of the former's Sonata and the latter's *Poème* (and the Sonata by Lekeu), he never fully surrendered to their musical language. Menuhin recalls him once remarking that he never tired of Brahms but sometimes did tire of Franck; and to Gavoty he explained that 'Franck's enthusiasm sometimes goes off the rails, because he quite often abandons himself to the facile procedures of improvisation'.[26] In some early works, such as the First Piano Quartet, there are what seem to be mild

[26] Information from Sir Yehudi Menuhin; *Contrepoint*, p. 54.

attacks of Chaussonitis, the compulsive filling-in of the
piano part with tremolo and arpeggio figurations. But the
closest affinity with the Franckian school which his works
show is with Duparc, in three French songs, Op. 4, written
in 1898 on verses by Jules Lemaître and Sully Prudhomme.
Two of the poems (*Le Galop* and *Soupir*) had in fact already
been set by Duparc; but Enescu was unaware of this when
he wrote his settings, so it is possible that he did not know
any of Duparc's three published collections at that time.[27]
If, then, one can only speak of an affinity here, it is
remarkably close. But it is clearly an affinity with that side
of Duparc which was closest to Fauré (as shown in the
modal coloration of songs such as Duparc's *Chanson triste* and
Phydilé), rather than with his Chaussonian style of chromatic
suspensions. And Fauré's direct influence can be heard in a
lighter and more carefree setting by Enescu of another poem
by Sully Prudhomme, *Si j'étais Dieu*, which is undated but
probably also belongs to this period.[28]

Fauré's influence suddenly blossoms with Enescu's
Second Violin Sonata, Op. 6, which was written in April
1899. There is a paradox here. The extraordinary thing
about this sonata is the qualitative leap which separates it
from Enescu's previous works, and which also means that
one can no longer speak of influences in the sense of models
which directly explain aspects of the work's character. This
music is no longer the *result* of its models or sources; the
music simply has its own character, which is primary, and in
terms of which one can only try to explain why certain
models or sources are used. And yet Fauré's influence
clearly had a decisively liberating effect. At best one might
say that Fauré's musical language gave Enescu resources
which were suited to his needs: linear fluency, sonorous but
delicate keyboard textures and an elliptical harmonic idiom

[27] *Ibid.*, p. 36, referring to *Soupir*; even at this stage Enescu seemed not to
know of Duparc's earliest published collection, the *Cinq Mélodies*, Op. 2, in
which *Le Galop* had appeared.

[28] This song, issued originally by Hachette and now one of the few works
still available from Salabert, is inexplicably omitted from all published
lists or surveys of Enescu's music.

in which hints of chromatic voluptuousness could suddenly be transformed, chastened or rendered poignant by modal progressions and cadences. And the writing is masterly throughout. One would never guess that this was written by someone fresh from the composition class at the Conservatoire – still less that he was only seventeen years old. It is certainly a work that deserves to become better known. More than fifty years ago Carl Flesch described it as 'one of the most important works in the whole literature of the sonata, and one which is most unjustly and entirely neglected'.[29]

Enescu described its genesis to Gavoty as follows. 'At the age of fourteen, when I was walking by myself in Prince Maurouzi's garden, a theme came into my head. I carried it inside me for three years; then, at seventeen, I wrote my Second Violin Sonata in the space of a fortnight.'[30] The work does have an extraordinary unity, mainly because of the way in which the long opening theme pervades the Sonata, not only making cyclical reappearances but also generating other themes in a manner much more fluid and germinal than in previous works. The theme itself is a characteristic piece of Enescian monody; it is pregnant with harmonic implications, and yet the melodic line is absolutely primary. This is emphasised in the opening bars, where the theme is stated by the violin and piano in unison (with the two piano lines two octaves apart: Ex. 5).

---

[29] Flesch, *The Art of Violin Playing* (trans. H. Martens), two vols: Vol. 1, Carl Fischer, New York, 1924, rev. edn. 1939; Vol. 2, Carl Fischer, New York, 1930; here Vol. 2, p. 124n. Heifetz also included it in his repertoire: see Herbert Axelrod (ed.), *Heifetz*, Paganiniana Publications, Neptune City (New Jersey), rev. edn. 1981, p. 265.

[30] *Contrepoint*, p. 71. I have corrected the text, which gives 'un rythme' instead of 'un thème', (a mistranscription which influences the otherwise fine analysis of this sonata in Mihai Rădulescu, *Violinistica Enesciană*, Bucharest, 1971, pp. 67–91). Firca mentions an earlier MS, which I have not seen, of a 'Moderato' for violin and piano which apparently sketches a similar theme: 'From Manuscript to Finished Composition', *Romanian Review*, Vol. 35 (1981), No. 8, pp. 64–71 (p. 67).

Ex. 5

Enescu's own recordings of this work with Céliny Chailley-
Richez and Dinu Lipatti show what a strangely hypnotic
effect of rhythmical disorientation can be achieved by
the first half of this opening statement, if it is played
without any accentual clues as to the time-signature and
bar-lines. Elements of this theme are developed
throughout the sonata, in ways which not only vary the
rhythmical pattern but also compress or expand the intervals between the notes, until one is left with a sense of a
powerful but indeterminate musical *shape* behind the theme
itself.

No sooner had Enescu completed this sonata than he
embarked on another major work, which shows equal assurance but is astonishingly different in musical character: the
massively contrapuntal Octet for Strings. This is an extraordinary composition. It is difficult to avoid the use of
architectural metaphors in discussing it, since it represents
such a feat of colossal and intricate musical construction.
But there is nothing drily intellectual about it; the effect is
rich, sonorous and unceasingly melodic. Enescu himself
used metaphors of building to describe the task he set
himself:

> I was gripped by a problem of construction: I wanted to write
> this Octet in four connected movements, in such a way that
> although each movement would have its own independent
> existence the whole piece would form a single movement in
> sonata form, on a huge scale. I was crushing myself with the
> effort of keeping aloft a piece of music in four sections, of
> such length that each one of them seemed about to fall apart
> at any moment. No engineer putting his first suspension

bridge across a river can have agonised more than I did as I gradually filled my manuscript paper with notes.[31]

The four movements certainly differ widely in character. The first, 'très modéré', is a grand, spacious exposition of themes and counter-themes in $\frac{3}{2}$ time; the second is an explosive fugato, and the third was described by Enescu as a sort of nocturne.[32] It leads without stopping into the last movement, which, improbably enough, is written in the tempo, and to some extent the character, of a waltz. It must have been here that Enescu agonised most over his construction: as it gathers force it becomes an extravaganza of cyclical form, with restatements, combinations and superimpositions of all the main thematic elements of the previous movements. The energy with which this happens is such that, to switch metaphors, it seems at times like a whirlpool in which fragments of melody appear suddenly at the surface, collide with other fragments and are then sucked down again. Underneath it all is an insistent triple beat, which settles for the last ten pages or so onto a hypnotic repetition of dominant and tonic, bringing the work to an end with an explosion of C major chords and a final statement in unison.

Not all the combinations and superimpositions of the last movement have the character of violent collisions. In the course of this movement Enescu brings out some of the half-hidden connections which unite the melodies he has used. Sometimes it is a matter only of an interval (a ninth, for example), which has been toyed with in some of the phrases of his long and sinuous melodic statements.[33] Many of the principal melodies have this in common, that they have something of the character of narrative: they are lengthy and fluent, they engage in some exploration of smaller patterns of intervals or rhythmical units, and they

---

[31] *Contrepoint*, p. 38.

[32] *Entretiens*, tape 9, 'une sorte de nocturne'.

[33] See the analysis in Pascal Bentoiu, *Capodopere enesciene*, Bucharest, 1984, pp. 19–37, and Ştefan Niculescu, *Reflecţii despre muzica*, Editura Muzicală, Bucharest, 1980, pp. 117–43.

return eventually to their starting-points. The opening
melody of the first movement, for instance (Ex. 6), given in
typical Enescian unison, lasts nearly a minute. Its sense of
extended narrative statement suggests a kinship with some
of Bach's opening paragraphs, such as that of the Third
Brandenburg Concerto.

The melodies of the Octet have a modal character, and
this is not mere colouring. The use of complex modes with
shifting seconds, thirds, sixths or sevenths dissolves the
listener's diatonic expectations and makes possible that
intimate fusion of the techniques of chromaticism with
those of counterpoint which gives the work its peculiar
character. Occasionally there are superficial harmonic
resemblances to Schoenberg's *Verklärte Nacht* (which, written
in 1899, was almost certainly unknown to Enescu as he
worked on the Octet in Paris and Moldavia in 1899 and
1900); but the two works are fundamentally far apart.
Enescu's own comment on his piece was that it was like how
one might imagine chamber music by Berlioz.[34] Here he
was also thinking of the orchestral quality of the work; and
years later he sanctioned the idea of playing it with a full
string orchestra ('on condition that certain singing parts be
entrusted to *soloists*').[35] With rare exceptions, this suggestion has not been taken up. The work would pose taxing
problems of ensemble and balance; but it would certainly be
a major addition to the repertoire.

[34] *Contrepoint*, p. 36 – prompted, perhaps, by Stan Golestan's review of the
premiere, which compared it to the *Symphonie Fantastique* (*Monografie*,
p. 354).

[35] Preface to 1950 edition (Enoch, Paris).

Ex. 6

V

1900–1914

The Second Violin Sonata and the Octet marked a turning-point. With these works, Enescu told Gavoty, 'I felt that I was developing rapidly, that I was becoming myself'.[1] In the years between the completion of these pieces and the outbreak of the First World War Enescu did indeed develop rapidly as a composer – though in so many different stylistic directions that it is difficult to take the phrase 'becoming myself' in the narrow sense of settling into a single individual idiom. Composition was his consuming interest. But his reputation as a performer was growing quickly; the time he could devote to composition was increasingly eroded by concert tours and other forms of music-making. In the circumstances, his output was impressively large; he was always prepared to find the necessary energies and powers of concentration for the task of composition, even in the middle of a busy concert tour. However, there was one thing for which he could never summon up the energy, either now or later in his life: the business of promoting his works and getting others to perform them.

At the outset he had benefited from Edouard Colonne's patronage, but this could not always be relied on. Soon after the completion of the Octet, Colonne began to rehearse it with members of his orchestra for a concert performance. But after five rehearsals he was persuaded by his son that the piece was too incomprehensibly modernistic, and he abandoned it.[2] Enescu had to wait till 1909 for its premiere.

[1] *Contrepoint*, p. 36.

[2] *Ibid.*, p. 38.

There were other disappointments in the field of orchestral music. A *Pastorale-Fantaisie*, written in 1899 and given its premiere by Colonne in the same year, met with little success and remained unprinted; the *Symphonie Concertante* for cello and orchestra, composed in 1901 but not performed until 1909, was greeted at its first and second performances with outright hostility, as we shall see. (The years 1908–9 must have given Enescu's self-confidence a heavy battering. In 1908 he had to abandon a concert he was conducting in Rome because of the audience's hostile reaction, and on his return to Paris he fell ill with scarlet fever. The disastrous premiere of the *Symphonie Concertante* came less than two weeks after the death of his mother on 2 March 1909.[3]) It was not until the very end of the decade that Enescu's reputation as an orchestral composer gradually began to gather weight, with performances in various European and American cities of the First Orchestral Suite and the First Symphony. Unfortunately, much of the impetus for this came from the growing popularity of the *Romanian Rhapsodies*, which were already starting to overshadow the rest of Enescu's work. In the field of chamber music the Second Violin Sonata did enjoy some initial success, and a few of Enescu's piano works met with acclaim in Parisian musical circles.

Enescu was based in Paris throughout these years, though he regularly visited Romania and often stayed there for several months in the summer. His closest friends were in the French capital, and it was often through their assistance and encouragement that his chamber music was performed in public there. They included Casals, Cortot, Thibaud, Casella, the cellist Joseph Salmon, the pianists Edouard Risler and Lucien Wurmser, the flautist and conductor Philippe Gaubert and the violinist Henri Casadesus. In 1901 Enescu formed a Trio with the cellist André Bloch and the pianist Louis Abbiate (himself a prolific composer); in a series of concerts they performed works by Haydn, Mozart, Beethoven, Weber, Schumann, Brahms, Saint-Saëns and

[3] *Ibid.*, p. 49.

Gédalge.[4] The following year saw the formation of another Trio with Casella and Louis Fournier: they played pieces by Arensky, Lalo, Gédalge and Grieg, and in 1904 they gave what was still something of a rarity in Paris, an all-Brahms concert.[5] 1904 also saw the birth (and rather brief life) of the 'Quatuor Enesco', with Fritz Schneider, Casadesus and Fournier; they were especially praised for their performance of the Debussy Quartet.[6] Enescu frequently played violin sonatas on the concert platform with Casella or Risler, and at one concert in 1904 he was accompanied by Ossip Gabrilowitsch. He also appeared as a pianist, playing two-piano music with Fauré or Wurmser, or accompanying other violinists; in 1907 he was the pianist in a performance of his First Cello Sonata with Casals. And on one extraordinary occasion, at a concert for the young composer Léon Moreau in Romania in 1903, he sang several songs by Moreau, accompanying himself at the piano.

Much of the Parisian music-making of this period was semi-public, in the form of performances at salons, soirées and receptions. These were often serious musical forums, with audiences as discerning as those at any of the concert-halls. Leading musicians such as Louis Diémer and Colonne had their own salons, at which Enescu sometimes played; at one of Colonne's soirées in 1906 he performed Strauss' Violin Sonata, with Strauss himself at the piano. In 1910 he accompanied Yvonne Astruc in a performance of his own Second Violin Sonata at a reception given in honour of the aging Auguste Rodin. Sadly, Elena Bibescu had died prematurely in 1902; in the last year of his own life Enescu was to pay her a final tribute, by dedicating to her memory all those of his compositions which did not already bear dedications.[7]

---

[4] Oprescu and Jora, *Enescu*, p. 143. All the following details of performances and concert-tours, unless otherwise stated, are given in the chronological surveys in this book and in Zeno Vancea (ed.), *George Enescu. Omagiu cu prilejul aniversării a 100 ani de la naştere*, Bucharest, 1981.

[5] *Monografie*, p. 272.

[6] *Ibid.*, p. 274.

[7] Elena Piru, 'À propos de quelques lettres de Georges Enesco', *Revue roumaine d'histoire de l'art*, Vol. 5, 1969, pp. 177–82 (p. 178).

Enescu in 1905: a portrait by F. Cormon

Besides these semi-public concerts there were many occasions on which Enescu joined his friends for long sessions of chamber music. Alfredo Casella later recalled frequent meetings, from 1907 onwards, with Enescu, Cortot and Thibaud at Casals' villa at Auteuil on the western side of Paris. Casals himself remembered in particular the summer before the outbreak of war in 1914, when 'Ysaÿe, Kreisler, Enesco, Thibaud and myself used to gather at Thibaud's place'.[8] Enescu spoke warmly of Casals in his conversations with Gavoty, and called him, rather untranslatably, 'mon maître à penser'. But this remark was a piece of typical humility on the part of Enescu, who had his own ideas on the interpretation of music, ideas which, as we

---

[8] Casella, *Music in my Time*, p. 80; J. M. Corredor, *Conversations with Casals* (trans. André Mangeot), Hutchinson, London, 1956, p. 47.

shall see, differed markedly from those of his friend.[9]
Enescu had made Kreisler's acquaintance when they coin-
cided on concert-tours of England in 1903. He often played
Kreisler's so-called 'arrangements' of miniatures by early
composers, but seems to have been one of the few musicians
who were not taken in by them.[10]

Ysaÿe was the Olympian deity of the violinists of this
period. In the interviews with Gavoty Enescu expressed
nothing but admiration for his fiery, impetuous playing, and
said that he was like a force of nature – referring not only to
his musical character but also to his physical size and his
astonishing appetite for food and drink. Once Enescu went
backstage after a concert by Ysaÿe to offer his congratula-
tions, and received this memorable piece of advice: 'Mon
petit Enesco, if you want to play as well as I do when you're
my age, you must eat up your food'.[11] Enescu claimed to
have had only a slight personal acquaintance with the elder
violinist;[12] but this seems to understate the importance of
their relationship. Ysaÿe's musical testament was his great
series of Six Sonatas for Solo Violin, Op. 27. Each was
dedicated to a younger violinist, and was designed to bring
out the characteristic qualities of the dedicatee's style of
playing. The third, a passionate *Sonate-Ballade*, was
dedicated to Enescu. It has become the most popular of the
six; one reason for this may be that it is the most quintessentially Ysaÿean of them all. It seems likely that Ysaÿe

[9] *Contrepoint*, p. 76. They remained firm friends up till Enescu's death; but
Grindea records Enescu's disappointment at never being invited to
conduct Bach at the Prades Festival, and his comment that conductors
never want to let the baton out of their own hands ('Notes on a Genius',
Adam, Year 43 (1981), Nos. 434–6, pp. 1–12 (p. 7)).

[10] Lochner, *Fritz Kreisler*, pp. 105 and 293; the revelation in 1935 that these
pieces were entirely Kreisler's own work caused a scandal among
offended music critics. Enescu did once, in an unguarded moment, refer
to Kreisler's 'petits machins sans intérêt' (Doda Conrad, 'Maître', *Adam*,
Year 43 (1981), Nos. 434–6, pp. 37–9 (p. 38)).

[11] *Contrepoint*, pp. 43–44.

[12] *Entretiens*, tape 10: 'Je l'ai souvent entendu, mais je n'ai eu que très peu
de rapport personnel avec lui'.

Enescu with Casals (and an unidentified woman) in 1904

considered Enescu to be the one young violinist who came closest to his own ideals of violin-playing. This in turn raises the possibility of a further link between Enescu and Ysaÿe's friend, Chausson. The *Sonate-Ballade* is filled with passages of the sort of sinuous double-stopping for which Ysaÿe was famous. Chausson, with Ysaÿe's collaboration, had written such passages into his *Poème*, Op. 25, which he dedicated to Ysaÿe and intended as a tribute to Ysaÿe's style of playing. Enescu himself was to be praised by all the critics, after Ysaÿe's death, as the finest living interpreter of the *Poème*; so one is perhaps entitled to feel, when listening to his recording of that work with Sandford Schlüssel (or indeed to the recording by Menuhin conducted by Enescu), that what one hears represents a special line of

musical and personal filiation which goes back to the
genesis of the *Poème* itself.[13]

Enescu's concert-tours took him several times to
Belgium, and it is possible that he visited Ysaÿe's country
house there, where chamber music was played by Kreisler,
Thibaud, Ysaÿe, Casals and the pianists Cortot, Raoul
Pugno or Busoni. Unfortunately it is not known whether
Enescu and Busoni ever met. In view of the strange parallels
between their musical lives – both inheriting more than one
musical culture, both struggling to compose under the
burden of a reputation as a virtuoso instrumentalist – it
would have been an interesting encounter. Enescu did play
Busoni's Second Violin Sonata, and was one of the few
violinists to keep it in his concert repertoire.[14] The other
pianist, Raoul Pugno, was Ysaÿe's favourite accompanist,
and in 1907 he accompanied Enescu on a concert-tour of
Scotland. Among the audience at a concert in Edinburgh
was the young Joseph Szigeti. He had gone to hear Pugno
and 'Pugno's protégé', but found that the great pianist's
playing was completely overshadowed by the violinist's
performance of unaccompanied Bach.[15]

[13] For Ysaÿe's collaboration with Chausson see Szigeti, *With Strings
Attached. Reminiscences and Reflections*, Knopf, New York, 1947, pp. 117–8
and n. Szigeti also gives a fine account of the impression made by Ysaÿe
on a younger violinist. He too was a dedicatee of a sonata (the others
being Thibaud, Kreisler, Crickboom and Quiroga). Sir Yehudi Menuhin
has pointed out to me, however, that Enescu did not use Ysaÿe's edition
of Chausson's *Poème* because he disagreed with many of its markings. He
also tells me that this is the one work in which he has always adhered
most closely to the bowings, fingerings and expression marks imparted to
him by Enescu.

[14] Oprescu and Jora, *Enescu*, p. 291; Vlad, 'Enescu şi Italia', p. 315. Vlad
has some suggestive remarks about the similarities between Enescu and
Busoni – for example, the importance they accorded to Bach, and their
distrust of any avant-gardism that demanded a break with the musical
past.

[15] Szigeti, 'One of the Least "Promoted"', *Adam*, Year 43 (1981),
Nos. 434–6, pp. 13–14. The programme is recorded in *The Musical Times*,
Vol. 49, No. 780, 1 February 1908, p. 114: Mozart A major Sonata (K526),
Grieg C minor, 'and M. Enesco performed movements from Bach's
Sonata in B minor, for violin alone'.

Enescu's international career as a violinist was gathering pace. In 1909 he went to Russia and played under the batons of Alexander Siloti and Mikhail Ippolitov-Ivanov; in 1910 and 1911 he gave several concerts in Holland, where he not only played concertos but also conducted the Berlin Symphony Orchestra and the Concertgebouw in some of his own works. In 1912 he visited Budapest and took part in an extraordinary concert, conducted by Oskar Nedbal, with the following programme: Schumann's Cello Concerto (Casals); Brahms' Double Concerto (Casals and Enescu) and Beethoven's Triple Concerto (Casals, Enescu and Donald Tovey).[16] There was nothing odd then, of course, about including more than one concerto in an evening's programme. At one concert in 1908, under Colonne, Enescu played concertos by Bach, Mozart and Beethoven; in November 1911 he played two concertos, by Bruch and Ernst, in a performance conducted by Hans Pfitzner at Strasbourg. His repertoire, needless to say, was huge, and hugely adaptable to the demands of concert organisers and conductors. The one work which he made a special effort to promote was the newly discovered Seventh Violin Concerto by Mozart, to which he felt a personal attachment, having been the first person to perform it after a copy was found in Berlin and published in 1907.[17] Enescu was also well known for his interpretation of the Beethoven Concerto. Weingartner repeatedly performed the work with him on his visits to Paris. But, sadly, Weingartner's patronage did not lead to any major performances of concertos in Germany; and for the rest of his life Enescu was always to be insufficiently promoted or recognised as a violinist in that country. He made several visits to Berlin during these years,

---

[16] *Monografie*, p. 384.

[17] For the strange history of this score see *The Musical Times*, Vol. 48, No. 778, 1 December 1907, p. 808, and C. H. Mahling, 'Bemerkungen zum Violinkonzert B-dur KV 271 i', *Mozart-Jahrbuch 1978/79*, Basel, 1979, pp. 252–68. The attribution to Mozart is still disputed, but the consensus is that this work is substantially by him, with some modifications by other hands (Alec Hyatt King, *Mozart Wind and String Concertos*, BBC, London, 1978, p. 31).

A letter from Enescu to Carl Flesch, 29 June 1907, concerning two performances by Flesch of Enescu's Second Violin Sonata (courtesy of Carl F. Flesch)

but his performances there were usually limited to a handful of chamber concerts.

Enescu was not without honour in his own country, however. Although the main purpose of his longer stays there was to devote himself to composition, he became closely involved in the musical life of Bucharest and gave frequent performances as a violinist and as a conductor. In France and other countries he was usually entrusted with the baton only to conduct his own works, but here he could spread his wings more widely, conducting, for example, an entire programme of Brahms, Wagner, Debussy and Strauss in January 1910. He often stayed in Peleş castle at Sinaia, and was naturally obliged to take part in concerts at the royal court. During these years he became more closely acquainted with Princess Marie. She ceased to regard him as one of Aunty's dubious discoveries, and in 1908 she presented him with a large signed photograph of herself (which still survives), bearing the inscription, in English, 'And he awakes the music of our souls'.[18]

One fruit of his court patronage was the composition in 1906 of a *Hymn Jubiliar* (*Jubilee Hymn*) for choir, military band and harp, a setting of patriotic verses in praise of King Carol. It is a rather solid, four-square piece, with occasional folk-colouring in the woodwind ornamentation; one senses that Enescu's heart was not in it – not because he lacked loyalty to the King, but because he did not take to writing commissioned works of this sort.[19] Enescu was not lacking in patriotism. Much of his concert-giving at Sinaia and in Bucharest was undertaken for local or national charitable causes, or out of his sense of a duty to help raise musical standards. He had been named an 'honorary director' of the Romanian Musical Association, and he gave large donations to the Association to pay for grants to musicians.[20] In 1912 he went on a concert tour of Romania to raise money for a national prize for composers. The huge sum of 27,000

A poster for the Berlin premiere of Enescu's
Second Violin Sonata

lei was raised (approximately £1,000 at the time), and he presided over the first biennial competition in 1913.[21] And Enescu had already shown his interest in training young Romanian musicians by accepting in 1906 an uncharacteristically academic appointment, that of honorary Professor of Composition at the Bucharest Conservatoire.[22]

Two years before this, Enescu had been persuaded by Fauré to serve on the competition jury at the Paris Conser-

[21] *Ibid.*, pp. 167, 169, 335.

[22] *Ibid.*, p. 153.

Princess (later Queen) Marie

vatoire. He performed this duty almost every year until 1910, judging pianists as well as violinists; his fellow jurors during these years included Pugno, Schmitt, Paul Dukas, Charles Tournemire, Harold Bauer and Lucien Capet.[23] In 1904 and 1906 he was also persuaded to write four pieces, for flute, harp, viola and trumpet, for use in the instrumental competitions. Of these pieces the *Cantabile and Presto* for flute and piano and the *Concertstück* for viola and piano are sometimes played today, but the *Allegro de Concert* for chromatic harp has suffered from the fact that this instrument never obtained the general acceptance which its manufacturer, Pleyel, was hoping for. The *Légende* for trumpet and piano is the most musically complex of the four, engaging in a ballade-like evolution of themes; and it awakened an interest on Enescu's part in the trumpet's powers of soft and muted evocative expression, which he

---

[23] *Ibid.*: see the entries from 1904 to 1910.

explored further in the same year with an improbably
scored 'poème', entitled *Au Soir*, for four trumpets.

Enescu's loyalty to Fauré and his continued links with the
Conservatoire offer some clues as to how he was placed in
the uncertain and shifting world of French musical politics
in this period. There was, roughly speaking, a three-
cornered antagonism at work. The Fauréans included
Ravel, Schmitt and Roger-Ducasse; Fauré represented a
connection with the Conservatoire, though Ravel's
treatment over the Prix de Rome had been one of the *causes
célèbres* against that institution. The d'Indyists, based at the
Schola Cantorum, were hostile to the Conservatoire and
unsympathetic to the Fauréan approach to music, which
they felt represented an effete aestheticism; they wanted to
revive a national tradition, anchored firmly in choral music
and early polyphony. And in the third corner were the
Debussyists, who were regarded as perniciously modernistic
by the d'Indyists, but shared with them some common
criticism of the Conservatoire and the Fauréans.

The d'Indyists controlled the National Music Society,
and when they refused in 1910 to allow the performance of a
work by Ravel's friend Maurice Delage, Ravel helped to
found a new 'Société Indépendante Musicale' ('S.I.M.'),
with Fauré as president.[24] One of their first concerts, on
18 May 1910, included a performance of Enescu's First
Piano Quartet, with the composer at the keyboard. There
was no hostility at the S.I.M. towards Debussy, whose works
Ravel was keen to promote: at their next concert, on 25
May, the programme included not only Enescu's Octet,
conducted by its composer, but also a performance by
Debussy of four new *Préludes*. It was a strange juxtaposition,
and few of Enescu's works of this period can have been more
foreign to Debussy's taste than the Octet. But Debussy had
probably already formed a favourable impression of

[24] See the account by Casella, one of the co-founders, in *Music in my Time*,
p. 91. What is said here of Debussyists and d'Indyists does not fully apply
to d'Indy and Debussy themselves: within a few years they were both
writing contrasting columns for the *Revue S.I.M.* (Edward Lockspeiser,
Debussy. His Life and Mind, two vols., Cambridge University Press, Cambridge, rev. edn. 1978; Vol. 2, pp. 56n and 285).

A meeting of the 'Société Indépendante Musicale' (from left to right, standing: Louis Aubert, A. Z. Mathot, Maurice Ravel, André Caplet, Charles Koechlin, Émile Vuillermoz, Jean Huré: seated: Gabriel Fauré, Roger-Ducasse)

Enescu's music: in 1908 he attended a special concert devoted to works by Enescu, consisting of the Second Violin Sonata, the Second Piano Suite and the premiere of the *Sept Chansons de Clément Marot* – a work which must surely have touched Debussy's heart (if he had one).[25] Enescu, for his part, took an interest in Debussy's music but could not be described as a Debussyist. He was later to include the Violin Sonata in his repertoire; he had several orchestral pieces in

[25] *Monografie*, p. 346.

his repertoire as a conductor; and, as we have seen, Debussy's String Quartet was one of the few works chosen for performance by the 'Quatuor Enesco'; but we have also seen that he was dissatisfied by *Pelléas*.

An interesting picture of Enescu's musical taste at this time is given in an article by an American journalist who interviewed him in July 1912. It is obviously a recollection rather than a transcript of what Enescu said, and its outspokenness seems very untypical. But even if Enescu's words have been gingered up by the writer, they probably do still broadly represent the judgements he expressed:

> Debussy I find growing cold at present. He seems to me to be becoming more and more like d'Indy – merely pedantic [. . .]. But better than Debussy I like Dukas, who is more substantial and generally stronger, and whose works are more perfect and solid than Debussy's in their structure. D'Indy I have never liked [. . .]. In Germany there is Strauss, who would have been the greatest composer in the world since Wagner if he had something more to work upon than mere shreds of ideas. Reger! *Ah! c'est horrible!* I cannot endure him! (And Enescu threw up his hands and grimaced as if violently nauseated.) In him you have an example of icy coldness, of want of heart, of bad counterpoint – for I do not admit that one whose polyphony is as harsh, as badly joined and as totally devoid of beauty as Reger's, can be called a good contrapuntalist. Strauss' counterpoint, you will notice, has almost always an elegance and is not devoid of smoothness.[26]

Enescu's own compositions in the years leading up to the First World War are hard to classify. He was exploring several different musical idioms. At times it looks as if he was cultivating entirely different species of music; there was, however, much cross-fertilisation between them. The easiest way to distinguish one group of his works is to use the label 'neo-classicism'; but the term is misleadingly

---

[26] Peyser, 'Enesco Analyses Himself', p. 195. See also Enescu's praise of Dukas in 'Hommage à Paul Dukas', *La Revue musicale*, No. 166 (special number), May–June 1936, p. 119. The hostility to Reger is confirmed by a letter of 1924: *Scrisori*, Vol. 2, p. 68.

narrow. The sequence of these works begins with the First Piano Suite, written as early as 1897. It is an exercise in deliberate archaism, and bears the title *Suite dans le Style Ancien*. The second movement, a three-part fugue, is almost perfectly Bachian, and in the other movements there are reminiscences of Bach, Handel, Couperin and Scarlatti. Enescu's Second Piano Suite was written six years later, and shows the development of his understanding of how to use the 'style ancien'. In February 1903 the French journal *Musica* announced a competition for composers, divided into ten different categories of which one was a suite for piano; an imposing jury had been assembled, including Debussy, Cortot, d'Indy, Pierné and Hahn. Enescu set to work during the summer and wrote a Sarabande, a Pavane and a Bourrée. He also wrote a Prelude and Fugue, which, although in a different key, may have been originally conceived as an attempt to find a suitable opening movement for the suite; but in the end he turned instead to a Toccata which he had written two years before.[27] Submitted anonymously under the motto 'Des cloches sonores', the suite won not only the prize for its category but also the Pleyel prize (consisting of a grand piano) for the best piano piece.

It might be thought that in choosing the character of his movements Enescu had engaged in deliberate flattery of Debussy, whose own *Pour le Piano* (Prélude, Sarabande and Toccata) was first performed in 1902. There are occasional Debussian inflections in Enescu's piece; but the character of the work is profoundly different. Where Debussy cultivates the repetition and juxtaposition of small-scale phrases, Enescu shows his love of lengthy melodic development, and in several of the movements there are threads of contrapuntal writing woven into the inner parts. In contrast with the First Piano Suite, Enescu no longer confines himself to the harmonic language of his historical models. Here and there in the Toccata one finds turns of phrase that seem

[27] *Monografie* p. 286; Oprescu and Jora, *Enescu*, pp. 144 and 147–8; the Prelude and Fugue is dated 11 September 1903, two-and-a-half weeks after the Bourrée.

positively Chopinesque, and in its overall effect this
movement is like a rather galvanised version of one of
Fauré's *Barcarolles*. There are also moments of extraordinary
rhythmical fluidity, especially in the development of the
'quasi flûte' melody of the Pavane. The distinguished
members of the French jury could hardly have known that
this melody, under its neo-classical trappings, bears the
unmistakable hallmarks of a Romanian doina. With this
Suite the term 'neo-classical', given the narrow sense in
which it is normally applied to pieces of twentieth-century
music, begins to lose its point. Enescu is not drawing
attention to a sense of musical-historical distance in order
to make a statement about music. Rather, he is closing the
gap between past forms and present needs. Perhaps the
same should be said of Ravel's *Tombeau de Couperin*, to which
this Suite is sometimes compared. In his radio interviews
Enescu modestly admitted that he was influenced by Ravel
as well as Debussy, and added that the second subject of his
Toccata 'reproduces' the rhythm of Ravel's Toccata in the
Tombeau. It was left to Gavoty to point out that Ravel's work
(begun in 1914) was not published until 1917.[28]

Between writing the Toccata in 1901 and the rest of the
Suite in 1903 Enescu had completed another work in a
similar spirit: the First Orchestral Suite, Op. 9. The
movements here are Prélude, Menuet Lent, Intermède and
Finale. The whole work is in one way closer to Enescu's
usual practice: each of the last three movements develops
thematic material taken from the Prélude. The two middle
movements are perhaps too similar in character because of
this, and they are both dominated by a warm string sound
which is lavished on the gradual development and amplification of the melody. (The second of these, the Intermède,
or Intermezzo, has a strong kinship with the second of two
Intermèdes for string orchestra which Enescu wrote in 1902
and 1903.) The most striking movement of the Suite is the
Prélude, which is played entirely in unison by the strings
only; the melodic statements here come in huge paragraphs,

---

[28] *Entretiens*, tape 9. Enescu was referring to the accented notes in bars
20–6 of his Toccata.

and Enescu proudly told Gavoty that Kodály used to get his pupils to study this piece as an outstanding example of monody.[29] Romanian musicologists have devoted an immense amount of attention to this Prélude, and have traced not only its roots in folk melody and its partial anticipation in the theme of the Op. 5 Variations (both of which seem plausible claims), but also its numerical dependence on the Fibonacci series.[30] But they have not noticed what is surely the greatest and most direct influence of all: the cor anglais solo, 'die alte Weise', in the Prelude to Act 3 of *Tristan*. The rhythmical character of the phrasing, and some of the implied harmonic progressions it undergoes, are both too similar for this to be mere coincidence. Enescu's Prélude does have special qualities of its own, however – notably the way in which the phrasing is designed to embody the sinewy feeling of physical tension which an entire string section playing in unison can produce.

Oddly enough, Fauré made no mention of this movement when he reviewed the Suite's French premiere for *Figaro* in 1904: 'The two movements which seemed the most attractive to me were the Minuet, which is very originally thought out and generously expressive, and the Finale, which is a sort of tarantella with changing rhythms, full of life, brilliance and colour – it was warmly applauded'.[31] But other reviewers were less favourable, and the score was not published till 1909. Once it became available, the work did find its advocates: in January 1911 its American premiere was conducted by Mahler; two months later Frederick Stock played it at Chicago; and in September Henry Wood introduced it to English audiences at a Promenade concert.[32]

[29] *Contrepoint*, p. 39.

[30] See, for example, Bentoiu, *Capodopere*, pp. 63–8. The Fibonacci series is the series of numbers discovered by the mediaeval Italian mathematician Leonardo Fibonacci, in which each number is the sum of the two previous numbers.

[31] Concert Review in *Le Figaro*, Series 3, No. 347, 12 December 1904.

[32] Oprescu and Jora, *Enescu*, pp. 164–5.

One other work can be added to this group of so-called neo-classical pieces: the *Sept Chansons de Clément Marot*, Op. 15, written in 1908. This is a setting of a contrasting sequence of poems chosen by Enescu from the *Epigrammes*, *Chansons* and *Rondeaux* of the sixteenth-century poet, who was famous for his delicate and ingenious metrical constructions. Each poem is a love-poem of a different sort: some are in Marot's favourite style of amorous-humorous badinage, and others are tinged with Petrarchan heart-ache. Enescu's settings explore this range of emotions while keeping to the same musical idiom throughout; deft Gallic humour alternates with Fauréan reverie. The music is coloured with a sort of affectionate archaism. There are often, for example, progressions of bare fourths and fifths in the piano accompaniment, which has a light texture of chords, rhythmical patterns and simple elaborations of the melodic line. In the last of the seven, a poignantly beautiful song of resignation to unrequited love, the piano part has almost the character of lute music. There is a very touching recording of these songs made in Bucharest in 1943 by Enescu and the tenor Constantin Stroescu, who had given the second performance of the work in Paris in 1909. But it is incomplete: the fifth song, for some reason which Stroescu later could not recall, was never recorded.[33] This song must have had a special significance for the composer, since he had dedicated it to Maggie Teyte: when she had been in Paris for her first season at the Opéra-Comique in 1906–7 she had had an affair with Enescu. Strangely, she knew nothing of the dedication of this song to her until she was asked about it more than sixty years later. Interviewed at the end of her life she explained that she had never broken the secret of this love affair 'because I wouldn't want them to say, "Oh, Teyte, . . . she would go to bed with anybody"'.[34] Perhaps this remark was not intended to sound quite

---

[33] Stroescu's account is in his sleeve-note to a record of these songs by his pupil Dan Iordăchescu (ECE 0412). His own recording has been re-issued by Electrecord as ECE 01976.

[34] Gary O'Connor, *The Pursuit of Perfection. A Life of Maggie Teyte*, Gollancz, London, 1979, p. 71.

Enescu in 1904

as dismissive as it does; one has only to look at photographs of the strikingly handsome young composer to know that he was certainly not just 'anybody'.

Enescu's other compositions during the period cover a wide stylistic range. The *Symphonie Concertante*, Op. 8, for cello and orchestra of 1901 contrasts strongly with the Octet of the previous year. There is little contrapuntal activity in the score, which is dominated by the cello's non-stop unfolding of seamless (and at times rather contourless) melody. The choice of title is surprising. Enescu seems to have been the first modern composer to revive this term (predating Szymanowski, for example, by thirty years). He was obviously not thinking of the original use of the Italian word 'concertante' in Baroque music; nor can he have meant that the solo cello was to be treated simply as a principal instrumental part within the orchestra – the score would be largely meaningless without it. In the original manuscript of the cello part the work is called a Cello Concerto.[35] Enescu must have felt that such a title would arouse false expectations of a virtuoso showpiece, à la Saint-Saëns or Lalo. The name he chose was, unfortunately, a gift to hostile critics at the first performance, who found the work too harmonically advanced and too deficient in recognisable, clear-cut melodic material: it was dubbed the 'Symphonie Déconcertante'. The audience's reaction to the second performance (4 December 1910) was vividly described by the music critic of the *Écho de Paris*:

> Well before the end, the public were giving clear signs of boredom: rustling their programmes, coughing and so on [. . .]. Suddenly, someone gave a whistle. Providential whistle! It was immediately applauded. The whistling was repeated: the applause grew. The whistle screeched: the applause thundered; the whistle howled: the applause became an avalanche. Unfortunately, someone shouted 'Encore!'; the applauders recovered themselves and began to cry 'No! No!' [. . .][36]

[35] Library of the Romanian Academy, MS R 987.

[36] A. Boschot, Concert Review in *L'Écho de Paris*, 5 December 1910.

Enescu's next major orchestral composition, after the *Romanian Rhapsodies* and the First Suite, was his most ambitious work so far: the First Symphony, completed in 1905. This did meet with universal enthusiasm at its premiere in the following year, and it is not difficult to see why. The Symphony is a sweepingly romantic work, with broadly stated themes which even conservative music critics would have been able to grasp and enjoy at first hearing. But there is nothing facile about it; needless to say, there is a complex set of inter-relationships between the thematic elements from which it is constructed. The harmonic language would not have shocked any audience brought up on Wagner and the French Wagnerian tradition. In the slow movement there is even a direct and powerful tribute to the 'Liebestod'. This symphony is sometimes compared to Chausson's, but it is less densely written and it lacks the sense of anguished introversion which Chausson's constant modulations produce.[37] Pascal Bentoiu has complained bitterly of the tendency of some commentators to seek comparisons with Germanic music, and insists that the work expresses the clarity of a Latin temperament. If a French comparison must be found it should perhaps be with the symphony written in 1897 by Dukas – or even with some of the orchestral music in d'Indy's *Fervaal*. But there are direct Germanic influences undoubtedly at work. Apart from the debt to Wagner, there are also some strong echoes of Brahms, especially in the last movement.[38] If one adds that there is a direct quotation of Schubert's 'Unfinished' Symphony in the first movement, and that there are touches of Mahler in the scoring, the Symphony may begin to sound like a rag-bag; but this would be quite misleading. What strikes the listener is the stylistic unity of the work, and the confidence with which it is carried through.

[37] For Marcel Mihalovici's comparison with Chausson see Cornel Țăranu, *Enescu în constiința prezentului*, Editura pentru literatură, Bucharest, 1969, p. 170.

[38] The cello solo at the close of the slow movement is also very similar to Brahms's use of the cello at the end of the slow movement of his Second Piano Concerto. Bentoiu's comments are in *Capodopere*, p. 94.

After the spacious grandeur of the Symphony Enescu's next major works were in a more intimate vein. In the following year, 1906, he completed a wind *Dixtuor* (the French term for a piece for ten instruments – there seems to be no usual English word for this). It was given its premiere that year by the 'Société moderne d'instruments à vent'; this was the group which had been founded by Paul Taffanel (the flautist, Professor at the Conservatoire and dedicatee of Enescu's *Cantabile and Presto*), and which had done so much to promote a French tradition of composing for wind ensembles. The *Dixtuor* has an obvious affinity with works in that tradition such as d'Indy's septet, entitled *Chansons et Danses* – with which it also shares a debt to Wagner's *Siegfried Idyll*. But by comparison with d'Indy's work Enescu's piece is much more intricate and polyphonic. It is scored for two flutes, oboe, cor anglais, two clarinets, two bassoons and two horns; there is a constant interchange of themes and ornamental motifs between the voices, and the work is beautifully balanced throughout. But despite its unmistakably French grace and vivacity, the *Dixtuor* is clearly influenced at a deep level by Romanian music. Sometimes this comes to the surface, as at the opening of the second movement, where a haunting oboe and cor anglais melody ('expressif et triste') is followed by the modal flurry of doina ornamentation shown in Ex. 7.

The last two bars of Ex. 7 also make use of a characteristic technique of Romanian folk music which was eventually to play a vital part in Enescu's mature musical language: heterophony, the superimposition of differing versions of the same material (often at a slight distance in time, though without creating the effect of canon). And the sense of cadence achieved here, as the music is stilled and clarified into the tonic note and finally 'placed' with a bare descending fifth, was also to become quintessentially Enescian.

Enescu followed this in 1907 with a strange but important transitional work which remained unknown until after his death, when its manuscript was sent with other pieces from Paris to the Romanian state music publishers in

Ex. 7

Bucharest.[39] It is a *Nocturne* in D flat major for piano, written
in three large sections. The two outer sections do belong to
the familiar genre of the nocturne, though they are unusually dense and substantial pianistically. The middle
section, however, is sinister and tempestuous, with demonic
scurrying trails of chromatic scales in the left hand; it has
something of the explosive menace of Ravel's *Scarbo*. The

[39] Aurora Ienei, 'Nocturna în Re bemol major de George Enescu', in
Speranţa Rădulescu (ed.), *Centenarul George Enescu 1881–1981* pp. 247–61
(p. 248).

effect of the whole piece is unsettling, and rather unconvinc-
ing; Enescu himself was evidently dissatisfied with it, since
he gave it no opus number. Nevertheless it does anticipate
some later developments in his piano music. It is laced with
heterophony and achieves in places an extraordinary rhythmical fluidity, with shifting sequences and superimpositions
of groups of notes with different rhythmical values – as in
the single bar given in Ex. 8.

Ex. 8

After this, the chaste simplicity of the *Sept Chansons de
Clément Marot* (written a year later, in 1908) is all the more
striking.

Another unpublished work from this period is of less
musical interest. Entitled *Cantate pour la Pose de la Première
Pierre du Pont à Transbordeur de Bordeaux* ('Cantata for the
Laying of the First Stone of the Transporter Bridge at
Bordeaux'), it is a setting of a rather pedestrian ode written
for the occasion by the poet Albert Bureau. The manuscript,
35 pages of almost-full score, is dated 'Paris, 27 May 1908'.
But since work on the transporter bridge in Bordeaux was
delayed until 1914 and then halted by the war, it seems
unlikely that the Cantata was ever performed; and the top
four staves of the score are marked 'military band – to be
orchestrated'. Apart from the band, the score requires two
harps, a five-part string orchestra, a solo cello, a four-part
chorus and a baritone solo: and on the final page there is an
extra stave marked 'cannons'. The opening choral section,
in E flat major, has a broad, hymnal melody in $\frac{4}{4}$; the
baritone's solo modulates to B major; the chorus returns,
passing through G major and G minor back to E flat, and
the work ends with an antiphonal chanting (marked

'majestueux') of the phrase 'Gloire à Bordeaux!' By the standards of Enescu's harmonic language of this period, the Cantata seems a very routine work – a reminder of the fact that he was temperamentally opposed to writing 'commissioned' works of any kind.[40]

In 1909 Enescu wrote another chamber work which in part shows an affinity with the quiet, meditative world of the string *Intermèdes* and the *Dixtuor*: the First Piano Quartet (Op. 16). But only in part. It is, by chamber music standards, a large work, lasting the best part of 40 minutes in performance, and the long coda to the first movement piles up the most imposing and dramatic climax in Enescu's entire chamber oeuvre. Some critics have written almost apologetically about this Quartet, saying that it is retrogressive and fails to press forward to a more 'advanced' style.[41] It is true that much of its character is Fauréan (this is most clear in the slow, pensive unfolding of the first movement); but the affinity seems to be with Fauré's late chamber works, such as the Second Piano Quintet of 1921. And the sparse and rhythmically hypnotic opening of the second movement (Ex. 9, pp. 108–9) gives a foretaste of some of Enescu's later writing (such as the slow movement of the Second Piano Quartet of 1944). But the hunt for stylistic advances can become a distraction. This work is self-sufficient, and can be enjoyed for its lyricism and its richness of construction, regardless of the imperious demands of musical 'progress'.

It was the last major work that Enescu was to complete for nearly five years. The blows and disappointments of 1908–9 may have been taking their toll; and the pressures of concert schedules were becoming stronger each year. For someone who had completed so many ambitious works over the last ten years, this period presents a sorry spectacle. A piano quintet (with double-bass and one violin) on which he had

---

[40] This manuscript, which is unknown to Romanian scholars, is in the Stiftelse Musikkulturens Främjande, Stockholm. I am very grateful to the Stiftelse for permitting me to study it, and to Martin Anderson for drawing it to my attention.

[41] E.g. *Monografie*, p. 556.

Ex. 9

Andante mesto

been working in 1909 was abandoned: the only surviving fragments are the 'Scherzino' and a sketch of an 'Aria'.[42] The year 1910 is a complete blank in Enescu's output. In 1911 he embarked on an orchestral suite; he gave it the title *Suite Châtelaine* and the opus number 17 (which he later transferred to his Second Symphony), but he got no further than orchestrating one movement, 'Entrée', and sketching another, 'Chasse'.[43] A violin sonata in A minor was begun in October 1911 and abandoned after eighteen pages.[44] In July 1912 he wrote the first movement of a piano sonata; the work was taken no further, and even this movement appears not to have survived in manuscript.[45] Only when he began his Second Symphony later in 1912 did Enescu embark on a major work which would eventually be carried through to completion, in the final weeks before the outbreak of the war.

[42] Vancea, *Creaţia muzicală*, pp. 254–5; Titus Moisescu, 'Lucrări inedite de George Enescu', *Muzica*, Vol. 25, No. 3, March 1975, pp. 11–15 (p. 14).

[43] *Monografie*, p. 356.

[44] Moisescu, 'Lucrări inedite', p. 14.

[45] The evidence, which seems to be unknown to Romanian scholars, is in the interview with Peyser ('Enesco Analyses Himself', p. 195), who says that Enescu played a piece which he described as 'the first movement of a piano sonata which I completed less than a week ago. It is my maturest work. Does it sound incomprehensible to you?' Perhaps Enescu said 'suite' rather than 'sonata'; but the first movement of the Third Piano Suite is clearly dated 1 June 1913.

VI

FIRST WORLD WAR

The violent uproar which greeted the premiere of Stravinsky's *Rite of Spring* in 1913 has entered the folklore of twentieth-century music. It should really belong to the folklore of twentieth-century choreography: Nijinsky, not Stravinsky, was the main object of the abuse. The story of the first *concert* performance of Stravinsky's score, on 5 April 1914, is much less well known. This time the music was wildly applauded and the composer was pursued by his cheering admirers into the street. Even less well known, however, is the programme for the rest of that concert. The second half also included a performance of *La Tragédie de Salomé* by Florent Schmitt; the first half consisted of Mozart's Seventh Violin Concerto, played by Enescu and conducted by Pierre Monteux, and the two *Romanian Rhapsodies* under the baton of the composer. What Stravinsky thought of these two pieces is not known, but it is known that Enescu was so intrigued by *The Rite of Spring* that he went to hear Monteux's next performance of it three weeks later.[1]

Enescu was to remain an admirer of Stravinsky's music, though with some reservations – he characterised *Oedipus Rex*, for example, as 'insolent cubism'. Asked about Russian music in 1928 he singled out Mussorgsky as 'a genius, set apart from the others', and described Stravinsky as continuing Mussorgsky's line of development.[2] Interviewed on the same subject in 1946 he said:

---

[1] *Monografie*, p. 408.

[2] On *Oedipus Rex*: Tomaziu, '"Mosh" Georges', p. 30; on Mussorgsky: Broşteanu, 'De vorbă cu Enescu', p. 2.

I think Stravinsky is a genius. I like *Petrushka* best, and also *The Firebird*, although it's stylistically rather more French than Russian. As for *The Rite of Spring*, I think it is marred, from the point of view of the emotional progression of the work, by the fact that the two parts are too closely similar in character. All the same, it's an outstanding work.[3]

And in 1926 he took part in Leopold Stokowski's extra-ordinary American premiere of *Les Noces*, in which the piano parts were played by four composers: Enescu, Tailleferre, Salzedo and Casella.[4]

There were plenty of conflicting musical currents to absorb on the eve of the First World War. Despite his remark about 'shreds of ideas'[5] Enescu was obviously deeply interested in the music of Richard Strauss. In 1912 the young Romeo Drăghici was having a violin lesson with Caudella in Iaşi when they were interrupted by the arrival of Enescu (an encounter which marked the beginning of Drăghici's long and faithful friendship with the composer). Enescu saw the score of *Elektra* lying on the piano and called it a wonderful work. Caudella protested that it overthrew all the principles of classical music: 'if it has no melody, it can't be music'. Enescu laughed, and asked if he might play through some passages at the piano; when he had finished, the 71-year-old professor exclaimed: 'Well, what a beautiful piece of music!'[6] And on the other hand, the influence of *Pelléas* was still working itself out: Enescu went to a perform-ance at the Opéra-Comique in June 1914, five weeks after listening to *The Rite of Spring*.[7]

After the outbreak of war, however, Enescu was to spend the next four years almost exclusively in Romania, increas-

[3] Oprescu and Jora, *Enescu*, p. 68 (from an interview in *Scînteia*, 6 April 1946).

[4] *Ibid.*, p. 204.

[5] See above, p. 96.

[6] Drăghici, 'Cînd şi cum l'am cunoscut pe Enescu', in Victor Crăciun and Petre Codrea (eds.), *Gînduri închinate lui Enescu*, Comitetul pentru cultură şi artă al judeţului Botoşani, Botoşani, 1970, pp. 219–22 (pp. 219–20).

[7] *Monografie*, p. 409.

ingly cut off from cosmopolitan musical influences. At the beginning of September 1914 he returned to his country, which was persisting uneasily in neutrality despite the sympathies of its Prussian-born king. Romania was tied by treaty obligations to the Central Powers (Germany and Austria-Hungary), but in the minds of the ruling political class, led by Ion Brătianu, these obligations were outweighed by pro-French sympathies and hostility to Hungary over the issue of Transylvania. Much of Romanian history has been dominated by territorial concerns, and never more so than during this period. Russia promised to give Romania possession of Transylvania in return for remaining neutral. The death of King Carol in October 1914 helped to promote the general alignment of Romania on the side of the Allies: King Ferdinand's wife, Marie, was fervently pro-English. But it was not until August 1916, after the Russians had launched a major new offensive and the Allies had issued further territorial promises, that Romania entered the War.

For much of this period of neutrality Enescu devoted himself with immense energy to the musical life of the capital, not only performing and conducting but also organising major new musical events. In December 1914, at a concert in aid of the Romanian Red Cross, he conducted the first integral performance of Beethoven's Ninth Symphony ever to be given in Romania.[8] In February he joined a committee to draw up proposals for a national opera company; in March he conducted a concert performance of Act 2 of *Parsifal*.[9] In a newspaper article later that year he wrote:

A Romanian Opera! It has been my dream for a long time. An Opera where you could hear, in our language, with our singers and players, the great masterpieces of Gluck, Mozart, Beethoven, Weber and the superhuman Wagner; and fine modern works such as *Pelléas, Ariane et Barbe-bleu, Boris Godunov*

[8] *Ibid.*, p. 410 (it had never been performed with the chorus).
[9] Oprescu and Jora, *Enescu*, pp. 173 and 174. As before, details of concerts are from the chronologies of this book and Gheorghe Firca (ed.), *George Enescu. Omagiu cu prilejul aniversării a 100 ani de la naştere*, Bucharest, 1981, unless otherwise stated.

and *Salome*; and, later, works by Romanians – when there are some good ones.[10]

In the early months of 1915 he toured the country, playing to raise money for the building of an organ in the Atheneum, the main concert-hall in Bucharest. By April he had collected the sum of 30,000 lei.[11] In May he returned to Paris for a few weeks, where he took part in another concert with Debussy and several performances in aid of soldiers and refugees. Back in Romania, he was at last able to devote a few months to composition, completing most of the Second Orchestral Suite; but in the autumn the concert season began again. Between 16 November and 31 December he gave no fewer than 24 concerts. The range of these performances is even more impressive than their sheer quantity. In November, with his old pianist friend Theodor Fuchs, he embarked on a series of concerts designed to illustrate the history of the violin: in the course of nine concerts he played roughly 60 different pieces by composers from Corelli to Kreisler. (Similarly in 1919 he was to give sixteen concerts, in seven weeks, entitled 'The History of the Sonata', in which he played 48 different violin sonatas, from Bach and Handel to Paderewski and Pierné.) Among his frequent appearances as a conductor one of the high points was a full-scale performance (repeated three times) of Berlioz's *Damnation of Faust*, in May and June 1916.

Amidst all this exhausting work and constant music-making, this period also saw the flowering of the one great passion of Enescu's personal life: his love for Marie Cantacuzino, whom he was eventually to marry. Born Marie Rosetti (and known to all her friends as Maruca), she was the daughter of a rich noble landowner in Moldavia, whose

[10] Enescu, 'A propos de l'opéra chez nous', *L'Indépendance roumaine*, Vol. 38, No. 12229, 26 October/8 November 1915, p. 1 (also printed in part in *Monografie*, pp. 416–7). He complained of endless performances of *Rigoletto*, *Un Ballo in Maschera*, *La Traviata* 'and other fossils', adding: 'If you must have Verdi, why not put on his masterpiece: *Falstaff*?'

[11] Oprescu and Jora, *Enescu*, pp. 172 and 174; 30,000 lei was worth approximately £1,100 at the time.

Marie Cantacuzino

estates were centred on the imposing villa of Teţcani or Tescani, near Bacău. She had married into one of the richest families in Romania: her husband, Michael, was the eldest son of Prince George 'Nabob' Cantacuzino. But the marriage had not been a success, and they now lived separate lives. She was a friend of Princess (later Queen) Marie, and it may have been through her that Maruca first made Enescu's acquaintance in the years before the War and began to invite him regularly to play at her soirées. She was evidently a fascinating woman in her youth, with a combination of great beauty and an unusual (and at times bizarre) vivacity of spirit. Queen Marie later wrote that 'she was rich and independent and lived exactly as she pleased'. She also had 'an almost perverse liking for the absurd in every form'; her soirées were lit only by the fire in the hearth, and on one occasion a short-sighted guest, groping among the armchairs for her furs, found that she was tugging away at the tousled hair of an exhausted pianist – 'whereupon shrieks of

Enescu in 1907, in a photograph inscribed to Carl Flesch (courtesy of Carl F. Flesch)

delighted laughter on the part of our hostess'.[12] Enescu fell passionately in love with the Princess Cantacuzino, and the affair was an open secret. A letter he wrote to her in 1915 begins 'Mon adorée', and goes on to describe his passion for her in terms which should bring a blush to the cheek of any casual reader.[13] They adopted a private mythological language of terms of endearment for each other, which they continued to use for the rest of their lives. Her favourite name for him was 'Pynx', a name derived apparently from the word 'Sphinx' and applied to him originally by Carmen Sylva, long before Enescu began to write the opera in which his own terrifying musical vision of the Sphinx was to appear.

[12] Queen Marie of Romania, *The Story of my Life*, Vol. 2, pp. 183–4.

[13] *Scrisori*, Vol. 2, pp. 37–8.

Carmen Sylva, Enescu's 'second mother', died on 3 March 1916. Enescu was ill at the time, and was staying at a hotel in Bucharest. Remembering her request that her favourite piece of music, the *Andante con moto* from Schubert's E flat major Piano Trio, should be played at her funeral, he decided to orchestrate the movement. He worked through the night without stopping until he had completed the task in 38 pages of full score.[14] Another death which occurred in the same year was that of the 39-year-old Stefan Luchian, Romania's finest painter, whom Enescu had got to know in 1915. The story of his final years is a tragic one: crippled by a paralysing disease, he had made an immense effort to take up his brush again, only to find himself being sued by art dealers who were convinced that he was signing canvases which he could not have painted himself. The poet Tudor Arghezi tells a moving story of Enescu's friendship for Luchian. In the last weeks of the painter's life, when he was paralysed, bed-ridden and scarcely able to speak, Arghezi called on Luchian one morning and found him crying. He learned that as he had lain there late the previous night, Enescu had come into his room, had taken out his violin and, without speaking or lighting the lamp, had simply played to his friend two hours of uninterrupted music.[15]

There was more pain and suffering to be witnessed. Romania entered the War against Germany, Austria-Hungary and Bulgaria at the end of August 1916, when the Russian summer offensive was already beginning to falter. As the Central Powers began to advance again on the

---

[14] The instrumental parts were copied out as he worked by Dimitrie Cuclin. See Emil Riegler-Dinu, 'George Enescu. În al cincizecilea an de viaţa', *Facla*, Vol. 10, No. 422, 7 September 1931, p. 2. The manuscript, with Enescu's note that it was orchestrated in a single night, is Romanian Academy Library MS R 986. Queen Marie reveals the extent of her knowledge of music when she writes that Enescu transcribed 'a certain Haydn quartet' for the funeral (*Story of my Life*, Vol. 3, p. 15). Elsewhere she calls Lekeu's Violin Sonata 'Lequeux's symphony'.

[15] Lucian Voiculescu, *George Enescu şi opera sa Oedip*, Editura de stat pentru literatură, Bucharest, 1956, pp. 39–40.

Eastern Front, the Romanian position rapidly became hopeless. Romanian losses were heavy, and a tide of wounded soldiers flowed back into the make-shift hospitals. Enescu was now giving concerts for, and to, the wounded almost every day. On the evening of 8 November he was due to give a concert in the St Spiridon hospital in Iaşi. The young Mihail Jora, who was later to become Romania's best known composer after Enescu, had a leg amputated in a two-hour operation that evening, without anaesthetic. Enescu delayed the start of his concert till Jora came out of the operating theatre; Jora later wrote that this concert gave him back the will to live which he had lost.[16] Twenty years later Enescu was asked in an interview about the concerts he had given during the War. He said: 'I have often noticed how great an uplifting of the spirit could be seen in the faces of the wounded after the first few notes. This transformation of the soul is the supreme raison-d'être of music. If it did not have this wonderful effect of calming and purifying the human spirit, music would just be a meaningless sequence of sounds.'[17]

It was in November that Bucharest fell to the enemy; the government and court had retreated northwards to Iaşi. 1917 was a black year. The early spring brought a typhus epidemic which ravaged the population. Enescu had found a small house in a street near the National Theatre in Iaşi, and during the winter and spring he took part in concerts at the Theatre, as well as touring hospitals and refugee camps during the day. At some of these concerts he had a new accompanist, Niculae Caravia, who had first come to his attention in the previous year as a competitor for the composition prize which he had founded. They quickly established an intuitive musical rapport, and Caravia remained Enescu's favourite accompanist for the rest of his life. In the course of 1917 and 1918 they gave innumerable

---

[16] *Ibid.*, p. 39. Jora was related by marriage to the Princess Cantacuzino.

[17] Ranta, 'Sub vraja': 'Mi-a fost dat nu odată să observ câta înseninare înflorea pe obrajii suferinzilor după primele note. Această transformare în suflet e suprema raţiune de a fi a muzicei. Dacă n'ar exista minunatul ei ecou pacificator, purificator, muzica ar fi o absurdă înşiruire de sunete'.

Enescu (seated, left) at a hospital in 1916

concerts, and went on tours of Moldavian towns and villages. Caravia has described the difficulties they encountered, and also the gratitude of the audiences, who would follow Enescu back to his hotel and wait for him to appear on the balcony. 'He always thanked them and tried to find some excuse for the performance, explaining that the piano was very out of tune and he had to tune his violin accordingly.'[18]

In early March 1917, at the suggestion of the Romanian G.H.Q., Enescu made a short trip to Russia, where he gave concerts for the Red Cross in St Petersburg. On 10 March (25 February, old style), while the city was paralysed by strikes and rioting was breaking out in the streets, Enescu played to a packed house in the Maryinski Theatre. The rest of the year he spent in and around Iaşi. Maruca was there too, in the Cantacuzino town residence; she had been

---

[18] Caravia, 'Fifty Years of Friendship', *Adam*, Year 43 (1981), Nos. 434–6, pp. 25–8 (p. 26); see also his article 'A Collaboration of more than 40 Years', *Romanian Review*, Vol. 35 (1981), No. 8, pp. 127–8.

working as a nurse since the outbreak of hostilities. On a few occasions in the despairing autumn and winter of 1917 she gathered a handful of friends there, and they listened to Enescu playing the violin or performing long sections of *Parsifal* at the piano.[19] Enescu did not give way to despair. Late in 1917 he formed what must have seemed an absurd project, that of assembling a complete symphony orchestra out of refugees and local players and training it for public performance. With the help of Caravia, Drăghici and others he assembled 60 musicians and began to rehearse. Their first concert was in December, and it was followed by 26 more in early 1918. They borrowed scores from the Conservatoire and each player copied out his own part. The rehearsals, taken by Enescu and lasting four hours each day, were held in the machine-room of the Theatre building.[20] And throughout this period of hectic organising and playing, Enescu was working steadily on his own Third Symphony.

The collapse of the Russian war effort, culminating in the Bolshevik-German Treaty of Brest Litovsk in March 1918, made it impossible for the Romanians to keep up even their tenuous position in Moldavia. Years later Enescu was to speak bitterly of what he felt was a Soviet betrayal of his country.[21] Romania was forced to come to peace with the Central Powers in May. The only consolation was the acquisition of the neighbouring Russian territory of Bessarabia, which had a majority population of Romanians. The Germans agreed to let Romania annex the area; and the Bessarabians, having declared their own independence after the breakdown of Tsarist government, had soon felt threatened by their other neighbours, the newly independent Ukrainians, and voted in April for unification with Romania. In late March and early April Enescu and Caravia took part in a special concert-tour of Bessarabia, arranged

[19] Queen Marie, *Story of my Life*, Vol. 3, pp. 252 and 297; *Contrepoint* p. 56.

[20] Drăghici, 'The Great Friend in my Life', *Romanian Review*, Vol. 35 (1981), No. 8, pp. 130–40 (p. 132); Caravia, 'Collaboration', p. 127.

[21] *Contrepoint*, p. 56.

Enescu at Iaşi in 1918

by the Romanian government to promote a favourable attitude to unification. In Chişinău (Kishinev), the Bess-arabian capital, they were obliged to woo their partly Russian audience with two concertos by Tchaikovsky – Enescu's least favourite composer.[22]

After the treaty was signed in May, Enescu refused an offer of a place in the French diplomatic party which was leaving the country by train, and stayed on in Iaşi. He continued to take part in concerts there, including one in honour of Caudella, but he was at last able to devote more time to composition. By early September he had finished his Third Symphony. The war ended with a surprising twist: on 10 November, a week after the surrender of Austria-Hungary and a day before the German capitulation, Romania cannily re-entered the War on the side of the Allies. This action was eventually to earn the Romanian state huge territorial gains at Trianon. For Enescu per-sonally, the ending of the war brought two long-term

[22] Caravia, 'Fifty Years', p. 26.

anxieties. One was financial. His ambition had always been that, after repaying his father and accumulating a reasonable amount of savings from his concert-tours (savings which were invested by his father, partly in land), he would retire to the country and dedicate his time to composition. But the collapse of the Romanian economy in the War had worn away his savings, and the land reforms promised to the peasants by King Ferdinand during the War were to lead shortly to the expropriation of a large part of his father's estate. Costache Enescu died in December 1919. There was little for Enescu to inherit, and he had to reconcile himself to starting again at the beginning and returning to the concert platforms of Europe.[23]

Enescu's other anxiety also involved a crushing sense of having to start all over again. In the summer of 1917 the Romanian government had sent its gold reserves by train to Moscow, intending them to be passed on to London. Among the various crates of documents which accompanied the bullion was a big wooden box labelled 'Musique Manuscrite Georges Enesco'. It contained a large collection of his manuscripts, including even the childhood pieces which he had fondly preserved. It also included the only copies of several recent works: the Second Orchestral Suite, the Second Symphony, and all Enescu's sketches for the opera *Oedipe*, which he was now hoping to complete. The box reached Moscow and disappeared. Nothing was heard of it for seven long years. Then in 1924, as Miron Grindea has recently revealed, it was Bruno Walter who intervened with the Soviet authorities on Enescu's behalf; he described Enescu as 'like a father who assumes his sons are missing in action', and offered to bring the box back from Moscow himself.[24] Eventually it was located in the Kremlin and returned to Paris with French diplomatic help. Perhaps it seems odd that Enescu, with his prodigious memory, should have felt so crippled by the loss of his manuscripts. In fact it

---

[23] *Contrepoint*, p. 22; Dianu, 'Cu d. George Enescu', p. 3.

[24] Grindea prints the entire letter by Walter (who describes Enescu as 'an unusually gifted musician, and, moreover, an extremely endearing and dignified person') in 'Notes on a Genius', p. 9.

simply helps to show that his gift was not a mere photographic memory: music spoke to him as a kind of statement,
and he remembered what it said. The finished works of
other composers, if they were well said, would remain
indelibly in his mind. But in the case of his own works the
music was a palimpsest in which there lay, behind every
achieved musical statement, innumerable layers of earlier,
less finished and less clearly stated drafts – drafts both
physical and mental. To recover these pieces might involve
retracing all the steps of revision and reduction over which
Enescu had agonised so much during the long and painstaking process of composition.

When the First World War broke out Enescu was coming
to the end of two years' work on his Second Symphony;
when it ended he was completing his Third. In later years
Fourth and Fifth Symphonies were projected, but the
sketches for them were abandoned. So these two symphonies of 1912–18 remain, with *Oedipe* and the Third Orchestral Suite, the summits of his large-scale orchestral writing.
And they are certainly conceived on a grand scale. The
Second Symphony lasts more than three-quarters of
an hour and is scored for large forces, which grow as
the work progresses: the celesta and 'one or more harps'
are joined in the last movement by castanets, tambourine,
tamtam, glockenspiel, piano and harmonium. In this
movement in particular the work shows an intense concern
with timbre. Different shades and gradations of orchestral
colour are constantly shifting, overlapping and dissolving.
The orchestration has many of the Enescian finger-prints
which one finds (applied with a lighter touch) in
the scoring of *Oedipe*. Intricate fragments of melodic
and ornamental material are entrusted to inner instrumental voices – sometimes to solo strings – which can all
too easily become drowned in performance. To anyone who
has first got to know the work from a recording, reading
the score comes as a revelation: there is so much going on
in what Bentoiu[25] has called this 'magic jungle' on the

[25] *Capodopere*, p. 156.

page. Each part is filled with Enescu's minutely detailed instructions; the string players are often told not only which bowing to use but also which string or which position; and there is a wide range of indications of mood and expression, including *mormorando* ('murmuring'), *bisbigliando* ('whispering'), *lusingando* ('flattering' or 'fawning'), *con calore, con grazia* and *con impeto*. This is certainly Romantic music, but it is far more dense and intricate, far harder to place or pin down, than the First Symphony. There is a strong and evident debt to Strauss, not only in the *Heldenleben*-like opening of the first movement but also in the perpetual chromatic transformations of the harmony; the harmonic effect here becomes more richly kaleidoscopic than in any of Strauss' tone-poems, and is a reminder of the admiration Enescu expressed in 1912 and 1915 for *Elektra* and *Salome*.

Enescu told Gavoty that he had written much of this Symphony without the help of a piano (which he would normally make use of when composing to check the effects of chords and harmonic progressions).[26] We can believe him when he says this cost him 'an appalling effort' – even though his inner ear was, as this score shows, prodigious. The harmonic realm he had entered was beyond the horizon of the critics who attended the first performance in Bucharest in 1915: they accused the work of 'impressionism', of 'futurism' and of sounding 'foreign'.[27] Their failure to notice that the first movement is in classical sonata-form is understandable; their lack of response to the work's generous fund of melodies (especially the hauntingly graceful second subject) is not. However, one can sympathise with their puzzlement over the last movement (Ex. 10, pp. 126–7). The constant re-combining here of fragments of the earlier themes must have seemed transparently clear to Enescu himself, with all the preceding music present to his mind, but to the listener it may pose a demanding or even bewildering task. And Enescu himself was not fully satisfied with the work: he told Gavoty in 1952 that it was far from

[26] *Contrepoint*, p. 72.

[27] *Monografie*, pp. 426–7.

finished ('loin d'être au point').[28] After the recovery of the manuscript in 1924 he had intended to make a thorough revision of the work, but other commitments had intervened. The first performance remained, sadly, the only one in his lifetime.[29]

The Third Symphony was begun at Sinaia in May 1916, in the last few months before Romania entered the war. The second movement was finished in January 1918 in Iaşi, at the blackest period of the fighting, and the third was written during the rest of that year.[30] Emotional intensity may therefore be expected, but it would be foolish to derive a sort of psychological-historical 'programme' from this sequence to explain the music – as if Enescu had no idea, at the time of writing each movement, what the character of the following movement would be. There is little point either in trying, as many critics have done (starting with Pierre Lalo in 1921), to identify the programme of a 'Dantesque trilogy' in the work, although the paradisal serenity of the last movement may make this a tempting pattern to apply.[31]

The Third Symphony follows Enescu's usual practice of developing in different ways the same melodic material; the only 'explanation' of how he uses this material in the later parts of the work must be sought in how he does so in the earlier parts. This is not, of course, causal explanation. The overall pattern of moods is as follows. The first movement is alternately brooding, questioning, heroic and lyrical; the second is a sort of scherzo, often blackly sinister but including, fragmentarily, a sprightly march (which, though it certainly never becomes triumphal, is not treated with Mahlerian sarcasm); and the third is serene in a solemn,

[28] *Entretiens*, tape 18 (Gavoty has altered this phrase in his text).

[29] The second was in Romania in 1961; the Symphony was published (in score only) in 1965.

[30] Oprescu and Jora, *Enescu*, pp. 180, 183 and 184.

[31] See the reports of the French press in *Muzica*, Vol. 3, 1921, Nos. 5–6, p. 119, and Bălan, *Mesajul-Estetica*, pp. 120–1. Most accounts have required the awkward sequence Purgatory–Inferno–Paradise. Alessandrescu suggested the more sensible but less Dantesque Earth–Hell–Paradise (*ibid.*).

Ex. 10

An example of the orchestral texture of the last movement of the Second Symphony

almost liturgical way.[32] It ends in a sort of quiet ecstasy, with gossamer-thin orchestral textures and the use at one point of a little bell which, Enescu specifies in the score, 'should have the same sort of sonority as the bells which are used in Catholic churches at the Elevation of the Host'.

The scoring is even more lavish than in the Second Symphony. It requires, in addition to piano, two harps, organ, celesta and glockenspiel, a xylophone, a wind-machine and a four-part chorus. The chorus, which is wordless, is employed in the last movement only, as an additional instrument in the texture of timbres. Enescu even specifies that boy altos are to be used if possible. The large brass section includes six horns (sometimes divided into six different voices), a piccolo trumpet and a valve trombone (the equivalent of the Wagnerian bass trumpet). For the climax of the second movement Enescu instructs the entire brass section to stand up for 48 bars, playing from parts attached to their instruments. Despite this proliferation of resources, the broad marshalling of strings and wind forces in the score often seems almost solid and stable by comparison with the complex fragmentation of voices and timbres in the Second Symphony. The harmonic language draws heavily on that of the previous Symphony, but the modulations and transformations seem somehow less Straussian: they are connected instead to a sense of an interlocking set of complex modes, with their shifting 'mobile' notes. In this way the Symphony looks forward to *Oedipe*; and there are indeed melodic cells in this work (especially in the second movement) which present, in germinal form, some of the principal motifs of the opera.

The first performance, conducted by Enescu in Bucharest

---

[32] Bentoiu makes an interesting comparison between this march and Tchaikovsky's in the third movement of the *Pathétique* (the only movement Enescu liked in that work): *Capodopere*, p. 208. I cannot agree with the identification of Mahlerian sarcasm here (Bălan, *Mesajul-Estetica*, p. 128; *Monografie*, p. 472); there are no distancing effects of irony or pastiche in Enescu's music. Gabriel Grovlez wrote, rather deliciously, of a performance in 1924 that it 'fait penser à Gustav Mahler – un Mahler qui aurait du goût' (Anon., *Georges Enesco. Notes biographiques*, Bucharest, 1928, from a review in *Le Courrier musical*, 15 March 1924).

in May 1919, was a great success.[33] No doubt this partly reflected the admiration which Enescu had earned in Romania during the war years. But it is also true that this Symphony, though more advanced than its predecessor, is somehow less difficult to grasp. Yet the composer was not satisfied with it, and spent several months in 1920 revising the orchestration. Again the work was well received when the revised version was played in Paris at the end of February 1921; but again Enescu became dissatisfied. He was still revising the Symphony more than thirty years later.[34]

While Enescu had been working initially on the Symphony in 1916 he had begun to sketch two other ambitious orchestral works which, unfortunately, were never finished. One of these, a 'Symphonie en fa mineur pour Baryton seul, Choeur et Orchestre, sur les paroles du Psaume LXXXVI', of which only ten pages survive, may eventually have been subsumed under the project of the Third Symphony.[35] The other was a setting for orchestra, choir and soloists of a work by the great nineteenth-century Romanian poet Mihai Eminescu. The poem, entitled *Strigoii* (*Ghosts*), is a sort of heroic ballad of the supernatural. The first part shows King Arald in the royal chapel, kneeling by the body of his dead bride Marie, and recalling their love. Then he visits an old magician, who takes him into the earth and summons up her ghost. Then, with each successive nocturnal meeting, death gradually strengthens its hold on the young king. In the last part death finally claims him as they ride together through the forest, and the light of dawn destroys the newly regained life of his bride. If this seems an unpromising subject for a musical setting, one should perhaps think of *Orfeo* and the *Erlkönig*. What is more, the poem is full of evocations of sounds: the priests singing in the chapel, the

[33] *Monografie*, pp. 469–70.

[34] *Scrisori*, Vol. 1, p. 396 (12 June 1951).

[35] See Moisescu, 'Lucrări inedite', p. 14 and Wilhelm Berger, *Muzica simfonică*, Vol. 4, *Modernă-contemporană 1930–50*, Editura Muzicală, Bucharest, 1976, p. 26.

murmuring cries of spirit voices, the rustling of leaves in the wind. Enescu's setting uses the whole poem (59 stanzas of five lines each); soprano and tenor soloists sing the parts of Marie and Arald, and the narrative is entrusted to a baritone, treating some stanzas *parlando*. Only a very rough version of a short score was completed, and from this the Romanian musicologist Cornel Țăranu has painstakingly reconstructed the work for piano and soloists alone.[36] Even in this reduced and partly conjectural form some features emerge. The accompaniment is richly imitative of the sounds described in the poem, while still constructing these effects out of the music's store of motifs (as at the line 'Vîntul geme prin codri cu amar', 'The wind groans bitterly through the forest', after the death of Arald). And the writing, though harmonically close to the language of the Third Symphony, is in places filled with the sort of trailing chromatic figures which give a strangely Skryabinesque quality to the piano accompaniments of the Fernand Gregh Songs.[37]

Between the two massive symphonies which Enescu completed during these years there lies a group of oddly contrasting works. The so-called Third Piano Suite is really not a suite at all but a set of separate pieces. It is sometimes referred to under the title *Pièces Impromptues*. The pieces were all written between 1913 and 1916; Enescu later thought he had lost the manuscript, and it was rediscovered only after his death, by Romeo Drăghici. No one hearing this group of pieces could possibly guess that it was composed under the threat of war. It contains some of Enescu's most limpid and untroubled piano music, written with what seems at times (in the opening piece, 'Mélodie', for example) like ingenuous simplicity. A wistful 'Mazurka Mélancolique' has something of the character of Franck's *Danse Lente*; and there

---

[36] See Țăranu's account in 'Enescu în lumina unor lucrări inedite', *Simpozion George Enescu*, pp. 231–4. The manuscript (Romanian Academy Library MS R 7.378; dated October–November 1916) is very rough indeed, and in places quite indecipherable.

[37] See below, p. 132.

is humour too, in a 'Burlesque' which chatters with acciaccaturas and contains fragments of popular dances, cymbalom music and a fairground waltz. The most fascinating piece is the last, which begins as a 'Chorale' and then passes into a 'Carillon Nocturne', imitating the sound of monastery bells echoing over the mountain pastures at Sinaia. The sonority of the bells is captured in an extraordinary way: above the main ringing notes, the impure harmonics are conjured up with clusters (spread over two octaves) of simultaneous fifths, sixths and sevenths, *pianissimo*. But the piece is not mere onomatopoeia. It points forward to the structure and harmony of the third movement of the First Piano Sonata, eight years later.

The *Three Songs on Poems by Fernand Gregh*, Op. 19, offer an almost complete contrast to the Third Suite. Only the *Carillon* seems to approach them in terms of complexity and of distance from normal harmonic procedures. They were written in June 1915 and February 1916, the third song being later revised in 1936. (A fourth song on words by Gregh, *De la Flûte au Cor*, is mistakenly included with the Op. 19 songs in the modern Bucharest edition; it was written in 1902. It was probably at that period that Enescu became personally acquainted with Gregh, who was a leading literary figure in the world of the Paris salons.[38]) The poems are all similar in character: atmospheric expressions of tristesse, resignation or longing – a French symbolist equivalent of Romanian 'dor'. Lines such as these gave Enescu an opportunity to use his most delicate palette of harmonic and pianistic devices:

> Seulement, sur un fond d'indéfinis murmures,
> L'égouttement léger de la pluie aux ramures.[39]

---

[38] Gregh was a friend of Proust; he also knew Ravel and Debussy, and was the person who broke the news to the latter that he had been made a 'chevalier' of the Légion d'honneur. The composer's first words, Gregh recalled, were 'Il faut télégraphier aux Debussy' – meaning his parents. See Gregh, *L'Âge d'or*, Paris, 1947, p. 11.

[39] 'Only, in a background of vague murmurs, the light sound of rain dripping in the branches.'

The final poem (*L'Ombre est Bleue*) elicits an unearthly rippling of cross-rhythms and suspensions (Ex. 11, pp. 134–5) to accompany its image of the gentle beating of angels' wings:

> Qui lentement, parmi les ombres embaumées,
> Et le sommeil immense et bleu de toutes choses,
> Eventent le silence et font pâmer les roses.[40]

Enescu has here developed further the style of rhythmical fluidity foreshadowed in the *Pavane* of the Second Piano Suite and experimented with in the 1907 *Nocturne*. It is not just rhythmical 'coloration', however; it is integrally bound up with the harmonic patterning of the writing, where modulations and quasi-cadences are lightly hinted at, passed through or passed by, as the suspensions overlap and dissolve against one another. Sometimes the use of trailing chromatic figures reminds one of Skryabin (in, for example, the *meno vivo* passages of the Fifth Sonata). But there is no sense of Skryabin's chordal system at work here. The best comparison, though it is a very lame one, might be to describe this music as a sort of liquidised mixture of Fauré and Messiaen.

After the exotic dream-world of these songs the Second Orchestral Suite, Op. 20, comes again as a complete contrast. It is the culmination of Enescu's 'neo-classical' series; the outer movements ('Ouverture' and 'Bourrée') are based on a theme of bustling mock-Baroque violin figurations, and the inner movements are a 'Sarabande', a 'Gigue', a 'Menuet grave' and an 'Air'. The writing in the fast movements is crisp and sometimes humorous, in a manner which might seem indebted to Prokofiev's *Classical Symphony* (1917), Ravel's *Tombeau de Couperin* (1917) or Stravinsky's *Pulcinella* (1919) – except that Enescu's Suite predates all of these. It was mainly composed in August 1915 (one month after writing the second of the Gregh Songs and the 'Mazurka' and 'Burlesque' of the Third Piano Suite); as with the Second Symphony, the initial short score was

---

[40] 'Which, in the embalmed shadows and the immense blue slumber of all things, slowly fan the silence and make the roses swoon'.

written without the help of a piano.[41] The orchestration was completed by December, and the Suite was performed twice in 1916 in Bucharest before it underwent its long hibernation in Moscow. It remained one of Enescu's favourite works, and there is a recording, dating from 1946, of him conducting the 'U.S.S.R. State Orchestra' in one movement, the 'Gigue'.[42] One sign of his affection for this Suite is his constant desire to revise it: he promised the conductor George Georgescu in 1935 that he was reworking the score for the last time, but in 1951 he was still planning to make further changes.[43] By comparison with the Symphonies the Suite is a simple work, with clear, open textures. Enescu's obsession with revision reflects his sense of how precisely the balance and clarity of the score are obtained. There is nothing casual about this simplicity, and the work is not a mere sequence of separate pieces thrown together; there are explicit thematic links between the movements. Nor is it one-dimensionally mock-Baroque. The 'Air', for example, breathes the modal atmosphere of a Romanian doina and builds up suddenly into a romantic climax which reveals the kinship of its central motif with the figure which dominates the accompaniment of the first Gregh Song, 'Pluie'.

The same motif recurs in a work written in the early months of the following year (1916): the Piano Trio in A minor. Enescu never got beyond the rough draft of this piece; he thought it was lost, and it was only found among his papers after his death. The pianist and musicologist Hilda Jerea has edited the Trio, and it turns out to be a peculiarly transitional work. The outer movements (*Allegro moderato* and *Andante – Vivace amabile*) carry the style of the First Piano Quartet forward into the harmonic world of the Third Symphony; the meditative-rhapsodic opening of the piece is closely akin to that of the Piano Quintet, written 24

---

[41] See the chronology in Oprescu and Jora, *Enescu*, pp. 175–7; *Entretiens*, tape 14 (saying it was written 'à la montagne').

[42] Listed by Gavoty in *Yehudi Menuhin – Georges Enesco*, Kister, Geneva, 1955, p. 32 (U.S.S.R. 013664/Supraphon 40064), but mis-identified as an arrangement of a (non-existent) 'Gigue' in the Op. 10 Piano Suite.

[43] *Scrisori*, Vol. 1, pp. 340 and 396.

Ex. 11

Enescu, around 1920

years later. The central movement is, surprisingly, an
Allegretto con variazioni – the last time Enescu was to write a
set of formal variations. Here, especially in the first variation, (*Presto, scherzando*), the writing is much less harmonically demanding, and is closer in spirit to some of the pieces
in the Third Piano Suite.[44]

Enescu told Gavoty that, naturally, he had composed
'rather little' during the War.[45] Yet the tally is an impressive one, and after the unproductive period between 1909
and 1913 the war years seem to have provoked a burst of
creativity. The character of these new works, however, is
often astonishingly untouched by the atmosphere of crisis
and suffering which surrounded the composer. Nowhere is

[44] The Trio is Romanian Academy Library MS R 7.397. The first
movement is dated (from Enescu's sickbed in a Bucharest sanatorium)
5 March 1916, the second 20 March and the third 22 March.

[45] *Contrepoint*, p. 58.

this more true than in the opening movement of the First String Quartet (Op. 22, No. 1), which Enescu started writing in 1916. (He resumed work on the Quartet in mid-1918 and completed it in December 1920.) The first movement is pervaded by a mood of serene, gentle nostalgia; there is fierceness and passion elsewhere in this work (with expression marks such as *feroce* and *stridente*), but the whole Quartet goes far beyond any possible explanation in terms of its origin in wartime. It offers, in the course of its 47 minutes, a complete and self-contained world of feeling. The writing, especially in the later movements, is immensely resourceful, making enormous demands on the players' powers of ensemble as well as on their individual techniques. Even the opening movement, which is at first deceptively simple in its construction, is hugely complex when compared with the surviving sketch of a quartet movement of 1906 in which some of its material first appeared.[46] In that sketch Enescu seems to have been influenced by a Debussian technique of rhythmical repetitions of motifs; here his writing is rhythmically sinuous and supple. It is also highly complex thematically: a very long and detailed analysis would be needed to show how all the themes are constantly adapting a central stock of note-patterns and intervals, building melodic lines out of combinations of these patterns and flooding the score with half-heard reminiscences and anticipations.[47] And in formal terms the Quartet also shows Enescu's ability to absorb and transmute traditional structures: the first movement is fundamentally in sonata form, the second (*Andante pensieroso*) is a sort of lied, with variations woven into it, the third is a scherzo (in which the harsh and resonant use of folk elements comes at times curiously close to Janáček), and the fourth is an unprecedented combination of cyclical re-development, sonata form and a sequence of variations on a new, chorale-like theme, culminating in a tumultuous

---

[46] The sketch, Enescu Museum MS 2863, has been published in photo-reproduction by Titus Moisescu (Bucharest, 1985).

[47] The best analysis so far is in Bentoiu, *Capodopere*, pp. 221–41.

climax and a massive chordal ending. This is a work which needs repeated hearings if the listener is to find his bearings in it. The parts (though, frustratingly, not the score) are still available from Salabert; but the Quartet has received few, if any, performances outside Romania since its French premiere was given in 1921 by the Flonzaley Quartet – to whom, in gratitude, Enescu dedicated the work.

VII

OEDIPE

In the years which followed the ending of the war Enescu was plunged once again into the life of an international virtuoso. But for Enescu himself the 1920s were dominated by one great task: the writing of *Oedipe*. As we have seen, he had already been working on this during the war, writing sketches which were then lost for seven years in Moscow. But the origins of the work go back to several years before the war. Enescu told Gavoty that he had first conceived the idea of writing an opera in 1906, and had considered and rejected a number of sub-Maeterlinckian libretti. Then, in 1909, he saw the great French actor Mounet-Sully in Sophocles' *Oedipus Tyrannus* at the Comédie Française. He was transfixed by this performance – years later when he composed the passage where Oedipus blinds himself, it was Mounet-Sully's terrible cry of pain that he was trying to capture – and he became obsessed with the idea of writing an opera about Oedipus.[1] His first sketches of the music date from early 1910.

Immediately, of course, he felt the need of a libretto. Enescu had a particularly strong belief in the importance of the words and the dramatic action in opera. Years later (and with, perhaps, a touch of his characteristic humility) he compared the opera-composer's task to that of a jeweller making a setting for a precious stone: 'the jewel itself is the

---

[1] *Contrepoint*, pp. 59–60. Octavian Cosma discusses the early chronology, and cogently argues that Enescu must have seen the play in 1909 (*Oedip-ul Enescian*, Editura Muzicală, Bucharest, 1967, pp. 29–30); Enescu says 1910, but several of the dates he gives in his discussion of *Oedipe* with Gavoty are wrong.

action, the dramatic conflict'.[2] In another interview he gave a fuller account, in which the music's role seems less subordinate, but that of the play remains primary:

> The substratum of music gives the whole play not only an atmosphere but also an important psychological commentary. The silences of the actors, as well as their words, can be underlined and reflected in music. The same goes for gestures, feelings, intentions [. . .]. In *Pelléas* Debussy follows this principle – which is basically Wagnerian [. . .]. The words are respected by the music, but at the same time the music doesn't merely underline the substance of the text, it transforms it: although music is an abstract language, it heightens the effect of the text with features which speak more directly to the audience's feelings.[3]

And when Enescu explained to Gavoty the rules which he had tried to follow in writing his opera, he produced a list of three requirements which seem either to apply primarily to the librettist or to reflect the importance of the librettist's work: 'One: it must keep going. No pathos, no repetitions, no unnecessary talk. The action must take shape quickly. Two: the public mustn't get bored (this follows directly from rule one). Three: the listener must understand the text'.[4]

Through the music critic Pierre Lalo, Enescu was put in touch with a well-known poet and dramatist, Edmond Fleg, who had recently written the libretto for Bloch's opera *Macbeth*. Fleg was a remarkable person; Menuhin has described him as 'one of the most admirable human beings I have ever known, gentle, idealistic, dedicated to service [. . .]'.[5] He was a man of wide European culture. Born Edmond Fleigenheimer, he was brought up in Geneva, where his father was Professor of Comparative Philology. Both parents were devoutly Orthodox

---

[2] Vasile Christian, 'Un geniu autentic al artei romîneşti, George Enescu', *Femeia şi caminul*, Vol. 2, No. 22, 6 May 1945, p. 7.

[3] Interview with Ticu Archip in *Dimineaţa*, 1945, quoted in Oprescu and Jora, *Enescu*, p. 35.

[4] *Contrepoint*, p. 66.

[5] *Unfinished Journey*, Macdonald and Jane's, London, 1976, p. 106.

Enescu (aged 70) imitating the actor Mounet-Sully in the role of Oedipus

Jews. Fleg later abandoned most of the formal observances of
his faith, but he was influenced by the more hellenistic
mysticism of the cabbalistic tradition, and he remained a firm
defender of Judaism against all the various movements of
antisemitism from the Dreyfus case to the 1930s.[6] Enescu met
him some time between 1910 and 1912, and fired him with
enthusiasm for the project. They decided that the opera
should be based not only on *Oedipus Tyrannus*, the play in which
Oedipus makes the discovery that he has killed his father and
married his mother, but also on Sophocles' other Oedipus
play, *Oedipus at Colonnus*, which presents his final self-
justification and his death in an aura of sanctity. In 1912 Fleg
duly presented the composer with a libretto divided into two
halves, which would be performed on two successive nights.
Enescu was a little dismayed by this; no doubt he was
thinking partly of the stamina of the audience, but he must
also have felt the demands of his own musical character,
with its striving to make each composition a single organic
whole. He pleaded with the poet: 'Do what good chefs do.
Put it back on the stove and let it reduce'.[7] Fleg went back to
work, but it was only after the long interruption of the war
that he was able to give Enescu a new, reduced and
concentrated version of his work.

The new libretto was not only reduced in length; it was
also expanded, so to speak, in content. Fleg was now
offering a single play in four acts, of which the last two
corresponded to the two plays by Sophocles. Fleg's first act
is set in Thebes soon after the birth of Oedipus (son of King
Laios and Queen Jocasta). It presents the moment where
fate first begins to imprint its pattern on his life: the
moment where the joyful baptism of the infant Oedipus is
interrupted by Teiresias' prophecy of parricide, causing
Laios to have the child taken away and (as he thinks)
abandoned to his death. The second act is in three scenes.
First, Oedipus appears as a young man at Corinth (where,
having been taken as a foundling to King Polybos and

---

[6] See especially his book *Why I am a Jew* (tr. L. Wise), New York, 1929.

[7] *Contrepoint*, p. 60.

Queen Merope, he has been brought up as their son);
he tells Merope that Apollo has prophesied that he will
commit parricide and incest, and says he has therefore
decided to leave Corinth and travel to the ends of the
earth. In the second scene his wanderings have brought
him to a crossing of three paths. He is about to turn
back when a storm breaks, and Laios enters with his
servants, arrogantly striking out at Oedipus to make
him stand aside. In an instant Oedipus has killed them all.
The third scene presents his encounter with the Sphinx,
which is terrorising Thebes, lying at the gate of the city and
killing all those who cannot answer its riddling question.
Oedipus gives the answer; the Sphinx dies; and he is
crowned king by the grateful Thebans and given Jocasta's
hand in marriage.

By adding these two acts to the material directly supplied
by Sophocles, Fleg was subtly altering the emphasis of the
work. His libretto enables us to see the life of Oedipus not
as an exceptional and terrible example of the workings of
the gods, but rather as a symbol standing heroically for the
nature of human life in general, with its processes of
suffering and knowledge. We are shown a complete cycle of
infancy-youth-adulthood-old age. In Sophocles, as Oedipus
comes to understand his past, it takes on the nature of an
objective pattern, existing, as it were, outside him, and
confronting him. In Fleg's libretto we go with him from the
start through that pattern, and our sense of it is centred on
his intentions, his hopes and his fears. This is a more
anthropocentric, more humanistic work.

Fleg neatly underlines this with his treatment of the
Sphinx's riddle. In the Greek myth the question was: 'What
goes on four legs in the morning, two legs in the day and
three legs in the evening?' The answer was 'man' (who
crawls as a baby and walks with a stick in old age). In Fleg's
play the answer is the same, but the question is different.
The Sphinx gives a chilling description of how its father,
all-powerful Destiny, is gradually destroying all things and
dragging the gods from their thrones. It asks the question: is
there anything in the universe that is stronger than Destiny?
Oedipus cries 'Man', and the Sphinx begins immediately to

die. But it is not necessary to conclude, as Romanian commentators have tended to do, that the message of the work is one of straightforward humanist optimism. The Sphinx's paroxysms are made to sound like laughter, and its final taunt to Oedipus is: 'The future will show you whether the dying Sphinx is crying at its defeat or laughing at its victory'.[8] Oedipus' answer may have been correct, but it is precisely this solving of the riddle which brings about the next stage of the fulfilment of his destiny, with his crowning by the Thebans and his marriage to Jocasta. Oedipus does not defeat destiny in the sense of breaking the pattern it imposes; his victory is an inner one, a redemptive process of suffering and understanding. Maruca Cantacuzino made a perceptive comment on the finished opera when she observed how odd it was that Enescu, the profoundly Christian believer, had evoked through his music a world of pagan classicism, while Fleg, the liberal intellectual Jew, had instilled into the final scene an essentially Christian sense of redemption.[9]

Enescu was satisfied with this libretto and started work again on the opera in 1921, having finally completed his First String Quartet and his revision of the Third Symphony at the end of the previous year. His first draft of the entire opera, written on two or three staves as a sort of piano reduction, was composed in a villa at Sinaia in July and August. The speed at which he did this is staggering. The last act, which in its finished form takes 36 minutes in performance, was written in six days; Act Three, which takes 45 minutes, was written in 24 hours.[10] Obviously he was drawing on the memory of his wartime sketches. But those sketches, written without this libretto, can only have supplied a store of musical material; the precise application of it to the text had to be thought out anew, bar by bar. The concentration of this work helped to ensure the overall

---

[8] 'L'avenir te dira si la Sphinge en mourant pleure de sa défaite, ou rit de sa victoire!'

[9] Marie Cantacuzino-Enescu, 'Pynx – le créateur', *Adam*, Year 43, 1981, Nos. 434–6, pp. 25–8 (p. 26).

[10] See the dates of completion in Octavian Cosma, *Oedip-ul Enescian*, p. 74.

structural unity of the opera, which Enescu was later to describe as 'constructed like a symphony'.[11] Explaining to Gavoty the difficulty he had faced in writing the opera, he said: 'It is a terrible thing: *you have to think of everything at the same time. If you could just attend to each detail in turn, it would be no trouble. But no, you have to give your audience the feeling that the whole work holds together because it all came from a single flow of ideas* [. . .]'.[12] Despite the brevity of this initial period of composition, the difficulty Enescu felt most keenly was, typically, that of economy and compression: he abandoned a large orchestral section which he had at first intended for the scene with the Sphinx in Act Two, because he realised that it would overbalance the work and detract from the climax of the whole opera in Act Three.[13]

Later in 1921 Enescu embarked on the second and final draft in piano reduction. Gradually the work was completed during the course of 1922. Enescu played through some of the acts, as he finished them, to a select group of musical friends which included Jora, Alessandrescu and Emmanoil Ciomac (who was later to write the Romanian translation of the libretto). Sometimes he made changes at their suggestion. Ciomac once complained that there was no special melodic element to accompany the appearance of Oedipus' daughter Antigone at the end of Act Three. Enescu duly wrote in a new theme, and when Ciomac asked him how he had done this 'he replied that it was derived from one of the principal leitmotivs in the score, and that in any case there was not a single note that wasn't logically conditioned by the rest of the symphony'.[14] On 19 November 1922 they heard, for the first time, a complete play-through of the

[11] 'Oedipe e clădit pe un plan simfonic': Cardine-Petit, 'Oedipe de George Enescu la Opera din Paris' (anon. tr. of interview by Cardine-Petit in *Paris Midi*), *Adevĕrul*, Vol. 50, No. 15994, 12 March 1936.

[12] *Contrepoint*, p. 72.

[13] *Ibid.*, pp. 66 and 72.

[14] Ciomac, article in *Revista fundaţiilor*, 1 June 1936, quoted in Cosma, *Oedip-ul Enescian*, p. 118.

score by Enescu, at Maruca's house in Bucharest.[15] The work of composition was finished at last. Long years of orchestration and detailed elaboration now lay ahead.

During the following years the reputation of the work gradually spread, as further glimpses of it were offered either in private or in the concert-hall: in 1923 Enescu once went through the opera at the piano in the École Normale de Musique in Paris, and a few years later he played it to a group of musicians and critics at the premises of *La Revue musicale*.[16] The orchestrated Theban Dances in Act One were played by the Colonne Orchestra in 1924, and the Cleveland Orchestra played them under Enescu's baton in the following year.[17] Interviewed in November 1924, Enescu said that the orchestration would take approximately one more year to complete; but in fact it was to drag on, with painful, painstaking slowness, until 1931.[18] Of course this delay is partly to be explained by Enescu's heavy schedules of concert tours during these years. But it also reflects the minute care and attention with which he worked out the polyphonic complexity of the scoring and tried to capture the precise nuances of timbre that he needed. While working uninterruptedly on *Oedipe* in the summer months he would take a whole day to complete a page, or even half a page, of orchestration.[19]

Enescu's first concern was with the balance between singers and orchestra. In a letter to Philippe Gaubert, who conducted the premiere, he wrote: 'The role of Oedipus is demanding. I've orchestrated as lightly as I can, so that he

[15] *Monografie*, p. 518.

[16] *Ibid.*, p. 524; Henri Prunières, review of *Oedipe* in *La Revue musicale*, Vol. 17, No. 164, March 1936, pp. 202–4.

[17] *Monografie*, p. 530; Oprescu and Jora, *Enescu*, p. 201.

[18] Massoff, 'Enescu vorbeşte'. Enescu dated his completion of Act Four 27 April 1931, but in September he was still making revisions (*Monografie*, p. 655).

[19] Alexandru Petrovici, 'Maestrul Enescu are aproape terminata opera Oedip', *Rampa*, Vol. 14, No. 3494, 14 September 1929 ('Am lucrat cu foarte mult spor in cursul verei şi chiar acum orchestrez cam o pagina pe zi'); Massoff, 'Enescu intim', p. 2.

can husband his strength'; and in an interview of 1931 he exclaimed:

> If I had an ideal stage and orchestra-pit like that at Bayreuth, I would orchestrate *Oedipe* quite differently. Oh, if only I could be sure that human voices could easily produce the effects I want – that would be a different matter! As it is, I'm trying to supplement the deficiencies of the human voice by means of combinations of instrumental timbres.[20]

The lightness of the scoring is not simply a matter of balance, however; it reflects Enescu's growing obsession with polyphonic and heterophonic textures in which each line needs to be heard as an individual voice. This follows on from the tendency of the Symphonies, especially the Second. But unlike the Symphonies, the writing in *Oedipe* eschews grand romantic gestures and constantly seeks effects of sparseness and concentration. As Enescu untranslatably remarked to Gavoty, he tried to resist 'les séductions de la facilité'.[21] There are grand climaxes in this score, but they are kept on a very short leash.

The forces Enescu requires may suggest a huge romantic score when they are listed together: they include several of the additional resources familiar from his Symphonies (piano, harmonium, celesta, glockenspiel), and the wind sections require Wagnerian families of instruments (three B flat clarinets, one high E flat clarinet, one bass clarinet; tenor, bass and contra-bass tubas). But Enescu applies them sparingly and precisely, to obtain exact shades of orchestral colour. An alto saxophone is used for a single phrase (*lamentoso*) in Act Two, and returns only at the end of Act Three to accompany the lament of the blinded Oedipus. Here and there are special effects: a pistol-shot, a whip against a drum, a nightingale (probably requiring a bird-

---

[20] Letter to Gaubert in Piru, 'A propos de quelques lettres', p. 182; Riegler-Dinu, 'George Enescu': 'Dacă mi-ar sta la dispoziţie o scenă şi o orchestră ideală ca ceea dela Bayreuth, a-şi orchestra altfel "Oedip". Ah, dacă aş fi sigur că vocile omeneşti ar atinge uşor efectele voite, ar fi alt ceva! Aşa însă caut să supleez insuficienţei materialului uman prin combinaţia de timbre instrumentale.'

[21] *Contrepoint*, p. 66.

The first page of the autograph full score of Oedipe

whistle rather than the HMV record used by Respighi in *The Pines of Rome*), and, most extraordinary of all, a saw, which takes over from the last shriek of the dying Sphinx and continues upwards in an unearthly glissando.[22] The entire scene with the Sphinx is a tour-de-force of orchestration, as well as of harmonic thinking. As the monster slowly awakes against a background of shifting wind chords and a bassoon solo, the piano part enters with *delicatissimo* runs in sinister, distorted chromatic modes, and there are strange runs and trills played by the violins *sul ponticello*. When the Sphinx speaks, the orchestral palette changes to a combination of bass flute, celesta, harmonium, four solo double basses and a tam-tam or suspended cymbal struck with a soft stick; other wind and string instruments are added very sparingly, the latter mainly *sul ponticello* or in harmonics. As Enescu told Gavoty: 'I tried to express the awakening of the Sphinx, in its smoky-black penumbral darkness, with music which was distant and nightmarish [. . .]. I had to invent its last scream, to imagine the unimaginable. When I put down my pen after finishing this scene I thought I would go mad [. . .]'.[23]

Elsewhere the orchestral effects Enescu achieves are more subdued. A pattern of flickering detail is created, with tiny phrases embroidered into the polyphonic texture of the music: here an isolated pair of harp chords, there a scurrying chromatic figure in the violins. But the overall pattern is often broadly sonorous nevertheless. The characteristic timbres of the work lie in the middle or lower strings and lower woodwind – especially the bassoon, the clarinets and the bass clarinet. Often there is a solo cello or viola doubling with a bassoon or a cor anglais; sometimes a solo double bass is paired with the contra-bassoon. Enescu knows how

[22] The saw is not mentioned in any standard work on orchestration. Enescu had probably heard it played by a M. Andolfi, who performed in a jazz band at a Parisian café and also played it at one of Jean Wiéner's concerts. Milhaud described it as 'a siren voice, ethereal, sobbing, trembling and uncertain; softer than the murmur of a saxophone, richer and more distant than the most exquisite human voice . . . '. (*Etudes*, Paris, 1927, pp. 83–4.)

[23] *Contrepoint*, p. 66.

to build powerful climaxes without relying on the brass; they contribute to but do not dominate the dark, sinewy sound which he achieves at these moments. Some instruments, including the flute, are used with conventional associations attached to them. In the 'Corinth' scene in Act Two Oedipus' troubled musings on stage are carried on against the background sound of a procession in honour of Aphrodite and Adonis: the music for this consists of an off-stage chorus accompanied by a harp and two flutes in the wings. A pastoral motif, reminiscent of a doina, is associated with shepherds from Act One onwards; it is played onstage, shortly before the entry and death of Laios in Act Two, by the shepherd who originally took the infant Oedipus to Corinth. This man eventually supplies the crucial missing link in the evidence which Oedipus acquires of his past in Act Three; the solitary intervention of this gentle flute phrase above the orchestra has a chilling effect when it appears there, foreshadowing the discovery. But, pastoral flute tunes apart, there is little or no specific evocation of 'Grecian' music. Enescu explained that he had decided to remain ignorant of ancient Greek modes, since 'nothing seems more tiresome to me than pseudo-historical reconstructions'.[24] The restraint and sombre sonority of this music does seem to match very effectively the spirit of Sophocles' plays; this, however, is a matter not of historical reference but of pure musical expression.

Modes are of course present (one might almost say, omnipresent) in this music, but they belong to Enescu's own individual language, with its fusion of Fauréan and Romanian modal elements with an advanced post-Wagnerian chromaticism. This modal style can be a powerful source of simplicity as well as complexity, as the serenity of much of the last act shows, with its gentle chanting in the sacred grove. But the complexity can be extreme, intensified as it is by the polyphonic cross-play of the writing and the fluid combination of different rhythms.

Some of the musicians who wrote reviews of the first performance were clearly disconcerted by their immersion in

[24] *Ibid.*

this strange, shifting sound-world. Milhaud was obviously completely out of his depth: 'We easily become lost in meanderings which appear to reflect a rather rhapsodic conception of the nature of music. We would prefer it if the melodic line were less fleeting, and if passages could be less episodic, more solidly constructed, with a more self-evident dramatic logic'.[25] Reynaldo Hahn similarly complained of Enescu's 'disdain for a whole range of normal musical resources, those which are drawn from melody, rhythm and tonal stability'.[26] No doubt one could find closely similar phrases in the early reviews of *Pelléas*. It is true that Enescu's score is a very complex one (more so than Debussy's, in the sense that it involves more types or levels of complexity); but a distinction must be made between complexity and difficulty, so far as the listener is concerned. What looks – and is – complex on these pages suddenly becomes clear when it is played: it speaks, and achieves its effect directly. To analyse exactly how the effect is achieved (as the critics and composers may have wanted to do) is indeed difficult. But the music itself, however strange, is not 'difficult' to listen to.

Possibly it was the vocal writing that Milhaud and Hahn had most in mind when they wrote their complaints. There are certainly no arias here which one could begin to whistle as one left the opera house. The writing for the singers often seems closer to Debussian practice than any other element of the score; this, however, may be a misleading resemblance, resting mainly on the fact that Enescu too has often fitted his notes precisely to the syllabic rhythms of spoken French. While Debussy's typical vocal patterns consist of step-like explorations of simple intervals with much repetition of notes on each step, Enescu's singing lines are perpetually in sinuous chromatic motion. Sometimes this is a sort of quasi-recitative, with semitonal shifts in the notes giving a colouring to the emotional contents of the words. But in most cases if one looks closely enough one can find

[25] Review in *Le Jour*, 12 March 1936, quoted in Darius Milhaud, *Notes sur la Musique* (ed. Jeremy Drake), Flammarion, Paris, 1982, p. 44, and in *Monografie*, p. 871n.

[26] Review in *Figaro*, quoted in *Contrepoint*, p. 66.

that the shape of these musical lines is determined by the working out of some of the great store of melodic motifs which run through the entire work (and which are often heterophonically working their way through other lines of music on the same page of the score).

Enescu makes considerable demands on his singers, in terms of precise nuances of expression and timbre. The Sphinx's part requires a fierce, chilling, sexless contralto voice of huge range. Enescu's instruction over its final line is: 'with a voice suddenly strong, colourless and metallic' ('soudain la voix forte, blanche et métallique'). Elsewhere, at special moments of fear or horror, a whole range of timbres somewhere between singing and speech are required: 'd'une voix rauque', 'voix blanche', 'à mi-voix', 'moîtié-parlé', 'quasi-parlé'. When, at the climax of Act Three, Oedipus reappears, blinded, before his people, his part is precisely notated on the stave, but with the instruction 'parlé' – a sort of 'Sprechgesang' which may possibly reflect the influence of *Pierrot Lunaire*.[27] Another advanced feature of the vocal writing is the use (again at special moments of stress) of quarter-tones; these first appear in the part of Oedipus when he is contemplating suicide in Act Two, Scene Two. By the time the opera was completed in 1931 Enescu had already written his Third Violin Sonata (1926), in which he made frequent use of quarter-tones as part of the folk-colouring of the violin part. This suggests that the origin, for Enescu, of this technique lay in Romanian music rather than in works or theoretical writings by Busoni, Ivan Vishnegradsky or Alois Hába.[28] One musico-

[27] Marcel Mihalovici recalls that this is one of the works by Schoenberg which Enescu knew; but it is not known when he first heard it. See the article by Sigismund Toduţa, 'Un aspect înnoitor al structurii vocale în tragedia lirică "Oedip', *Simpozion George Enescu*, pp. 94–110 (p. 104), which also makes some interesting connections between Enescu's semi-sung passages and techniques of Romanian folk music.

[28] Busoni advocated microtonal composition in his *Entwurf einer neuen Aesthetik der Tonkunst* (1907); the Russian émigré Vishnegradsky wrote microtonal music in Paris from the early 1920s onwards (he died in 1979); the Czech composer Alois Hába's first microtonal work (his Second String Quartet) was written in 1920.

logist has argued that Enescu's use of these intervals goes beyond ornamentation and involves writing the music in a quarter-tonal modal scale; he has managed to draw up such a scale (of eleven notes in the octave) for Oedipus' dialogue with the Theban watchman in Act Two, Scene Three, but it is difficult to do the same for other passages in the opera, where the quarter-tones seem to relate simply to the emotional tension of the part.[29] And in most of these passages the vocal lines are still developing, in a somewhat stretched or crushed form, the primary melodic cells of the whole work, which are not themselves microtonal.

These cells must inevitably be called leitmotivs; Enescu used the term himself in his conversations with Gavoty. In the context of his other symphonic and instrumental works, the way they operate is entirely familiar. It is the same process of perpetual thematic development, with the cells themselves being related to each other through shared intervals, chords, or sub-cellular patterns of notes. There is no explicit dramatic function, no reflex holding up of name-tags and subject-labels (of the sort that sometimes becomes tiresome in Wagner, and prompted anti-Wagnerians such as Nielsen to describe the whole system of leitmotivs as 'childish'). Enescu's motifs are so woven into the texture of the music that it is possible to listen to the whole work without becoming aware of their use – or at least, of their use as leitmotivs.[30] Nevertheless, some connections can be made. Some motifs are directly associated with characters, though they are associated also with emotions or actions which are in turn connected with those characters: the 'Laios' motif, for example, is also a 'parricide' motif and is associated with the elements of destiny

[29] J. Vysloužil, 'L'Origine, l'apparition et la fonction du quart de ton dans l'œuvre de Georges Enesco', *Studii de muzicologie*, Vol. 4 (1968), pp. 253–9 (p. 256).

[30] Anyone who has had the motifs spelt out will hear them everywhere, and may therefore doubt the truth of this claim. But is was certainly true of my first hearings of the work; and I have listened to the entire opera, following it in the score, with a composer who is also a musicologist and a Wagner-lover: he remained quite unaware of the operation of leitmotivs in the music.

and character, in both Laios and Oedipus, which bring
about the murder.

Oedipus's own primary motif is built round two intervals
(Ex. 12). The tritone is associated with Fate and its repre-
sentatives (such as the Sphinx), and the major third
expresses human affirmation – though it is often deformed
into a minor third.

Ex. 12

The 'Laios' motif is a sort of transposed enactment of that
deformation (Ex. 13). (Placing the C sharp an octave higher
will show the motif's affinity with that of Oedipus.)

Ex. 13

Jocasta's leitmotiv is a passionate, sweeping chromatic
melody, of which the first phrase contains the tritone-cell of
the Oedipus motif, and the final phrase repeats the outline
of the entire Oedipus motif but with the intervallic values of
Laios (Ex. 14).

Other motifs are associated with places (such as Corinth) or
themes (such as Fate). In fact several different motifs can be
connected with Fate: the long opening theme at the beginning
of the Prelude to Act One is traditionally identified as the
'destiny motif', but there is also a sinister phrase which
presents the tritone as a descending whole-tone scale, and
seems to express the gradual entrapment of Oedipus by Fate
and its agents (Ex. 15).

No study has yet achieved an exhaustive classification of
all the motifs in *Oedipe* (though Octavian Cosma puts his

Ex. 14

Ex. 15

tally at 21 so far).[31] Nor would it necessarily increase one's
enjoyment of the opera to have such a list before one. The
motifs are constantly interacting, and it is the resultant
large-scale patterns of melody that matter most. They, after
all, constitute the music we hear; to go behind them in this
way may be to analyse Enescu's creative processes rather
than analysing the music itself.

[31] *Oedip-ul Enescian*, p. 117.

After the completion of the orchestration in 1931, Enescu
continued to make minor revisions of the score as the parts
were prepared for publication by Salabert in Paris. He was
hopeful that the work could be performed in Paris before
long, and set his heart on persuading Chaliapin to take the
part of Oedipus. He met the great bass (who was now 59
years old) in August 1932; Chaliapin was busy with the film
version of Massenet's *Don Quichotte*, and arranged to meet
Enescu again, to look at the music, in two months' time.
Meanwhile he took away only a copy of the libretto. As
Enescu later understood, Chaliapin could feel his strength
waning and wanted simply to find out how large the part
would be; sadly, he decided that it was beyond his powers.[32]
Two years after this blow, however, Enescu's spirits were
raised again when the opera was approved by Jacques
Rouché, the adventurous Director of the Grand Opéra in
Paris. Enescu's old friend, the conductor Philippe Gaubert,
was assigned the task of preparing the work for the 1936
season. Enescu sent him the score and began corresponding
with him to explain some of its complexities. He also made
a plea which should perhaps be repeated for the benefit of
the Bucharest Opera, which has adopted the practice of
cutting most of the 'Corinth' scene from Act Two: 'Do you
think M. Rouché wants cuts to be made? It would be tragic
to do so, since I don't see where it would be possible. I leave
it to your experience to decide [. . .] and to the friendship
you feel towards me [. . .]'.[33]

Preparations got fully under way at the Opera at the end
of 1935, with Pierre Chéreau as producer. Huge forces were
used: the total number of players, singers, chorus and
dancers came, according to one estimate, to 350. (With the
exception of the dancers and a few special orchestral
players, there is in fact no reason why this work should need
greater forces than any normal modern opera.) The music
critic Pierre Berlioz interviewed Gaubert at a rehearsal on

[32] See *Contrepoint*, p. 67; Enescu's account in a letter to Fleg, 4 August
1932 (*Scrisori*, pp. 318–9); and Victor Borovsky, *Chaliapin*, Hamish Hamilton, London, 1988, p. 432.

[33] 4 November 1934: Piru, 'Quelques lettres', p. 182.

Enescu in 1932

1 March 1936, twelve days before the opening night. 'It's a magnificent opera', Gaubert said, 'but it presents enormous difficulties. [. . .] Just think – this is our eighteenth rehearsal, and we're still not ready.' And André Pernet, the bass who sang in the title-role, described his part as 'splendid, but exhausting'.[34] But the work was done, and the *répétition générale* on the 10th was followed by the official premiere on the 13th. For Enescu it was an immensely moving experience to see and hear his opera at last, having lived with the music as part of himself for so many years. In a later interview he described it as the most beautiful moment of his life; 'I was possessed by an extraordinary feeling – I felt like someone in a dream, or a legend [. . .]'.[35] The audience on both these nights was full of critics, composers and

[34] *Le Jour*, 2 March 1936, reproduced in *Monografie*, p. 840.

[35] Interview in *Duminica*, 27 September 1942, quoted in *Monografie*, pp. 867 and 610n.

musicians (including, on the 13th, Furtwängler).[36] When
the final curtain fell, the applause was thunderous.

The critics followed suit in the journals and newpapers:
they praised the opera almost unanimously for the grandeur
and individuality of its music, and the benign puzzlement of
Milhaud or Hahn was perhaps the most hostile sort of
comment on the music to be found in the reviews. The
composers Ibert, Auric, Aubert and Emmanuel were warm
in their praises; the influential critic and philosopher
Gabriel Marcel had already described it as 'one of the
summits of musical creation since Wagner'; and the
composer and critic Gustave Samazeuilh was so enthusiastic that he wrote no fewer than six reviews for different
journals.[37] Henri Prunières exclaimed: 'For how many years
have we been waiting to hear a masterpiece comparable
with Enescu's *Oedipe*, so full of music, so dense, so balanced,
so mature [. . .]'.[38] But the writer who, as Enescu thought,
came closest to grasping the spirit of the work was
Debussy's friend Émile Vuillermoz, who wrote:

> We do not have the right to judge whether it is orchestrated
> well or badly: there is no common standard by which it could
> be measured. The instruments here speak a strange lan-
> guage, direct, unaffected and serious, owing nothing to
> traditional polyphony [. . .]. In the early scenes the music
> does not make fine speeches. It has no use for rhetoric. The
> orchestra does not give expansive commentaries on events: it
> submits to them with a sort of trembling passivity [. . .].
> Then, in the last act, this technique gives way to concentrated
> lyricism [. . .].

And in a second review he wrote: 'Despite the apparent
austerity of this music, there are few scores which express

---

[36] Miron Grindea in the *Kensington Symposium* (the recording of a
symposium held at the Central Library, Kensington, London on 21 May
1982; the speakers were Alan Bush, Miron Grindea, John Amis and
John Ogdon: tape held at the National Sound Archive, London, T 5107
BW).

[37] *Monografie*, pp. 840 and 869–70.

[38] Review of *Oedipe*, p. 202.

such a force of feeling so sincerely and so powerfully'.[39]

Notwithstanding the welcome given to it by musicians and critics, *Oedipe* did not fire the imagination of the public. It was not a flop, but it was certainly not a great popular success. There are no love-duets in *Oedipe*. Eleven performances were given during 1936 and 1937. The next performance of the work was in a concert version conducted by Charles Brück and broadcast live on French radio in 1955. (Sadly, this came only a few days after Enescu's death; one can only imagine what happiness it would have given him, pinned as he was to his deathbed by a long illness, to hear again the one work which he loved best out of all his compositions.) In 1956 the opera was put on at Brussels, and in 1958 the first Romanian performance was conducted by Silvestri.[40] Since then the work has been played in various European countries by visiting Romanian performers, usually in an unstaged or semi-staged form. But none of the major opera-houses of the West has yet taken up the challenge it represents. It remains (like its exact contemporary, Busoni's *Doktor Faust*) one of the least performed masterpieces of twentieth-century opera.

[39] Review in *Excelsior*, 16 March 1936 (reproduced in *Monografie*, p. 872 and quoted by Enescu in *Contrepoint*, p. 67); and 'Oedipe à l'Opéra', *Candide*, 19 March 1936.

[40] See Bentoiu, *Capodopere*, pp. 296–7.

VIII

1919–1931

The pattern of Enescu's life between the end of the First World War and the completion of *Oedipe* in 1931 is a familiar one: several months each summer and autumn were devoted to composition, and the rest of the year (usually from November to June or July) was spent in a marathon of appearances as violinist, pianist and conductor. The summer was usually spent in Romania, but in 1919 and 1920 Enescu stayed in Switzerland with Maruca in a house she owned at Vers-chez-les-Blancs, east of Lausanne on the shore of Lake Geneva. Here he was able to lead a quiet and relatively simple life, with occasional visits from Queen Marie and other friends of Maruca; and it was here that he spent one of his longest periods away from the concert-halls of Europe, from June 1920 to February 1921, as he completed his work on the First String Quartet and the Third Symphony and began once again to tackle *Oedipe*. Even so there were interruptions: a performance of the Brahms Concerto with Ansermet and the Suisse Romande Orchestra, and a sonata recital with Risler at Geneva.[1] But in return there was also a concert of Enescu's music at the Lausanne Conservatoire, in which Clara Haskil played the Second Piano Suite and the premiere was given of the String Quartet, with Enescu playing the viola.

In the following years Enescu usually stayed either at

---

[1] Oprescu and Jora, *Enescu*, p. 189. As before, details of concerts, etc., mentioned in this and following chapters will be found, if not otherwise noted, in the chronology in this book and Gheorghe Firca (ed.), *George Enescu*.

Maruca's country house at Teţcani, near Iaşi, or at the villa
'Făget' in Sinaia. He came to love the peace of the mountain
scenery at Sinaia so much that in 1923 he bought a plot of
land there and commissioned an architect to build – in
accordance with Enescu's own sketches and designs – a villa
which was named the 'Villa Luminiş', 'glade of light'.
Enescu and Maruca were to spend some of their happiest
days there, she entertaining in the spacious ground-floor
rooms and he retreating up a small spiral staircase to work
in his monastically austere study with its spectacular views
across the mountains.

For the other two-thirds of the year, however, Enescu's
schedules were even heavier than they had been before the
War. In 1922, for example, his season in western Europe
began with a visit to Belgium in January (five concerts in
eight days); this was followed immediately by a tour of
Spain with Marcel Ciampi; in early February he returned to
Paris for four concerts, followed by a series of fourteen
concerts in other French towns; and in March he was
playing concertos under Guy Ropartz in Strasbourg and
André Caplet in Paris. Apart from Romania, these were the
main European countries which he was to tour during the
inter-war years. Germany remained unvisited (with the
exception of two concerts in Berlin which preceded a brief
tour of Poland in November 1928); and Vienna seemed
unappreciative of its former pupil. He gave one concert
there in 1930, arranged in conjunction with a performance
under Dohnányi's baton at Budapest. (When a tactless
invitation to perform in Vienna was sent to Enescu at
Bucharest during the Second World War, it caused one of
his rare outbursts of anger in the presence of another
person.[2]) There was, however, one major new addition to
Enescu's itineraries: the United States.

A tour in America had been planned for 1914, but was
then cancelled because of the War. Enescu finally took it up
in 1923, and his American tours (usually in January or

---

[2] Octav Onicescu, 'A Founder of Romanian Culture', *Romanian Review*,
Vol. 35 (1981), No. 8, pp. 149–51 (p. 150).

The young Romanian pianist Clara Haskil in 1920

February) were to become almost an annual fixture during the next ten years. Before he went he was already known there as a composer, through performances of his orchestral works by Mahler, Walter Damrosch and Frederick Stock. Under the batons of the last two conductors among others, his reputation as a violinist was quickly established with performances of major concertos. Another conductor was added to the list of his admirers: Leopold Stokowski, under whom, with the Philadelphia Orchestra, he played the Brahms Concerto in 1923 and Mozart and Chausson in 1926.[3] But America was also quick to offer Enescu the opportunity to appear as a conductor himself. The main part of his first visit there in 1923 was a tour of several East Coast cities as conductor of the Philadelphia Orchestra. His

[3] A few years after Enescu's death, Stokowski told Romeo Drăghici: 'I have known very many great musicians, and very few geniuses. Enescu was a genius' (information from Romeo Drăghici).

initial experience was not a happy one: the organisers had decided, without consulting him, that the first programme should include Tchaikovsky's Sixth Symphony, which he detested. (In a letter to a friend he wrote: 'Pathétique Tchaikowsky!!! voiciii!!!')[4] Afterwards he felt that he had conducted the work so badly as a result of this antipathy that he turned down engagements as a conductor for the next year's tour.[5] But later in the 1920s he did accept numerous invitations to conduct the orchestras of Cleveland, Boston and Cincinnati. Often he was asked to include one of his own compositions; sometimes he conducted one half of a concert and played a violin concerto in the other. And there were also many recitals in which Enescu played violin sonatas, accompanied by Edward Harris, or, later in the 1920s, Sanford Schlüssel. In 1924 he made a special trip to America to take part in the Berkshire Festival of Chamber Music, which was held at Pittsfield (Mass.), under the patronage of Elizabeth Sprague Coolidge. There he gave an all-Bach concert with Harold Samuel, and played the Chausson *Concert* with Carl Friedberg and the Rich Quartet (which included the cellist Hans Kindler, who was later to become an enthusiastic promoter of Enescu's works as a conductor).[6]

In March 1925 Enescu's itinerary took him to the West Coast for the first time, and he appeared with the San Francisco Symphony, conducting his own First Symphony and playing the Brahms Concerto. An eight-year-old boy in the audience became possessed by the impression that Enescu made on him at that concert. More than fifty years later he wrote:

Before a note was sounded he had me in thrall. His countenance, his stance, his wonderful mane of black hair – everything about him proclaimed the free man [. . .]. And the music he

[4] 5 January 1923 (to Ninette Duca): *Scrisori*, Vol. 1, p. 272.

[5] *Contrepoint*, p. 47; see Oprescu and Jora, *Enescu*, p. 198.

[6] Details from a bound volume of Berkshire Festival programmes in the Pendlebury Library, Cambridge University. Hans Kindler, the friend of Busoni and brother-in-law of Bernard van Dieren, founded the National Symphony Orchestra in Washington in 1931 and conducted it until 1948.

began to play had an incandescence surpassing anything in my experience. In afteryears when I knew him intimately, saw him at times almost daily, watched him age, I never had the least cause to qualify this first judgment – if judgment isn't too cold a word for my wholehearted response.

The boy's name was Yehudi Menuhin, and this concert was eventually to have a decisive influence on his musical life.[7]

Back in France, Enescu was not deprived of opportunities to conduct; Paul Paray, for example, willingly handed over his Lamoureux Orchestra to Enescu for a concert of Strauss, Dukas and Beethoven.[8] But it was, of course, in Romania that he had the widest scope for music-making of this kind. After the precedent he had set during the war years of conducting whole series of symphonic concerts, he was often asked to take up his baton; in April 1921, for instance, he conducted nine concerts at Bucharest, including works by Wagner, Rimsky-Korsakov, Glazunov, Franck, Debussy, Dukas and Ravel. He helped to organise not only the transformation of what had previously been the Orchestra of the Ministry of Education into the Philharmonia Orchestra, but also the establishment, at long last, of a national opera company: he rehearsed the company for its first production, *Lohengrin*, and conducted the Bucharest premiere on 31 December 1921. During these years he was elected to many committees and official bodies; some of these were merely honorary appointments, but to others he brought an immense practical enthusiasm for raising musical standards in Romania. Particularly important, he felt, was the encouragement of young composers. In 1921 he paid a large further sum into the fund for the composition prize which he had set up.[9] The names of the prize-winners during these years read like a roll-call of many of the future leading composers in Romania, too few of whom have become sufficiently recognised outside that country: Con-

---

[7] Menuhin, *Unfinished Journey*, p. 57. The concert is not listed by Oprescu and Jora, who do however mention two concerts at Los Angeles on 13 and 14 March (p. 201). Enescu did not visit the West Coast in 1924 or 1926.

[8] 27 April 1927 (Oprescu and Jora, *Enescu*, p. 208).

[9] *Ibid.*, p. 191 (23 June 1921).

stantin Nottara, Theodor Rogalski, Sabin Drăgoi, Mihail Andricu and Paul Constantinescu.[10] They also included, in 1919, 1921 and 1925, Marcel Mihalovici, who was to become a close friend of Enescu and, with his wife Monique Haas, a faithful supporter of him in his later years in Paris. Enescu helped also to promote the works of young Romanian composers outside his native country; in March 1920, for example, he played in a Paris concert devoted mainly to the works of Stan Golestan (who had won the Enescu Prize in 1915, and had gone to Paris to study under d'Indy, Roussel and Dukas).[11]

Enescu was also keen to help young musicians. Two names appear in rather different connections in the year 1921; both were later to develop close musical links with Enescu. The young Romanian pianist Clara Haskil had, as we have seen, taken part in the Enescu concert at Lausanne in early 1921. In November of that year he intervened personally with the Minister of Finance in Bucharest to make sure that she would be able to continue her studies in Paris.[12] The other musician, Dinu Lipatti, was born in 1917.

---

[10] *Ibid*, pp. 336–8. Constantin Nottara (1890–1951): violinist, conductor, and pupil of the Italian composer Alfonso Castaldi; his own compositions were mainly influenced by French 'Impressionist' music. Theodor Rogalski (1901–1953), composition pupil of d'Indy, but best known in Romania as a conductor, wrote a small number of works based on Romanian folk music, of which *Three Symphonic Dances* is the best known. Sabin Drăgoi (1901–1953), studied in Czechoslovakia under Vítězslav Novák and Otakar Ostrčil, and became a professor of music and folklore at Cluj (the capital of Transylvania) and Bucharest; he was a prolific composer of music in most genres, including four operas. Mihail Andricu (1895–1974), pupil of d'Indy and Fauré, pianist and occasional accompanist of Enescu, concentrated as a composer on adapting folk material to symphonic forms: he wrote eleven symphonies, three chamber symphonies and thirteen sinfoniettas. Paul Constantinescu (1909–1963), a pupil of Mihail Jora, Franz Schmidt and Joseph Marx, taught composition at Bucharest from 1937 until his death; regarded by Enescu as the most promising of the next generation of Romanian composers, he concentrated especially on reviving the tradition of Byzantine church music.

[11] On Golestan see Viorel Cosma, *Compositori şi muzicologi români.*

[12] *Scrisori*, p. 257.

His father, a fine amateur violinist who had studied under Flesch, asked Enescu to be Dinu's godfather, but the baptism was postponed till after the war. By the time it was held in 1921 the four-year-old child was sufficiently advanced to be able to give a piano concert to the assembled guests; he also played the violin, and there is a touching photograph of him standing with his half-size fiddle in his hand as Enescu, also violin in hand, places a small laurel wreath on his head.[13] Lipatti was also to win the Enescu Prize for composition in 1934, and was to be considered by Nadia Boulanger as one of her most outstanding pupils; the success of his tragically brief career as a pianist has now eclipsed his other talents, and has made it less easy to see how far he modelled himself on the universal musicianship of his godfather.

The Enescu Prize was the occasion of an intriguing meeting of minds in 1924, when Béla Bartók accepted an invitation to join the examining jury for the competition. Enescu headed the delegation which met him at the station in Bucharest, and afterwards he took him to his house, where they played through Bartók's Second Violin Sonata. On the next day the final meeting of the jury took place (with Enescu ceding the chair to Bartók); and on the following evening a concert of music by Bartók was given, in which Enescu played the Sonata. Years later a friend of the Hungarian composer recalled that Bartók had been deeply impressed by Enescu's powers of musical understanding, and told a story in which Enescu had read through one of Bartók's orchestral works in Bartók's presence, had given the score back to him and had then conducted a rehearsal of the work, on the following day, from memory, bringing out every nuance of the writing.[14] Unfortunately it has not been possible to reconcile this story either with the events of Bartók's visit in 1924 or with the known details of his other visits to Romania or Enescu's other performances of works

[13] Madeleine Lipatti (*et al.*), *In Memoriam Dinu Lipatti 1917–1950*, Geneva, 2nd edn., 1970, p. 11.

[14] The story, told by Iosif Willer, was printed in *Scînteia Tineretului*, 1955, and is reproduced in *Romanian Review*, Vol. 35, No. 8, 1981, p. 121.

Enescu and Dinu Lipatti, at the latter's baptism-cum-recital in 1921

by him.[15] It is likely, though, that when Enescu read through the Second Sonata with Bartók he was seeing the work for the first time; and his performance of it two days later, which may have been from memory, was probably the true origin of the story – earning praise from Bartók which later became mixed up with some other story of Enescu's prowess in the recollections of Bartók's friend.

There were other contacts with composers during these years. In March 1921 Enescu met Richard Strauss again at

[15] See Lajos Pinter's discussion in 'Enescu în presa budapestiană', *Centenarul George Enescu 1881–1981*, pp. 77–117 (pp. 80–83).

A poster for the Bartók-Enescu concert of
20 October 1924

Bucharest. Obviously they got on well together, for in the following year Strauss helped to arrange a performance of the *Dixtuor* at the Salzburg Festival, where he was on the committee, and also showed an interest in putting on some of Enescu's more recent compositions.[16] Earlier in 1921 Enescu had renewed his acquaintance with the aging

---

[16] 1921: Oprescu and Jora, *Enescu*, p. 190. 1922: letter of 19 July to Orchiş, *Scrisori*, Vol. 1, pp. 262–3.

French composer Louis Vierne, who had become a near neighbour of Enescu and Maruca in Switzerland. He had been sent there by his doctors to rest and undergo treatment for his glaucoma, which threatened to destroy the little sight he still possessed. Enescu could not help seeing a resemblance between this resigned and dignified old man and the blinded Oedipus at Colonus. He had long discussions with Vierne about his plans for the opera, and together they played Vierne's Violin Sonata, which was one of Enescu's favourite sonatas.[17] The 1920s also saw the growth of Enescu's friendship with Guy Ropartz, who dedicated his Third Violin Sonata to him in 1927; Enescu gave the first performance of the work that year with Marcel Ciampi, and in a special concert in honour of Guy Ropartz in 1933 he played all three of the Breton composer's Violin Sonatas with Robert Casadesus.[18]

Enescu's interest in the works of modern composers is illustrated by the programmes of the twelve concerts he gave with Alfred Alessandrescu in Bucharest in the spring of 1921. They performed 36 different sonatas; along with works by the classical Viennese composers they played sonatas by d'Indy, Busoni, Vierne, Emil Sjögren (who had dedicated his Fifth Sonata to Enescu in 1914), Weingartner, Sigismund Stojowski, Golestan, Jean Huré, Pierre-Onfroy de Bréville and Magnard. In similar sets of recitals in 1923 and 1926 they included works by Schmitt, Roussel, Milhaud, Korngold and Honegger, and in 1927 Enescu added Szymanowski's *Mythes* to his repertoire – a work of which he grew especially fond, and of which some echoes can be heard in his own later composition *Impressions d'Enfance*. It would be a difficult task indeed to draw up a complete list of Enescu's concert repertoire during these years, which con-

---

[17] *Contrepoint*, p. 64.

[18] *Monografie*, p. 727. Enescu had suggested such an all-Ropartz concert to the composer in 1928. For this, and a moving letter written at the end of Enescu's life to thank Ropartz for his 'belle et lumineuse musique', see Alfred Hoffmann, 'Lettres de Georges Enesco adressées à des musiciens français', in M. Voicana (ed.), *Enesciana*, Vol. 1, Bucharest, 1976, pp. 63–70 (pp. 66 and 70).

tained several extraordinarily taxing tours of Romania: 44 concerts from 9 April to 7 June 1923, for example, and 65 concerts between 3 January and 22 March 1927. These tours were, to a large extent, a labour of love for his country; he could have earned much more money more easily in the major concert-halls of Europe.

The inter-war years were the period when Enescu was at the peak of his fame as a violinist. Sadly, his hostility to the gramophone[19] meant that there are very few recordings from this period. His later performances on record, from 1941 onwards, are musically superb, but they are sometimes blemished technically by the physical disabilities of his final years. To an author who, like myself, was born too late to hear Enescu in the flesh, the task of describing his special characteristics as a violinist is a daunting one. And of course it would be absurd to try to find some technical 'secret' of his playing, isolated from the profound musical understanding which shaped his interpretations of the music he performed. This indeed, if anything, was the secret of his playing: that all his concentration was on letting the music speak, eliminating with complete self-effacement any sense in the listener's mind of his own virtuoso technique as an object of attention in its own right. An American critic in 1928 went so far as to write: 'Mr Enesco's technique fails, at first, to impress'. He explained: 'The output of the strings is so simply that of a singing voice that its grip is not immediate. Nothing is there except the sound – well-nigh perfect bowing eliminates the musician, the violinist, the bow. There is no sense of contact between bow and strings – except when deliberately done for effect'.[20] Enescu agreed that the violin should have all the expressive range of a

---

[19] See below, pp. 196–7.

[20] Extract from *The Bellingham Herald*, 25 January 1928, reprinted in Anon., *Georges Enesco*, p. 79. The editor of this book was almost certainly Maruca's relative, Maximilian Costin; Enescu referred approvingly to a biographical work edited by him in 1928 (Enescu, 'Ce ne-a spus', p. 9). The cutting of this review was thus probably obtained from Enescu or his agent, so it is likely that Enescu thought it an especially true comment on his aims as a violinist.

human voice.[21] (Some striking examples of this vocal expressivity can be heard in the recordings he made in 1943, with Lipatti, of his Second and Third Violin Sonatas.) Menuhin has commented that Enescu was the only violinist to produce on his instrument the interrupted 'sanglot' used by Italian tenors. He has also written that Enescu had 'the most expressively varied vibrato and the most wonderful trills of any violinist I have ever known.'[22]

If this emphasis on expression is taken to imply that Enescu's playing was 'romantic', in the sense of sentimentalising the music, the impression is a false one. His interpretation of Bach set new standards of clean and sober classicality: only in this way, he knew, could the full expressive power of the music be realised. The *New York Times* critic Richard Aldrich gave this assessment of his performance of works by Bach and Leclair in 1923:

> He is first and last a musician and an interpreter, devoted solely to expounding music and not at all to the display of his technical powers. These are indeed remarkable, but they are employed entirely as a means to an end [. . .]. There are violinists with a more beautiful tone than his. Sensuous charm is not its most conspicuous quality, though it has marrow and masculine vigor; and in dynamics Enesco cultivates a very wide range, being especially fond of an almost whispered pianissimo [. . .]. There is, undoubtedly, a certain austerity in Mr Enesco's playing, he is very little concerned with 'lascivious pleasings', or with obvious sentiment. But there is through it all a richly musical feeling, potently expressed.[23]

---

[21] Bocu, 'De vorbă cu Enescu', p. 8.

[22] 'My Great Master', *Adam*, Year 43 (1981), Nos. 434–6, pp. 19–22 (p. 20); *Unfinished Journey*, p. 71.

[23] Review of 23 January 1923, reprinted in Richard Aldrich, *Concert Life in New York, 1902–1923*, Putnam, New York, 2nd edn. 1941, p. 724. He added a comment which makes the flawed intonation of Enescu's last recordings especially poignant: 'Mr Enesco's playing is notable for its exquisite purity of intonation, especially in double stoppings [. . .]. His certainty in such passages is uncanny; and any deviation from the pitch, or any searching for it, most rare.' See also Boris Schwarz's description of Enescu's Bach playing in *Great Masters of the Violin*, Robert Hale, London, 1984, p. 365.

When sensuousness was called for by the music itself,
Enescu could supply it in abundance – as this review by a
French critic of a performance of Szymanowski's 'Dryades et
Pan' (the third movement of *Mythes*) makes clear: 'His
singing virtuosity, his brusque, fierce attacks with the heel
of the bow, his plaintive, sensuous harmonics, commu-
nicated all the desires and pursuits of Pan and the Dryads,
while at the same time being unrushed, clear and luminous
throughout'.[24]

The same critic, Dany Brunschwig, has left a long and
valuable account of the master-classes Enescu gave in Paris
in 1928. Enescu's motto was: 'technique can be summed up
in one word: music'. What he meant was that true technical
skill could not be acquired by learning some self-contained
system of bowing or fingering and then 'applying' it to the
music; the player must first of all understand the musical
effect which any device of bowing, etc., was designed to
produce.[25] Enescu's fingerings, as a result, were often
idiosyncratic, and in his teaching he was always concerned
first of all with his pupils' musical understanding of the
piece, encouraging them, if they were capable of it, to work
out their own fingerings or bowings to produce the desired
effect. The minutely detailed instructions which he wrote
into his own violin compositions were simply an attempt to
express in notation the nature of the effects he wanted his
players to seek. And in the notation which he used some
characteristic details of his own technique can be found –
especially the use of 'louré' bowing, in which each note in a
phrase is given a slightly separate emphasis with minute
extra pressure from the forefinger of the right hand, while
the whole phrase remains *legato* within a single bow.

[24] Daniel Brunschwig, Concert Review in *Le Monde musical*, 31 May 1928,
p. 190.

[25] Brunschwig, 'Cours d'interprétation de Georges Enesco', *Le Monde
musical*, 30 September and 30 November 1928, pp. 295–6 and 367–8; esp.
p. 295: 'La technique (doigté, coup d'archet) se résume en un mot:
Musique. D'abord technique *musicale*, donc moyen pour exprimer une
phrase, une intention, une douleur, une joie. Peu importe employer telle
position, telle élégance d'archet. Voyez l'œuvre, la couleur de chaque
idée, la construction harmonique, contrapuntique . . . '.

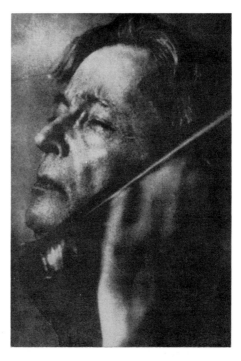

Enescu as violinist – a famous publicity photograph, in which he is said to have been playing Chausson's Poème

Enescu's emphasis on the subservience of technique to music might suggest that he had a slipshod, *ad hoc* approach to technical matters. This was certainly not so, as any of his pupils can testify. Some slightly resentful colleagues, such as Flesch, concluded that it must be so when they heard that Enescu gave his violin classes seated at the piano.[26] Of course, Flesch knew of these lessons only at second or third hand. One person who was in a position to make a comparison was Ida Haendel. After studying for many months with Flesch she found her musical and technical development transformed by her lessons with Enescu:

> Firm and uncompromising, he removed all the frills which had hitherto adorned my playing of Bach. [. . .] This emphasis on simplicity and purity of line served to bring out the true grandeur of the structure; I seemed to hear Bach the giant for the first time. Although Enescu gave precedence to the

[26] Flesch, *Memoirs*, p. 180.

musical thought above all else, he did not neglect technical imperfections, and the slightest inaccuracy never escaped his keen ear. I found it extraordinary that after these lessons with Enescu, I became even more attentive to technical precision than I had been before. This was inexplicable, as there was no doubt of Flesch's rigorousness in technical matters. Yet it seemed to me that Enescu went one degree further, for every note was of equal importance to him, even in the fastest scale, and had to be crystal-clear.[27]

The irony is that when it came to Bach in particular, it was Flesch's rigorous application of principles that introduced 'romantic' superfluities into his interpretations. His inviolable rule for Bach was that there must be unity of timbre: each melodic statement must be confined whenever possible to the same string. This led to the frequent use of romantic-sounding high positions, and sometimes to intrusive *portamenti* in order to get up and down the string. Enescu mainly preferred low positions for Bach, and his unorthodox fingerings avoided the use of *portamenti*, often stretching the hand to encompass the interval of a third between two adjacent fingers. The result was a style of playing which made use of the natural resonances of the instrument (instead of struggling, like Flesch, against its limitations), and which was sonorous, clear and always subservient to the intrinsic shape and structure of each musical phrase.[28]

Enescu was always reluctant to become a violin teacher.

[27] *Woman with Violin. An Autobiography*, Gollancz, London, 1970, pp. 90–91. This was in 1939. Ivry Gitlis, who also studied under Enescu and Flesch in 1937–8, writes: 'J'ai l'impression d'avoir plus appris avec lui (Enescu) que, par la suite, avec Flesch' (*L'Âme et la corde*, Editions Robert Laffont, Paris, 1980, p. 82).

[28] In several important studies the violinist George Manoliu has compared the solutions adopted by Enescu (noted by Manoliu at Enescu's Paris classes in 1937) with those given in standard editions such as Busch's edition of Franck and Flesch's edition of Bach. See especially, 'Bach în concepția interpretativă Enesciană', *Centenarul George Enescu 1881–1981*, pp. 45–55, and 'Enescu's Violin-Playing', *Romanian Review*, Vol. 35 (1981), No. 8, pp. 71–81. Flesch explained his principles in *The Art of Violin Playing* (e.g., Vol. 1, p. 147: 'Uniformly related phrases should be played whenever possible on the same string'; p. 121: 'I have a decided prejudice against stretching').

Between the Wars he gave several occasional courses, nevertheless: at Bucharest in 1921–2, at the École Normale in Paris in 1924–5 and 1928–30, and at Yvonne Astruc's 'Institut Instrumental' in 1937.[29] But he seldom took private pupils. Many violinists have described themselves as his pupils, having attended only a short course or a handful of individual lessons: this is a reflection not so much of exaggeration on their part as of the fact that even a few hours with Enescu could have a decisive effect on their musical development – as Ida Haendel's account shows. But there is, of course, one name that stands out for his long and special association with Enescu: Yehudi Menuhin.

At the end of 1926 Menuhin and his parents crossed the Atlantic to find a new teacher who could add to the high level of musical development which he had already attained under Louis Persinger in San Francisco. The parents' first choice was Ysaÿe, who had been Persinger's teacher when he was at the height of his powers. But he was now an aging and somewhat off-putting figure, and Menuhin's first and only meeting with him was a disappointment. Menuhin himself was nursing a secret desire of his own. Ever since hearing Enescu play in San Francisco, there was only one man in Europe that he wanted to study under. His parents had also given much thought to the matter and, fortunately, had placed Enescu near the top of their short-list. On Christmas Day, soon after the abortive visit to Ysaÿe, they took Yehudi to a concert given by Enescu at the Salle Gaveau in Paris. Enescu played the Mozart B flat Concerto with the Lamoureux Orchestra under Paray; the Menuhins needed no further convincing. After the concert they went backstage, and Yehudi asked Enescu if he could study with him. Enescu was obviously reluctant to agree, but he avoided making a blank refusal and simply explained that he was leaving for Romania at 6.30 the following morning. Finally he agreed to hear Yehudi at 5.30. The young boy appeared punctually with his father at Enescu's apartment; he played, with Enescu accompanying him, for half an hour;

---

[29] See Manoliu, 'Bach în concepţia', for 1937, and V. Cosma, *Enescu azi*, pp. 144–5, for the other dates and further details.

and Enescu turned to him and said: 'I shall be happy to make music with you, anytime, anywhere, whenever I am not on tour'.[30]

Enescu returned to Paris at the end of March, and for the next three months there were frequent sessions, at irregular intervals, in his apartment in the Rue de Clichy. On his return to Romania he invited the Menuhins to join him there, and the sessions were continued throughout the summer at the Villa Luminiş.[31] Enescu himself never referred to these meetings as 'lessons'; nor did he accept any payment for them. From the start he treated the boy almost as a colleague, discussing the music with him, listening to his interpretations and adding suggestions of his own. Sometimes he illustrated a technical point on the violin; more often it was a matter of sharing his understanding of the flow and structure of the music by playing the piano, or singing a phrase, or helping to mould Yehudi's interpretation as he accompanied him. His approach was, obviously, unacademic, in the sense that he theorised little about the violin. But he did insist on the need to study the whole range of a composer's work, and also on the importance of playing exactly what the composer had written – which, in a period still awash with unreliable nineteenth-century editions, often meant going back to the Urtext and if necessary seeking out the original manuscripts. (As Professor George Manoliu has shown, before the autograph manuscript of Bach's violin music was published Enescu was already playing the notes written there when they

---

[30] Faced with several different accounts of this episode (including two widely differing ones by Enescu), I have followed the version related by Menuhin's father, Moshe, in *The Menuhin Saga*, Sidgwick and Jackson, London, 1984, p. 100. Details of Enescu's concert on 25 December are in Oprescu and Jora, *Enescu*, p. 206; he also conducted a performance of his First Orchestral Suite.

[31] For what follows, see the accounts given by Moshe Menuhin (*The Menuhin Saga*, pp. 103–5) and Yehudi Menuhin (*Unfinished Journey*, pp. 70–72; 'Georges Enesco', *The Score and I.M.A. Magazine*, 1955, pp. 39–42; Robin Daniels, *Conversations with Menuhin*, Futura, London, 1980, pp. 136–7) and the letter from Enescu to Menuhin translated in I. Iampolski, *George Enescu*, n.p. (Moscow?), 1947, pp. 11–12.

Enescu and Menuhin

differed from the edited versions issued by Joachim, Hellmesberger, Flesch and Busch.[32]) Casals once heard
Menuhin playing a Bach Partita, and asked Enescu why his
pupil did not use *spiccato* bowing to liven up one of the
movements; Enescu's reply that it was not authentic for the
style of Bach's music left Casals shaking his head at the gulf
which this indicated between his own approach and that of
his old friend.[33]

It was during Menuhin's second month with Enescu that
he and his father witnessed the most extraordinary example
of Enescu's musical memory. Ravel burst in with the
manuscript of his newly completed Violin Sonata, and
asked Enescu to play it with him that evening for the
publishers. With the Menuhins' permission they read
through the work, Enescu stopping occasionally to ask for

[32] 'Bach în concepţia', pp. 46–8.

[33] Corredor, *Conversations with Casals*, p. 189.

clarifications. Then they resolved to play it through once more – and Enescu closed his part and played the entire Sonata from memory.[34]

Once Enescu had started work again on *Oedipe* in 1921, he had little time to devote to other compositions. In 1931, when he had finished the orchestration but was still occupied with minor revisions, he told an interviewer: 'I can't work on ten different compositions at once, as I did when I was young. I confess that I have several symphonies, string quartets and pieces for violin and piano in my head which are just in need of time'.[35] The harvest of the 1920s is a slender one: a short piece for piano, a Piano Sonata and a Violin Sonata. The piano piece was a tribute to Fauré written in 1922. In that year the *Revue musicale* prepared a special issue devoted to Fauré (who was now aged 77) and commissioned short piano pieces from seven of his former pupils – Aubert, Enescu, Koechlin, Ladmirault, Ravel, Roger-Ducasse and Schmitt – to be printed as a supplement to it. Each piece was to be based on Fauré's name, spelt musically as F, A, G, D, E, (with the values of U and R reached by continuing the alphabet up the scale above G: the letter H becomes the note A, I becomes B, and so on). Enescu's contribution is a gentle, meditative piece (*molto moderato e cantabile*) lasting only ten bars and a bit; but with delicious ingenuity it repeats the stipulated notes no fewer than twelve times. It would take a very sharp-eared listener to spot the recurrence of the motif more than three or four times after its initial statement, yet the piece almost consists of nothing else. Enescu hides the motif behind shifting veils of harmonic changes, which are lightly embroidered with minimal arpeggios and what might be described as ornaments in slow motion. Though the harmonies are

---

[34] Menuhin, *Unfinished Journey*, p. 70. Enescu gave the premiere of the sonata with Ravel on 30 May 1927.

[35] Riegler-Dinu, 'George Enescu': 'Nu mă mai pot împrăştia în compoziţia a zece opere diferite în mod simultan, ca în tinereţe. Iţi mărturesc însă că am în cap mai multe simfonii, cvartete de coarde şi bucăţi pentru pian şi vioară care îşi aşteaptă timpul'.

Menuhin and Enescu in 1952

elusive, the piece does not represent Enescu at his most harmonically challenging – it was, after all, a present for Fauré – but it does have all his characteristic fluidity of rhythm (Ex. 16).

The First Piano Sonata was written at Maruca's family house, Teţcani, in July and August 1924. This was when Enescu had only just begun work on the orchestration of Act Two of *Oedipe*. In an interview in November (the same one in which he said he thought *Oedipe* would take only another year to complete[36]) he explained: 'It may seem strange that I have interrupted my work on *Oedipe* to write a piano sonata. A creative artist has moments when he must obey his soul's impulses – so I had no choice. It's dedicated to Frey, a Swiss pianist. I had promised it to him eighteen years ago – it was about time I wrote it!'[37] Émile Frey was an old Paris friend and an accomplished pianist who had

[36] See p. 146.

[37] Massoff, 'Enescu vorbeşte'; printed also in *Monografie*, p. 532.

Ex. 16

studied under Diémer; but it was Enescu who gave the premieres of the work in Bucharest (November 1925) and Paris (April 1926). The Sonata demands pianistic skills of a high order: it covers a wide range of types of piano sonority, and often requires a variety of dynamics and kinds of attack within the same hand simultaneously. The last movement contains some tone-painting in a recognisably Debussian-Ravelian style, but the overall character of the Sonata is quite distinctive. The opening movement (*Allegro molto moderato e grave*) is severe and at times menacing, with angular themes and climaxes of crashing, rhythmically irregular chords. Although in sonata form, it has a meditative-episodic character which can generate swift changes of mood; among the episodes marked *tranquillo, dolce, delicatamente* or *amabile grazioso* there is a passage of hypnotically repeated dissonant notes which foreshadows the Third Violin Sonata, and a graceful dance which is the only section of this movement to have a recognisably folk-Romanian style.[38] Though different in character, this dance does have a distinct thematic affinity with the bell motif of the *Carillon Nocturne* in the Third Piano Suite; and there are bell-like sounds in this movement (one bar is marked *quasi campana*) which also look forward to the tintinnabulations of the last movement.

The second movement, in complete contrast, is *Presto vivace*, a helter-skelter rondo, rhythmically taut and precise. The sparks fly, but in stylised patterns which in places seem Stravinskian. The closest relatives of this piece of writing are the 'Burlesque' and 'Bourrée' from the Third Piano Suite. And it is the advanced style of the 'Carillon Nocturne' which is developed further in the atmospheric third movement of this Sonata. (The unorthodox sequence of movements – opening *allegro*, then fast *scherzando* movement, then a slow final movement, marked here *Andante molto espressivo* – is probably modelled on the Third Symphony.) This movement opens with a distant ringing (layers of quiet repeated notes superimposed in a rhythmically disorientating way), and then a phrase of bell-notes, marked *doloroso*, strikes heavily against the stillness (Ex. 17).

This is atmospheric music of a quite original kind. When Enescu began his interviews with Gavoty he wanted to evoke the scenery of his childhood memories: he played part of this movement, and explained that it attempted to capture the feeling of the Romanian plains at night. It is not simple tone-painting; the bell motifs are soon incorporated into a complex, glistening web of interwoven themes. In the way it combines imitative atmospherics and intricate musical development it looks forward to the *Impressions d'Enfance* of sixteen years later. But it also marks an important stage in Enescu's use of folk music. It is certainly the

---

[38] Bentoiu prints a strikingly similar tune from a folk anthology: *Capodopere*, p. 310.

Ex. 17

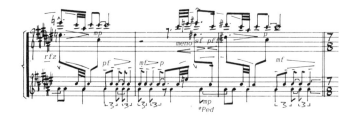

Romanian plains, rather than any other, that are conjured
up here; the music of this movement does have a distinct
folk character (despite the occasional washes of French
whole tones), but this is achieved without any real quotations of folk material, in a way that is elusively indirect.

This movement paves the way to the Third Violin Sonata
of two years later (written in August–November 1926). With
its exotic, explicitly Romanian character it has become
Enescu's best-known work apart from the *Rhapsodies*. In its
attitude to the use of folk music, however, it goes far beyond
those early works. Enescu's dissatisfaction with the idea of
subjecting simple folk tunes to .complicated musical development has already been mentioned; these were delicate

wild blooms, he felt, which would only be crushed and mangled by such treatment. In this Sonata there is no quotation, no arrangement of plucked flowers. Instead, he has invented not only folk material of his own but also an entire folk language, in which all the atmosphere and melodic colouring is deeply Romanian, but the themes are incorporated from the start into his own individual processes of melodic and harmonic development. Enescu has here distilled, in a highly personal way, a sort of quintessence of Romanian folk music, with its modes, its rhythms (either the *parlando rubato* rhythm of the first movement, or the spiky dance-rhythms of the last) and its opulent treasury of ornamentation.[39]

The title-page describes the Sonata as 'dans le caractère populaire roumain'. Enescu explained the significance of the term 'caractère' in an interview two years later, when discussing another violin piece which was in fact never completed.

> I'm working on a *Caprice* for violin and orchestra, in which I'm writing the equivalent of a dialogue between the playing of a gypsy lǎutar and the accompaniment of his band. I'm writing it in the character of folk-music. I don't use the word 'style' because that implies something made or artificial, whereas 'character' suggests something given, existing from the beginning. You should emphasise that the use of folk material doesn't in itself ensure an authentic realisation of folk character; it contributes to it, circumstantially, when it is done with the spirit of the people; in this way Romanian composers will be able to write valuable compositions whose character will be similar to that of folk music, but which will be achieved through different, absolutely personal means.[40]

[39] As a result, musicologists have had endless opportunities to find folk analogues for themes, etc., in this sonata. There are some interesting illustrations of the Moldavian character of Enescu's modes and themes in Bentoiu, *Capodopere*, pp. 324–43. Bentoiu also points to a minor mode found in Jewish synagogue music in Austria-Hungary; it is worth noting Moshe Menuhin's recollection that 'Enescu had made a thorough study of Jewish and gipsy music and it was from him that I learned that many of the traditional "Jewish" melodies I used to sing for him were of gipsy origin' (*The Menuhin Saga*, p. 106).

[40] Broşteanu, 'De vorbă cu Enescu', p. 2: 'Lucrez la un *Capriciu* pentru

These comments may be especially important if it is true
that Enescu first started work on the *Caprice* in April 1925 – a
year before he wrote the Violin Sonata.[41]

In his attempt to catch the spirit of Romanian music,
Enescu developed for this Sonata what is virtually a new
language of violin-writing. The music is full of extremely
detailed instructions such as *flautato sulla tastiera colla punta
del arco* ('flute-like, with the point of the bow, on the
fingerboard'); the ornamentation is elaborately notated, and
different degrees of vibrato are also specified. When this is
combined with the frequent fluctuations of rhythm, tempo,
dynamic and mood, the result is a score brimming with
expressivity of a peculiarly intimate kind. (One of Enescu's
most characteristic markings, which he borrowed from
Beethoven's A minor String Quartet, Op. 132 and used in
several of his compositions, is *con intimissimo sentimento*.)
Menuhin has written: 'I know of no other work more
painstakingly edited or planned. It is correct to say that it is
quite sufficient to follow the score for one to interpret the
work'.[42] What Enescu has done with this extraordinary
degree of specification is, paradoxical though it sounds, to
convey a spirit of improvisation. But this will only seem a
paradox to those who have not heard the work played.

Much of the violin technique used here is, of course, an

violină şi orchestră, în care traduc dialogul dintre cîntecul unui ţigan
lăutar şi accompaniamentul tarafului său. Il scriu în caracterul popular.
Nu întrebuinţez cuvântul de stil pentrucă el arată ceva făcut, în timp ce
cuvântul *caracter* exprimă ceva existent, dat dela început. Vă rog să
insistaţi asupra faptului că folosirea materialului folcloristic nu realizează
autenticitatea caracterului etnic, ci la aceasta contribuie numai împreju-
rarea cu spiritul rasei, următor căreia compozitorul român va putea să
creeze, paralel cu muzică populară, dar prin alte mijloace, absolut
personale, lucrări valoroase, asemănător caracterizate'.

[41] Moisescu refers to pages of sketches of the *Caprice* and *Vox Maris*, dated
April 1925, 'en route Chicago-New York' ('Manuscrisele lui George
Enescu. Doua cvartete de coarde', editorial note in Enescu, *Cvartete de
coarde, manuscriptum* (Op. 22, No. 2 and C major Quartet), Bucharest,
1985, pp. 109–13 (p. 110). I have not seen this manuscript, but I suspect
the date has been misread. In 1925 Enescu left America in mid-March,
and was in Strasbourg by 24 March: see Oprescu and Jora, *Enescu*, p. 201.

[42] 'Georges Enesco', p. 41.

imitation of the playing of Romanian fiddlers – though the
term 'imitation' here covers a whole spectrum, from the
direct reproduction of techniques (such as using a slight
upwards *portamento* to lean into the beginning of a note) to
the sort of 'imitation' Enescu engaged in when he used the
piano to paint a Romanian night-scene filled with bells. The
piano part here sometimes imitates a cymbalom (Ex. 18),
and there are other types of imitative writing; but the
overall effect is one of evocation, not transcription.

Ex. 18

The slow movement opens with a hypnotic repetition of a single B natural in the piano, above which the violin enters on a C sharp played as a harmonic (Ex. 19).

Ex. 19

The pianist Céliny Chailley-Richez, who recorded this work with Enescu, wrote down Enescu's comments in her copy of the music: the note against this passage is 'crapauds' – 'toads'.[43] This is not, however, directly imitative writing;

[43] Her copies of this and other pieces which she played with Enescu

Enescu no doubt told her to think of a still summer night, with the faint sound of toads squeaking in the background, as a way of giving her a more vivid image that might act as a correlative to the musical atmosphere of the piece. Cortot, who discussed and played the work with Enescu, described this movement as 'an evocation in sound of the mysterious feeling of summer nights in Romania: below, the silent, endless, deserted plain; above, constellations leading off into infinity . . . '.[44] Whether the listener thinks of toads, cicadas or the motion of galaxies is secondary. The music is primary.

(including the complete Beethoven sonatas) are now in the Library of the Romanian Academy. I am very grateful to Constantin Stihi-Boos for letting me consult them. The note at the start of the first movement of the Sonata is: 'Toujours écouter les basses'.

[44] Quoted in *Monografie*, p. 567n.

IX

1931–1939

In 1931 Enescu celebrated his fiftieth birthday. It was a busy year, with visits to Holland, Spain and Portugal, several concerts in Paris and a Romanian tour comprising 26 appearances in provincial towns. There were festivities in the capital; he was given honorary citizenship of Dorohoi and Bucharest; and a banquet was held in his honour, at which Professor Marinescu, a neurologist who made a speech on behalf of the Romanian Academy, caused scandalised embarrassment to all present by asking Enescu to bequeath his brain to the University laboratories.[1] Enescu celebrated with a special gesture of his own: he conducted four concerts in Bucharest, paying for the Philharmonia Orchestra out of his own pocket, and offering the tickets free to music students and subscribers to the orchestra's regular concert series.[2]

It is difficult to imagine the precise mixture of feelings with which Enescu must have contemplated his life at this point. Since the launching of his concert career more than thirty years before, he had always told himself that the demanding and distracting life of a performer was simply a preliminary to his real goal, a first step which would give him the necessary independence to retire from the platform and devote himself to composition. And now he was fifty – an age when many people are beginning to contemplate the prospect of retirement in the usual sense of the

[1] Alice Magheru, 'Being near the Maestro', *Romanian Review*, Vol. 35 (1981), No. 8, pp. 143–9 (p. 147).

[2] Drăghici, 'The Great Friend', p. 135.

word. Enescu was at last starting to cut down, slightly, his annual schedule of performances. In the late 1920s he remarked to Menuhin's father that he was beginning to find life easier now.[3] But at that time, with the task of completing *Oedipe* still hanging over him, he felt frustrated by his lack of time for other compositions. In 1928 he began to sketch a Fourth Symphony, which he would often return to but never complete, and in 1929 he started (or perhaps resumed) work on the symphonic poem *Vox Maris*, which would remain unfinished till the final years of his life.[4] He was already comtemplating a second opera: in the late 1920s he toyed with the story of 'Meşterul Manole', a Romanian folk hero about whom Carmen Sylva had written a play.[5] He also considered a dramatic poem by George Magheru and, in the late 1930s, two works by his playwright friend Horia Furtună.[6] But nothing ever came of these plans. *Oedipe*, though substantially finished in 1931, did still require further attention over the next few years. Enescu devoted more time to the Fourth Symphony in 1932–4, and it was not till 1935 that any new completed works appeared: the Second Cello Sonata and the Third Piano Sonata. The title of this last work says much about the frustration of Enescu's life as a composer: the Second Piano Sonata was never written, but up till the end of his life he explained that it was ready, entire, in his mind – 'elle est là dans ma tête'.[7]

In September 1934 Enescu wrote to the violinist Sandu Albu: 'I have begun to fulfil what has always been my dream – to retire with my scores for whole months at a time, with no more than 2–3 months of concerts each year. I think I

[3] Menuhin, 'Georges Enesco', p. 40.

[4] *Monografie*, p. 750; Oprescu and Jora, *Enescu*, p. 213; see below, pp. 244–6.

[5] Dianu, 'Cu d. George Enescu', p. 3.

[6] Magheru, 'Being near the Maestro', pp. 146–7; *Scrisori*, Vol. 2, p. 32n. Enescu was still contemplating 'Meşterul Manole' in 1936: see Cardine-Petit, 'Oedipe de George Enescu'.

[7] *Monografie*, p. 1076n.

deserve it, after more than 30 years of useless effort [. . .]'.[8] At this particular time of writing, however, he was in fact setting a brave face on what had been one of the blackest years of his life. One morning in September 1933 Enescu called on the Menuhins and explained that he had to go to Vienna or Bucharest, because of a grave personal obligation which had suddenly arisen. The young Yehudi was not told the exact nature of the crisis, though he understood that it was to do with Maruca. From Enescu's correspondence over the next few months it emerges that she had suffered some sort of severe illness, of a kind which could not be alluded to directly. The most likely conclusion is that this was when she underwent the mental collapse from which she was never to recover fully, remaining, for the rest of her life, at best demanding and hyper-eccentric and at worst simply mad.[9] The one great happiness of Enescu's life, outside the realm of music, thus withered away; but he was a man of his word, and having promised that he would eventually marry her after Michael Cantacuzino's death, he did so, on the eve of the Second World War – thereby ensuring that the final years of his life would be weighed down by a further burden of responsibility.

After tending Maruca through the winter of 1933–4, Enescu himself fell ill. He gave a few concerts in Bucharest in February and March, but then he retired to Teţcani to convalesce for the rest of the year. Enescu had always possessed colossal stamina and resilience; now, in the 1930s, some long-term medical problems were beginning to surface. In December 1936 an interviewer for a local news-paper in Oradea found him sunk in an armchair in the interval of one of his concerts, forbidden by his doctor to move. He wrote that 'Enescu has recently recovered from a dangerous heart attack. In his exhausted smile one can clearly see a spirit in torment'.[10] Enescu himself connected

[8] *Scrisori*, Vol. 1, pp. 331–2.

[9] Information from Sir Yehudi Menuhin; *Scrisori*, Vol. 1, pp. 326–30, e.g., the letter to Fleg from Bucharest, 26 September (p. 326): 'I did leave Paris very suddenly, after receiving some alarming news; and our worries are not yet over [. . .]'.

[10] Béla Katona in *Szabadság*, 19 December 1936, quoted in Lajos Pinter,

Maruca's family house, the villa at Teţcani

this trouble with the nervous angina from which he had suffered since his childhood.[11] And as the 1930s progressed, Enescu began to display the early symptoms of the chronic illness which was to cripple him in his final years: anky- losing spondylitis, causing a gradual and painful curvature of the spine.

After the black year of 1933–4 Enescu took on a lighter load for 1935; he confined himself mainly to concerts in France, and he gave more time to teaching at Yvonne Astruc's 'Institut Instrumental' in Paris.[12] The next year, 1936, was busier, with concerts in Holland, Algeria and Morocco and a taxing Romanian schedule in October– December: he gave 44 concerts in two months, including his first appearance in Bucharest with Lipatti. Despite his heart trouble that year, 1937 had an even heavier programme, with a long tour of the United States and Canada, numerous concerts and teaching engagements in Paris, and another exhausting stint of concert-giving in Romania at the end of the year. This time he gave 35 provincial concerts and seven

---

Mărturii despre George Enescu (transl. Tereza and George Sbârcea), Editura Muzicală, Bucharest, 1980, p. 61.

[11] Massoff, 'Enescu – omul'.

[12] See Oprescu and Jora, *Enescu*, pp. 226–7.

recitals in Bucharest; he also accompanied Casals when the latter visited the city in December; and during these months he conducted the Radio Orchestra in a complete cycle of Beethoven Symphonies. He also conducted four concerts of the Philharmonia Orchestra, in which he included (for the first time in Romania) a performance of Act Three of *Siegfried*. Alice Magheru attended all the rehearsals for this, and recalls that at the second one the bass was absent because of illness.

> From the desk, maestro Enescu sang perfectly the whole of Wotan's part with his incomparable full and exact voice, much to the surprise of the orchestra, which rewarded him at the end with ovations. On the next day, to everybody's delight, Enescu sang again. At the concert it was Goangă who sang. But in the ears of all those who had heard Enescu at the rehearsals his extraordinarily expressive voice was still resounding.[13]

Enescu's American tours were repeated in 1938 and 1939; but otherwise he gave himself a lighter load in these years. He devoted more time to teaching for Yvonne Astruc, but went on fewer concert-tours. A brief trip to Italy in November 1939 was his last foreign journey for many years. He returned to Romania and stayed there for the duration of the War.

There were many high points in his public life as a performer during this decade: concerts accompanied by Cortot, Marcel Ciampi or Yves Nat; a complete cycle of the Beethoven Violin Sonatas with Céliny Chailley-Richez; concerts in which he conducted performances by Menuhin or Rudolf Serkin, and concerts in which he accompanied Casals or Thibaud at the piano. In 1933 he took part in a special concert in memory of his old teacher Marsick, together with his fellow-pupils Thibaud and Flesch. Each played one of Marsick's compositions, and together they performed a triple violin concerto by Vivaldi – a rare, perhaps unparalleled, conjunction of three of the greatest violinists of the century. Flesch tells a characteristic story of Enescu's behaviour on this occasion, between the rehearsal and the concert. 'Enesco suddenly declared that he would

---

[13] 'Being near the Maestro', p. 147.

Enescu and Menuhin in 1934

not have dinner with us, he simply must "practise". Sure
enough, shortly after we heard him zealously doing finger
exercises (for which he had not the least use in the concert
itself) for an hour on end [. . .]'.[14] Enescu's perfectionism
must often have seemed obsessive in the eyes of others; the
nervousness he always felt before he gave a performance can

[14] *Memoirs*, p. 179.

Enescu playing in the
Marsick memorial concert
(courtesy of Carl F.
Flesch)

also be described as a sign of his extraordinary and genuine
humility – towards not only the audience but also, more
importantly, the music itself, which he felt he would be
betraying if he gave a less than perfect performance of it.

There were, of course, other less formal occasions for
music-making. Enescu often found that his transatlantic
crossings were a good time to draw breath and recover his
spirits; on one of these, in 1932, his fellow-passengers
included Szigeti. Each day they met, played and talked
about music, especially unaccompanied Bach. Once they
went through a Bach sonata, each at his violin, playing
alternate bars; and once, in the saloon before lunch, amidst
all the rattle and clatter of waiters laying tables, Szigeti
played through Enescu's Third Violin Sonata, with Enescu
accompanying him.[15]

[15] Szigeti, 'One of the Least "Promoted"', p. 14; Pinter, 'Enescu în presa',
p. 114.

Some of Enescu's happiest days of music-making were spent with the Menuhins, who returned to Paris in 1931 (after a period of two years during which, at Enescu's own suggestion, Yehudi had studied with Adolf Busch in Basel). At their house outside Paris, at Ville d'Avray, Enescu would join Yehudi, Hephzibah and Yaltah Menuhin to play chamber music, with Maurice Eisenberg playing the cello and Thibaud or Jacqueline Salomons also playing the violin. (Enescu usually played the viola, unless Pierre Monteux was there to play it.) It was at one of these evening gatherings that Enescu, having heard Yehudi and Hephzibah perform a Beethoven sonata, first raised the idea that they should appear together in public.[16]

Yehudi was still having frequent sessions studying music with Enescu; occasionally they also appeared together in the concert-hall. In December 1931 Enescu conducted the Beethoven Concerto and Mozart's Seventh Concerto, and also joined Menuhin for a performance of the Bach Double Concerto under Pierre Monteux. The HMV Gramophone Company heard such glowing reports of this performance of the Bach that they persuaded all those involved to make a recording of it. The resulting record won the 'Grand Prix du Disque' for 1932, and remains one of the most famous Bach recordings in the history of the gramophone. There now followed a series of recordings for HMV by Menuhin, in which he stipulated that the conductor must be Enescu (or, if he were not available, Monteux).[17] One famous exception was made, in favour of Sir Edward Elgar. Freddy Gaisberg of HMV, the king (some would say, tyrant) of the recording world, gave Menuhin the score of Elgar's Concerto and asked him to come to England to record it with the composer. Menuhin learned it on his own, and then had a couple of sessions with Enescu going through the work: Enescu too liked it immensely. After Yehudi's now famous meeting with the composer (in which he had been so satisfied with Yehudi's interpretation that he stopped the

---

[16] Menuhin, *Unfinished Journey*, p. 110.

[17] Moshe Menuhin, *Menuhin Saga*, p. 147.

A poster for a concert of Beethoven sonatas with Thibaud,
24 June 1938

rehearsal halfway through the first movement and took the
boy to the races instead), Elgar was persuaded to come to
Paris to conduct the work in 1933. In preparation for this
the Orchestre Symphonique de Paris was coached through
the concerto by Enescu, who knew that the French were
unmoved by Elgar's music and declared: 'We will *make* Paris
like it'. The concert, the rest of which was conducted by
Enescu, was a success – though it must be admitted that
Paris remained unconverted.[18]

Collaboration with Menuhin helped to overcome, to some
extent, Enescu's hostility to the gramophone. Under his
baton Menuhin recorded Chausson's *Poème*, Wieniawski's
Légende, Lalo's *Symphonie Espagnole*, two Mozart concertos
(the G major and the Seventh – the latter with cadenzas by
Enescu), the Bach A minor and E major Concertos, and the
Mendelssohn and Dvořák Concertos. As a fill-up to the last

---

[18] *Ibid.*, pp. 147–50. Menuhin played the Bach E major Concerto and
Lalo's *Symphonie Espagnole*. See Gerald Moore's recollections of the concert
in *Am I Too Loud? Memoirs of an Accompanist*, Hamish Hamilton, London,
1962, p. 105.

of these Menuhin played Paganini's Sixth *Caprice* (the 'Trills' *Caprice* in G minor) with Enescu playing a delicate piano accompaniment which he had written.[19] In America in the 1920s Enescu had recorded, as a violinist, Chausson's *Poème*, a Handel sonata and a small number of other pieces.[20] But he was never happy in a recording studio. He told Gavoty that 'recording sessions have always been my bête noire, because of the faults that stay for ever engraved in the wax, and because you're obliged to re-record a side if it's disfigured by a technical error, when it's perfectly satisfactory so far as the interpretation is concerned'.[21] And in an interview in 1936 he said: 'Apart from the distortions brought about through mechanical recording, the other thing I grieve for in these "simulated" performances is the lack of the physical presence of the player'.[22]

One further recording must be added to the list, though it is possible that it will never be found or identified. On 7 March 1933 Enescu played Mozart's Seventh Concerto (and Ravel's *Tzigane*) in a concert at New York, conducted by Léon Barzin. His next concert was at Washington three days later; in between, he stayed with a family in Baltimore. Late on the evening of the 9th his host switched on the radio, and Enescu was astonished to recognise the sound of his own interpretation of the Mozart Concerto – although he had never recorded the work. Eventually, after much questioning of the radio station by his host, the truth was revealed. A recording company had bribed the lighting engineer in the concert-hall at New York to conceal a

---

[19] Enescu wrote accompaniments to two other *Caprices*, Nos. 16 and 24, but the music seems to have been lost during the war (Oprescu and Jora, *Enescu*, p. 284; letter of 6 September 1949 in Enescu, 'Letters to Yehudi Menuhin. Master to Disciple', *Adam*, Year 43 (1981), Nos. 434–6, pp. 52–5 (p. 54).

[20] Details of all these recordings are in Appendix 3: Recordings by George Enescu, pp. 278–90.

[21] *Contrepoint*, p. 47.

[22] Ranta, 'Sub vraja lui Enescu': 'În afară de deformările legate de mecanizare, un alt factor ce mă face să deplâng "simularea" e lipsa fisică a interpretului'.

microphone in the wings; the music was picked up in a nearby studio, and the discs were on sale to the public the next day, with labels which did not mention the name of the violinist. The radio station ('Scanacted') had bought a copy and played it the next evening. Somewhere perhaps, in a basement or an attic in New York or Baltimore, there is a copy of this set of records – the only complete solo concerto ever recorded by Enescu, and, what is more, recorded when he was at the height of his powers as a violinist.[23]

Enescu's recordings with Menuhin may have served also to widen his fame as a conductor – though this was already well established, particularly in America. In 1936 he was considered as a candidate to replace Toscanini as permanent conductor of the New York Philharmonic; he was not in the end given the post, and the whole episode is a sorry story of high-handed treatment by Arthur Judson, the dictatorial director of the orchestra.[24] When Toscanini resigned (largely because of his quarrels with Judson) he suggested Fritz Busch or Furtwängler; Busch, however, was happy in Copenhagen and Furtwängler was vetoed by Judson on the grounds that he was too controversial. Judson announced that five conductors would be invited to perform during the winter, one of whom would then be selected for the permanent post. He then offered the first ten weeks of the season to Barbirolli, the last eight to Rodzinski, and the middle six to Enescu, Stravinsky and Carlos Chávez at a fortnight each – thus indicating perhaps where his own preferences lay. These became even clearer when he announced the selection of Barbirolli in mid-December, after hearing him for five weeks and before hearing any of

[23] Enescu tells this story in an interview of December 1936 (translated in Pinter, *Mărturii despre Enescu*, pp. 65–6). He does not specify which Mozart concerto, nor the date. But in all his American itineraries after the advent of electrical recording this is the only occasion I can find when he would have been in Baltimore two days after a Mozart performance in New York. For the dates and programme details see *Monografie*, p. 718.

[24] For the details which follow see Michael Kennedy, *Barbirolli, Conductor Laureate*, Macgibbon and Kee, London, 1971, pp. 105, 120, and Abraham Chasins, *Leopold Stokowski. A Profile*, Hawthorn, New York, 1979, pp. 199–201.

*Stravinsky, Enescu and Chávez as guest conductors
of the New York Philharmonic Orchestra*

the others. Enescu fulfilled his engagement, nevertheless, with ten concerts in January and February. By 6 February Barbirolli was writing anxiously and self-defensively to his wife: 'Some sections of the press have in an insidious way been hinting that Enesco would have been the conductor for the orchestra'. He went on to say that Enescu was a bad conductor and that 'in fact he has no pretensions at being one'; he also added, with barely concealed Schadenfreude, that the box office takings had gone down while Enescu was appearing.[25] If this last claim is true there is a simple explanation for it: Enescu, ever keen to promote the works of his fellow-countrymen abroad, had included substantial Romanian compositions in almost every programme. Conservative concert-goers probably did not rush to hear unknown works by Mihail Jora, Ion Nonna Otescu, Sabin Drăgoi, Marcel Mihalovici or Dinu Lipatti.

But what is one to make of Barbirolli's remarks that

[25] Letter quoted in Kennedy, *Barbirolli*, p. 133. The figures he gives seem to be sheer hearsay: he says Menuhin 'pulled it up with two sold-out houses', but one of these concerts was in fact a chamber recital with Enescu which had nothing to do with the orchestral series.

Enescu was a bad conductor and that he had no real claim
to be a conductor at all? The latter statement suggests sheer
ignorance. Enescu had performed a huge repertoire in the
last 38 years, and he had been conducting internationally
famous orchestras while Barbirolli was still a humble cellist.
And against the former statement must be weighed the
opinions of many competent judges who admired Enescu's
conducting – including Mengelberg, Elgar, Paray, Monteux,
Toscanini, Stokowski, Mitropoulos and Silvestri. Yehudi
Menuhin once said, after discussing Toscanini, Walter and
Boult, 'Of all the conductors I have ever known, the most
reassuring and inspiring was Georges Enesco. His
thoughtfulness and compassion were expressed in every
gesture'.[26] This gentleness is a theme which recurs in many
descriptions of his conducting; perhaps Barbirolli had only
seen, at a distance, the gentle, unassertive beat of Enescu's
baton and had lightly assumed that he was doing little more
than keeping up with the music. He would not, of course,
have attended any of the rehearsals, in which Enescu always
seems to have made such an extraordinary impression on
orchestral players with his prodigious ear, his total
knowledge of the score and above all his love for the music
itself. He might not, therefore, have noticed how devotedly
the players may have hung on Enescu's every gesture.
Whether this was true of these particular concerts cannot
now be said; perhaps the players were too busy deciphering
the works of Otescu and Drăgoi. But it is something that
emerges again and again in descriptions of Enescu's rehearsals and concerts.[27] In a world of histrionic star conductors,
Enescu must sometimes have seemed to belong to a
different species. Yet there was a historical precedent for
this unassertive lightness of touch. Enescu himself once
gave this description of the great Wagnerian conductor
Hans Richter, whom he had heard in Vienna in the 1890s
and at Bayreuth in 1901: 'His gestures were sparse – often a
mere nod of his beard – yet every player knew he had to do

[26] Daniels, *Conversations with Menuhin*, p. 89.

[27] See, e.g., Robert Simpson, 'He was Made of Music', *Adam*, Year 43
(1981), Nos. 434–6, pp. 34–6, and Amis, 'Master Classes', p. 40.

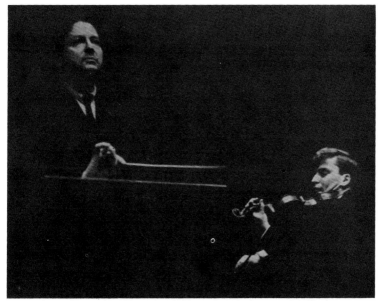

Enescu conducting a concerto with Menuhin in 1938

his best'.[28] But there is more warmth than this in Sergiu Comissiona's description of Enescu: 'His manner of conducting was to caress the music, not beat it. He moved his arms gently and gracefully. He truly held the orchestra like a madonna with a child in her arms [. . .]'.[29]

The Third Piano Sonata was Enescu's first finished work after the completion of *Oedipe*. A full draft was written between October 1933 and January 1934, and final revisions were made in May 1935. The Sonata is thus substantially the product of some of the most difficult months of Enescu's life; yet it is a work full of sparkle and delight. As Enescu

[28] Lochner, *Fritz Kreisler*, p. 92.

[29] Comissiona, 'The God-given', p. 31. See the Bibliography (p. 298) for several important articles on Enescu as a conductor by Eugen Pricope. John Amis has called Enescu 'one of the greatest two or three conductors I've ever heard in my life [. . .]. Always *communication* [. . .] with the least possible show' (*Kensington Symposium*).

wrote to Fleg at the end of January 1934: 'I console myself by taking refuge in composition. The result is a new piano sonata, freshly arrived after *Oedipe*. It's full of gaiety, in complete contrast with the atmosphere which surrounds it!'[30] The two outer movements have, initially at least, a similar character of light, open textures and quick tempos (respectively, *Vivace con brio* and *Allegro con spirito*). Whilst the last movement is more Romanian in character, the first is at the outset reminiscent of Enescu's neo-classical 'Bourrées', pointing in the direction of Couperin and Scarlatti. As it undergoes an elaborate sonata-form development the themes do take on a more distant, folk-pastoral appearance, and the simple textures begin to fragment into something more heterophonic.

It is the central slow movement, however, which displays Enescu's peculiar type of sublimated folk idiom in all its glory. These must be some of the strangest pages of piano music written this century. Long skeins of meditative 'doina' melody are wound round one another, overlapping, reinforcing one another or drifting slightly apart in a quiet riot of heterophony and polyvocality. The melodies quiver with ornamentation in every bar: grace notes, mordants and bird-like trills, not simply added to the phrases but growing out of them in a way which reminds us that in a doina there can be no ultimate distinction between ornamentation and melody. Yet all the time, this movement too is following an elaborate pattern of sonata form, with two development sections, a complex recapitulation and a coda.[31]

The last movement is even more of a formal triumph: what begins as a simple rondo turns into a tour-de-force of cyclical re-combination, in which material from the earlier movements is sucked in and transformed, in a sequence of passages which remain musically connected despite their frequent shifts in mood and style.[32] And it

[30] *Scrisori*, Vol.1, pp. 329–30.

[31] See the analysis in Niculescu, *Reflecţii*, pp. 20–28. Bentoiu offers a slightly different scheme: *Capodopere*, p. 379.

[32] See the comprehensive analysis of this movement in Bentoiu, *ibid.*, pp. 379–90, esp. p. 389.

goes without saying that throughout this Sonata the
notation is immensely detailed. John Ogdon, one of the
few great pianists to have played this work since the
famous recording of it by Lipatti, commented especially on
the precision of Enescu's instructions for pedalling and
half-pedalling.[33]

No sooner had Enescu put the final touches to this work
than he began to write another sonata, this time for piano
and cello. The first movement was completed in Bucharest
in early April 1935, and the last (fourth) movement was
finished at the end of November in Vienna, on the way back
to Romania from a busy concert tour in France. This is a
large work, but its character seems somehow more self-
enclosed than that of the Third Piano Sonata – in the outer
movements at least. In the first movement here the cello
carries an almost ceaseless melodic line in a way that
resembles Enescu's previous cello piece, the *Symphonie Concertante*; and here too the overall shape of the melody is
difficult to grasp at a first or second hearing. The harmonic
language is a refined version of Enescu's chromatic-folk-
modal idiom; the piano textures are fluid but clear, devoted
to accompaniment rather than response or counter-
challenge. There is more argument between the instruments in the second movement, a demonically scuttling
Allegro agitato in $\frac{6}{8}$: here there is less sense of folk-colouring
and more of a modernist exploration of dissonance and
rhythmical or melodic angularity. These are unusual pages
in Enescu's œuvre; and they contrast with the rest of the
sonata, too, which is not an experimental work and sometimes strikes echoes of the First Piano Quartet – in places
enabling us to see more clearly the latent folk-character of
some of the melodic shapes found in that piece. Folk-
character is strongly felt in the third movement here, a
gentle *Andantino cantabile* which begins with a doina-like
unaccompanied melody (Ex. 20), and it becomes completely
explicit in the last movement, entitled *Final à la roumaine*,
with its imitative cymbalom-writing for the piano and its
cello glissandi and quarter tones.

---

[33] *Kensington Symposium.*

Ex. 20

At one point the piano part is marked *rustico*. There are passages here which will remind the listener directly of Bartók's use of folk dances – it is Bartók's Romanian dances that spring to mind, so the resemblance is not surprising. And Enescu too has a quiverful of percussive discords and cluster-chords, usually formed out of the chromatic modes he is using; the penultimate piano chord is a wonderful accumulation of all the notes of a pentatonic Lydian mode on F, with a crunchy F sharp thrown in.[34]

1936 was a fallow year, with only the revision of one of the Gregh songs (*L'Ombre est Bleue*) to show for it. But 1937–8

---

[34] For analyses of the Sonata see Dumitru Bughici, *Repere arhitectonice în creaţia muzicală românească contemporană*, Editura Muzicala, Bucharest, 1982, pp. 70–86, and Bentoiu, *Capodopere*, pp. 394–416.

saw the writing of a major orchestral work, Enescu's first since the Third Symphony and *Oedipe*. This was the Third Orchestral Suite, which is entitled *Village Suite (Suite Villageoise)*. It is one of Enescu's most advanced orchestral works, but also one of his most immediately attractive. Like the *Poème Roumain* and the later chamber work *Impressions d'Enfance* it has a programme consisting of a day-night-day sequence. It is closer in many ways to the latter work; it shows to perfection Enescu's ability to transform imitative or descriptive writing, incorporating it into an autonomous realm of musical expression and development. The first movement sets the scene with a gentle *Allegro moderato* entitled 'Springtime in the country'; the second is a *scherzando* sequence of children's games called 'Children out of doors', with percussion imitations of whipping a spinning-top, muted sounds like toy trumpets or harmonicas and a discordant quick-march dance (marked *buffo*) which may remind the listener of the 'Giuoco delle coppie' in Bartók's *Concerto for Orchestra* – written five years later.

There are three more movements, of which the last is a sparkling folk-dance sequence (simply entitled 'Country Dances'). But it is the third and fourth movements that contain the most magical music of the Suite. The third has a detailed programme of its own: 'The old childhood home, at sunset. Shepherd. Migrating birds and crows. Evening bell'. An atmosphere of tranquillity and nostalgia is created with a slow, elusive melody which winds in and out of several different modes. (Versions of the Dorian mode predominate, with restful fourths and fifths and open, wide-eyed tritones.) The shepherd's tune, again harking back to the cor anglais in the Prelude to Act Three of *Tristan*, is played by an oboe out of sight in the wings; the migrating birds and crows are also played by off-stage instruments. Enescu achieves his effect here with an inventiveness which provokes comparison with the flock of sheep in *Don Quixote*. Four muted trumpets play dissonant clusters of semitones, and are answered by similar sounds from three muted trombones; the dissonances are also echoed by a harmonium. The beat-notes set up by these discords contribute tremors of interference to the sound, so that the listener

half-senses the distant beating of wings as the birds pass
high overhead in the twilight. The fourth movement is
simply called 'River in the Moonlight'. It explores a soft and
luminous combination of timbres: the main instruments are
soprano (or sopranino) saxophone, flute, oboe, celesta,
harp, strings, suspended cymbal and tam-tam. There is a
melodic line throughout, but it is so rarefied that the hearer
may scarcely be aware of it, listening instead to waves of
chords which sweep on in long, slow $\frac{5}{4}$ bars, with strange (but
also strangely restful) chromatic progressions such as Ex. 21
(which gives the simplified harmony of pp. 112–14 of the
score).[35]

Ex. 21

Apart from *Vox Maris*, of which a full draft had already
been written, this Suite was Enescu's last large-scale work
for full orchestra. He had been sketching a Fourth Symphony in 1928 and 1933–4, and he returned to it in the
spring of 1939, but then he abandoned it. Two orchestrated
drafts of the first movement survive, the later of them dated
20 December 1934; this manuscript also sketches the begin-
nings of an *Andante*.[36] Held up to the light, each page is a
mass of erasures: Enescu always wrote in ink and spent long
hours whittling the music down by scraping unnecessary
notes away with a sharp knife. Even so, from this first
movement it seems that he was returning to the more
abundant orchestral style of the Second and Third Sym-

[35] This simplified version is taken from Bentoiu, *ibid.*, p. 437.

[36] Enescu Museum, MSS 2909(b) and 2909(a) respectively. In the latter
the first movement is 51 pages long, and there are 45 bars of *Un poco
andante, marziale* in $\frac{3}{4}$ (For the other dates see the chronology in Oprescu
and Jora, *Enescu.*)

phonies: partly because of the emotional intensity of the work, the scoring shows less of the extreme lightness of touch which one associates with Enescu's late works for orchestra. The opening bars (simplified in Ex. 22) give some idea of the emotional character of the piece, which also seems to point back to those earlier symphonies.

Ex. 22

Finally, one other abandoned work must be mentioned which may belong to these years, though the dating of it is very uncertain. Enescu gave the title *Voix de la Nature* (*Voices of Nature*) to the whole projected work, but only part of one movement, 'Nuages d'automne sur les forêts' ('Autumm Clouds over the Forests') survives, in a fragment of 43 pages (lasting about eight minutes in performance). It is scored for a much smaller orchestra than the Fourth Symphony or even the Third Suite, and one interesting feature of it is the employment throughout of a group of soloists consisting of

two violas, two cellos and a double bass. It is a complex
score, but it sounds less polyvocal than most of Enescu's
other orchestral works; at any moment there is usually one
leading melodic section and much textural accompaniment – culminating in a shimmering passage of forest
murmurs. But there it breaks off.[37]

[37] The work is described briefly in Moisescu, 'Lucrări inedite', p. 14;
Bentoiu argues for dating it from the mid-1930s, though on stylistic
grounds I think it may be earlier than this (*Capodopere*, p. 555). My
account is based on a performance by Remus Georgescu and the
Timişoara Philharmonic Orchestra in Bucharest in 1981.

X

SECOND WORLD WAR

Once again Enescu was confined to his native land for the duration of a long and bloody war. He was a patriot, and would not have wished to be anywhere else; but he devoted himself to the musical life of the capital and kept his distance from the political developments of these years, not all of which were to the credit of his country. Politics had never interested him. He was a man of strong personal loyalties, and he remained faithful to the royal family which had done so much for him (though he was less personally close to King Carol II, who, after renouncing the throne in favour of his young son Michael, had reclaimed it in 1930 and developed an increasingly autocratic hold over the political life of the country). The closest Enescu ever came to making a political statement in an interview was when he once offered a vague remark about the value of order and hierarchy for the prosperity of mankind.[1] He did, it seems, express approval of Maniu's National Peasant Party, which governed the country in 1928–30 and aimed to reduce police control in the state and to improve the conditions of peasant smallholders.[2] But he was also sympathetic to Octavian Goga, whose more right-wing National Christian Party formed a shortlived government in 1937–8; in this case it was probably a matter of personal friendship and admir-

---

[1] Massoff, 'Enescu intim': 'Continui să visezi o lume care să se conducă după principiile ordinei şi erarhiei, singurele modalităţi pentru propaşirea acestei omeniri'.

[2] Tomaziu, '"Mosh" Georges', p. 30.

ation, arising from Goga's achievements as a poet.[3]

Otherwise Enescu showed a positive distaste for political movements. He disliked the strident Romanian nationalism which was increasingly active in the political life of the country in the 1930s, with its hostility to Jews and Hungarian-speaking Transylvanians. Sergiu Comissiona recalls a concert at which Enescu was due to play a sonata by the Jewish composer, Ernest Bloch. The audience was packed with student members of the Romanian fascist movement, the Iron Guard, who protested loudly. Enescu came onto the stage and said that he would not play the sonata. There was loud applause. Instead, Enescu continued, he would play a work by a French composer: Ravel's *Khaddisch*, the Jewish prayer. The audience fell silent – there was nothing they could say.[4] On another occasion in the early 1930s, in a town in Transylvania, Enescu said he would cancel his concert if the nationalist students used it to make an anti-Magyar demonstration: 'otherwise I could never look my old friends Bartók and Dohnányi in the face again'.[5] After another concert in the same town in 1937 he asked his interviewer if it were true that Bartók had forbidden the playing of his works on German or Italian radio. Yes, explained the journalist, it was because they had attacked him for his political opinions. 'Oh, politics . . . ', said Enescu bitterly. 'Bartók's music will still live on in the world when these people and their children's children have long been forgotten.'[6]

The position of Romania during the war years was governed as much by traditional territorial concerns as it was by the new political movements. As in the First World War, Romania was neutral to start with, poised between the hammer and the anvil. When Russia moved into Bessarabia

---

[3] Drăghici recalls that Enescu knew many of Goga's poems by heart ('The Great Friend', p. 131). It was Goga who proposed Enescu's election to the Romanian Academy in 1933.

[4] 'The God-given', p. 32.

[5] Pinter, *Mărturii despre Enescu*, p. 12.

[6] *Ibid.*, p. 69.

and Bukovina in 1940 the Romanians looked to Berlin for protection; later that year Germany did intervene to arbitrate between the territorial claims of Romania and Hungary, but forced Bucharest to cede a large part of Transylvania. This was so unpopular that King Carol was obliged to resign in favour of his son, Michael. German troops then moved into Romania to protect their supply of raw materials; a military government under General Ion Antonescu co-operated with them; and in 1941 Romania joined the German campaign against Russia, partly to regain territory from the Russians and partly to gain credit with Berlin in order to bring about a revision of the Transylvanian settlement. In 1943 the first Allied raids on the Romanian oilfields began, and in April 1944 Bucharest was heavily bombed. In August 1944, with Soviet armies rapidly approaching, King Michael dismissed and imprisoned Antonescu, declared war on Germany, and turned the Romanian army round to fight a final bloody campaign against the Axis forces. Within a few weeks the Soviet army had moved into Romania. King Michael remained in place for more than two years, though he found it increasingly difficult to co-operate with the Communist-dominated 'National Democratic Front' which, acting as a tool of Russia, came to control the government. By the time he abdicated in December 1947 it was quite clear what form the future government of Romania would take.

Enescu spent most of his time in Bucharest during the War, with occasional spells at his villa in Sinaia. In 1939, ten years after the death of Prince Michael Cantacuzino, he had fulfilled his vow to marry Maruca. Her town house was a huge and splendid mansion on the main street of the city; she entertained there in apartments of Oriental luxury, but he preferred to work in a small and sparsely furnished house in the rear courtyard. (The main house is now the Enescu Museum, and Enescu's little house was lived in by Romeo Drăghici, who lovingly preserved the rooms there exactly as his old friend had left them.)

Enescu was too pre-occupied with music to have much contact with the political events of the war years, but occasionally he intervened with the government on behalf of

Maruca's house in Bucharest

other musicians. In February 1943 he wrote to the Minister
of Education on behalf of his old friend and former accompanist Theodor Fuchs, asking that the government's ban on
performances by Jewish musicians should be lifted in his
case.[7] And later that year Enescu, Mihail Andricu and
Emanoil Ciomac wrote jointly to the Minister for the
Interior requesting that the young composer Matei Socor
should be released from an internment camp, to which he
had been sent as a 'militant anti-fascist'.[8]

[7] *Scrisori*, Vol. 1, pp. 372–3.

[8] *Ibid*, Vol. 1, p. 374 (10 August); T. Pintean, 'Enescu în apărarea

Enescu's schedules of concerts were at first less frenziedly demanding than they had been during the First War. 1940 was a comparatively blank year, enabling him to complete two major compositions, the *Impressions d'Enfance* and the Piano Quintet. In the following year he formed a string quartet, and during March they performed the complete cycle of Beethoven quartets in Bucharest. Enescu insisted that they play the *Grosse Fuge* at the beginning of each rehearsal; then they would practise for five or six hours. Enescu always played from memory. The violinist of the quartet, Alexandru Rădulescu, asked him if it were true, as d'Indy had once said, that if the works of Beethoven were destroyed Enescu would be able to reconstruct them all from memory. Oh no, said Enescu – only the Symphonies, Quartets and Trios, the *Missa Solemnis* and *Fidelio*.[9] Chamber music featured largely in Enescu's concert schedules of the following years: in early 1943 he took part in a long series of performances of piano trios and quartets. There were also many violin recitals, including several with Lipatti. Madeleine Lipatti has written a touching description of their appearance together on the platform: the young man frail-looking, timid and deferential, and Enescu 'strongly built, powerful, but with his back already bent, his head twisted over to the left as if he were perpetually playing the violin [. . .]'.[10]

It was during these years that Enescu and Lipatti made their recordings of the Second and Third Violin Sonatas at the radio studios in Bucharest.[11] Enescu's hostility to recording had been softened further by his musicologist friend Constantin Brăiloiu; in 1938 he had listened to 30

---

demnității umane', *Magazin istoric*, Vol. 8, No. 3, March 1974, p. 43. He wrote again, with Andricu, Ciomac, Brăiloiu and Jora, in October: *Scrisori*, Vol. 2, p. 107.

[9] See C. Răsvan, Interview with Rădulescu in *Muzica*, Vol. 25, No. 6, June 1975, pp. 12–13. No doubt one should add to this list the Violin Sonatas and most, perhaps all, of the Piano Sonatas.

[10] *In Memoriam Lipatti*, p. 13.

[11] *Ibid.*, p. 29; *Monografie*, pp. 994, 991 and n. The recordings were made in April–May 1943.

The house in the rear courtyard of Maruca's town house

recordings of folk-music made by Brăiloiu, and they were
both on the committee set up by Romanian Radio in 1943 to
plan a series of recordings of Romanian compositions.
Enescu and Lipatti also recorded the *Impressions d'Enfance* for
the series, but this seems not to have survived. However,
they made a recording which does survive of the Second
Piano Suite, in which they took turns at the keyboard:
Enescu played the slow movements and Lipatti the
'Toccata' and 'Bourrée'.

    Enescu's public concert-giving included several series of
symphonic concerts. In November 1943 the soloists he
conducted included Gieseking, in a special 'Beethoven
Festival' concert. At the end of 1944 he conducted all the
Beethoven Symphonies. Once the Soviet army had arrived
in Bucharest, it was judged fitting that Russian works
should be included in the Philharmonia's programmes. On

Shostakovich, Enescu and Maruca in Moscow, 1946

19 March 1945 Enescu conducted an all-Tchaikovsky programme, with Lev Oborin and David Oistrakh as soloists,
and on 1 April he conducted Shostakovich's Seventh Symphony. When Oistrakh came he brought the score and parts
of Khachaturian's Violin Concerto; Enescu performed the
work from memory ten days later.[12] At the end of the year
the Vuillaume Quartet (from Kiev) came to Bucharest and
played the Schumann Piano Quintet with Enescu at the
piano. But Enescu's concert-giving was not completely
dominated by Russian music or Russian musicians. In
March 1946, for example, he conducted the first performance of Paul Constantinescu's huge oratorio, *The Passion of
the Lord*, which was based on reconstructions of early
Romanian Byzantine church music.

In April 1946, in a strange repetition of what had happened in 1917, Enescu was invited to go and perform in
Moscow. There he met Oistrakh and Oborin again; in one
concert he played the Franck Sonata with the latter and
then accompanied the former in a sonata by Grieg. The
critics were divided on his interpretation of Tchaikovsky's
Fourth Symphony, which some found more reserved and
scrupulously classical than was usual in the Russian tradition; but all praised his performance of the Bach Double
Concerto with Oistrakh under Kondrashin. As a present for

---

[12] Voiculescu, *Enescu şi Oedip*, pp. 101–3.

A poster for a concert in Bucharest,
20 May 1946

Oistrakh he wrote out from memory his cadenza to the
Brahms Concerto.[13] The Russian violinist later wrote a brief
but moving memoir of Enescu's visit. In particular he
recalled going to his hotel room and pausing at the door
when he heard the sound of Enescu's violin. He pushed the
door slightly ajar and stood there, listening to Enescu

---

[13] *Monografie*, pp. 1025–9.

playing Bach's Chaconne 'in the faint light, sitting in the armchair, stooped, with his eyes closed'.[14]

On this visit to Russia Enescu was accompanied by his wife. A photo survives of them sitting at table with Shostakovich, who seems to be almost smiling; perhaps Maruca, who was becoming ever more bizarre and eccentric, had somehow pierced his usually impenetrable reserve. What Moscow thought of the Princess Cantacuzino-Enescu is not known, but what she thought of Moscow may easily be guessed: no doubt she saw life in the Soviet Union as a foretaste of what life would soon be like in Romania, and did not like what she saw.

After their return to Bucharest at the end of April, May brought the unexpected pleasure of a visit by Yehudi Menuhin, whom Enescu had last seen in early 1939. Menuhin has described the happiness of that brief visit: 'It was an Enesco festival, an Enesco orgy, an Enesco delirium, promoted by my coming. He and I gave concerts every day for nearly two weeks, with public rehearsals in the mornings, going through a good part of the violin literature, every day a different programme, Enesco either at the piano or conducting the orchestra'.[15] When Menuhin left, King Michael gave him a guard of honour at the airport. But the days of royal power were already numbered. Enescu and Maruca spent the summer months at Teţcani, settling their affairs. Romeo Drăghici visited them, in his professional capacity as a lawyer, to help draw up a plan to leave the Teţcani estate (which contained a very valuable library) as a cultural foundation where writers and composers could stay and work.[16]

In August Enescu paid a last visit to his birthplace, Liveni. The country had suffered a severe drought since March, and hundreds of the villagers at Liveni came to meet him, begging him for help; he gave them money, and promised to send more from abroad. 'After that moment',

[14] 'A Great Love of Art', *Romanian Review*, Vol. 35 (1981), No. 8, pp. 123–4.

[15] *Unfinished Journey*, p. 214.

[16] Drăghici, 'The Great Friend', p. 136; the plan was confirmed in a letter from Enescu to the Minister of Arts in October 1947 (*Scrisori*, Vol. 1, pp. 382–3).

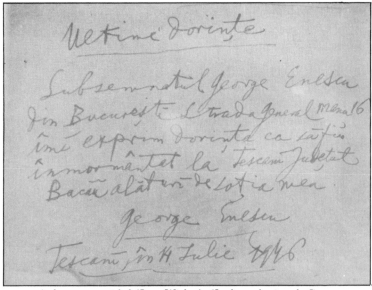

*A document entitled 'Last Wishes': 'I, the undersigned, George
Enescu, of 16, str. General Manu, Bucharest, express my wish to
be buried at Tescani, in the district of Bacău, beside my wife
[Signed] George Enescu, Tescani, 14 July 1946'*

Romeo Drăghici writes, 'Enescu asked to be left alone to go
into the garden at the back of the house. We waited,
respectfully quiet. On his return he was depressed,
melancholy, as when you part from someone you hold very
dear.' He went next to the graveyard in Dorohoi where his
father lay buried, and then to his mother's grave at Mihaileni
where, shaken violently by emotion, he stood for about a
quarter of an hour with his head bowed. On 3 September he
returned to Bucharest, and a week later he boarded a ship at
the Black Sea port of Constanţa. Romeo Drăghici, who was to
stay in Romania for the rest of his life, said his farewells. It
was the last time he would ever see his friend.[17]

Enescu's feelings as he visited his childhood home will seem
all the more poignantly vivid to anyone who knows his first

[17] Drăghici, 'The Great Friend', pp. 138–9.

Romeo Drăghici and Enescu on board the ship at
Constanța, shortly before they parted

major composition of the war years, the *Impressions d'Enfance*
for violin and piano. This is a continuous descriptive suite,
with a programme and a character partly similar to that of
the Third Orchestral Suite. But whereas in that work the
viewpoint from which the description is made is general,
abstract or authorial ('Children out of doors', 'The River in
the moonlight', etc.), in this piece everything is seen
through the eyes of the young child himself: the five- or
six-year-old George Enescu in his parents' whitewashed
house in the Moldavian plains. The music is, of course, of
an immensely sophisticated construction, with a gradual
cyclical accumulation of themes. Yet it succeeds in captur-
ing a child's freshness of vision; its character is one of

genuine innocence and wonder, untouched by the sort of knowing 'sophisticated' humour which one finds in Ravel's *L'Enfant et les Sortilèges*. Because of this, the descriptive writing in this piece is more directly imitative than anywhere else in Enescu's œuvre, with the violin producing magically accurate mimicry of a caged songfinch, a cuckoo-clock, a cricket, and the wind in the chimney – and making huge demands on the violinist's technique. Even at its most imitative, however, as in the chirping of the caged bird, the music is all the time weaving a delicate web of interconnected motifs and cellular intervals.

The programme is a simple one, and can be briefly described, with additional explanations taken from Enescu's remarks in his conversations with Gavoty. The piece opens with the sound of a fiddler outside in the street. Enescu remarked on the piece as a whole that it contained 'not the slightest trace of allusion to folklore' ('allusion folklorique'), meaning presumably no direct quotation of folk-music.[18] This fiddler is certainly a folk-fiddler, but what he plays is a sort of distillation of Central European fiddle-music. He is followed by an old beggar, murmuring 'Have pity on me, have pity on me . . . May the lord bless you'. The violin part here is marked *un poco raucamente, ma dolce e mesto* ('a little hoarsely, but soft and sad'). The next section is entitled 'The little stream at the bottom of the garden'. Here the music offers (Ex. 23) a delicate reminiscence of passages in Szymanowski's 'Fontaine d'Arethuse' (the first movement of *Mythes*).

The violin part is full of diaphanous chromaticised arpeggios and high, luminous harmonics, and the piano part is marked *dolcissimo, con una sonorità acquatica*. Enescu told Gavoty: 'I can still see it – a small stream which tinkled softly at the bottom of our garden, and sometimes grew into a little pond which shimmered in the light [. . .]'. The child comes indoors now; first the chirps and whistles of the caged bird are heard, then the striking of the cuckoo-clock (which is preceded by wonderful premonitory wheezes and

---

[18] *Entretiens*, tape 1. The phrase is incorrectly given by Gavoty as 'pas la moindre allusion folklorique, à peine de pittoresque'; Enescu only said 'pas la moindre trace d'allusion folklorique dans ce recueil'.

Ex. 23

thuds of the clock's mechanism in the piano part). It is seven o'clock: time to cover the bird's cage (there is a last faint chirp) and time also for bed. The boy's nurse sings an old lullaby ('You will grow tall, you will grow strong . . . '), and as he drifts off to sleep he hears a cricket in the hearth. Night has fallen, and the next section is called 'Moonlight through the window'; it is marked *molto tranquillo*, and at one point the instruction to the players is *quasi addormentato* – 'as if asleep'. Then 'The Wind in the Chimney' offers a tour-de-force of imitative writing, with hoarse, eerie, slithering tritones played *sul ponticello, un poco flautato* on the bottom two strings. A storm rises, breaks and dies away, and the last section is called 'Dawn'. In Enescu's words: 'Shafts of light enter, all through the room. Birds sing. All the themes of day and night come back, this time in the major, pacified and transformed'.

If any hint of tweeness is raised by this description of the music's programme, then the best disproof would be to let the music speak for itself. Sadly, it is almost never heard in the concert-hall; it seems to be quite unknown to most violinists, although it offers a fine chance to display technical skills of a high order. It should also prove instantly attractive to any audience; it can be listened to without difficulty by anyone who enjoys Szymanowski or Ravel, for it is much less harmonically elusive than Enescu's later chamber works. Given the special autobiographical nature of this piece, it is particularly sad that Enescu's own recording of it with Lipatti has not survived. But there is a consolation: he can be heard playing several sections of it with his old friend Caravia to illustrate his childhood memories in the recordings of his conversations with Gavoty.

The *Impressions d'Enfance* is at least easy to talk about insofar as it has a story. With Enescu's final chamber works – especially the Piano Quintet, the Second Piano Quartet and the Second String Quartet – the problem of description becomes acute. These compositions show Enescu's mature style at its most rich and rarefied. Of the three, the Piano Quintet, Op. 29, is the earliest, the longest, and the most luxuriously lyrical. Its history is slightly mysterious. It was not published in Enescu's lifetime, and

in the list of works added to Gavoty's edition of Enescu's
memoirs (which came out before Enescu's death) 'Op. 29'
is listed simply as 'Néant' ('Nothing') – but is correctly
dated '1940'. The manuscript bears the date 24 September
1940 at the end of the first movement, but the other
movement is undated; the two together do, however, form a
complete and finished work, and the manuscript is itself
incomplete only insofar as it lacks a few details such as the
pedal markings for the last section and the metronome
timings throughout. It is a large work, lasting at least 40
minutes, and it displays all the Enescian hallmarks of
rhythmical and harmonic flexibility, thematic transformation and cyclical re-combination. After the rich
lyricism of the *Molto moderato* first movement (Ex. 24,
p. 225), the second (*Vivace*) begins in complete contrast with
a crisp, clear, rhythmical dance.

Gradually reminiscences of the first movement begin to
break through, in the manner of the finale of the Third
Piano Sonata; there are turbulent alternations and shifts of
mood (in the manner of the finale of the Second Symphony),
and the energy of the *Vivace* movement is finally combined
with the yearning and passion of the *Molto moderato* in a huge
climax to the work. It is, in the end, the soaring lines of the
first movement that come out, literally, on top and seem to
predominate in the character of the work, with their long
rhapsodic melodies filled with wide intervals: sevenths,
sixths and, above all, augmented fifths. Often the violins are
in unison or some other parallel, with the first violin part
floating high above; perhaps to strengthen the sense of
soaring, there is surprisingly little heterophony (though
there is some genuine counterpoint and one remarkable
page of intricate fugato). The harmonies often lean in the
direction of some traditional late romantic progressions, but
they usually remain at one remove (at least) from the
familiar; and Enescu's sublimated modal language can
often be heard working through these progressions and
gently shifting them aside.

The Quintet is certainly a romantic work. By comparison,
the Second Piano Quartet and the Second String Quartet
seem more governed by a spirit of purity and restraint – a

Ex. 24

*An example of the fluid piano writing and soaring string lines in the
first movement of the Piano Quintet*

sort of innate classicism of expression, designed to serve more perfectly the same demands of expressivity. The Piano Quartet was written between July 1943 and May 1944. This was the worst period of the War for Romania, with heavy losses on the Russian front and the first Allied bombing raid on Bucharest. It will not be surprising to learn that this Piano Quartet contains some of Enescu's most radiantly tranquil music. It is dedicated with perfect appropriateness to the memory of Fauré; moving to this work after the Piano Quintet is rather like coming to Fauré after Chausson. (This dedication was not Enescu's only act of piety towards his old master: in December 1944 he organised a special concert in Bucharest to mark the twentieth anniversary of his death.) Although this work is in a more traditional (three-movement) form than the Quintet it undergoes a similar process of sifting and culmination in the last movement, where it offers an outstanding example of Enescu's love for endings which are almost endlessly prolonged, with an inventive succession of climaxes and postponements. But the glory of the work is its slow movement, *Andante pensieroso ed espressivo*, in which quiet bell-like piano sonorities combine with open, clear or delicately ornamented string writing to produce music which is somehow both intimate and distant, possessing an extraordinary quality of serenity. The piano part throughout this movement has been fined down to a bare and limpid minimum; a characteristic touch is the light repetition of notes in octave patterns, which helps to isolate and emphasise transitional moments of harmonic stillness in the music.

Of Enescu's other compositions during these years only two are known, fragmentarily. One was a song for a choir of three equal voices *a cappella*. It was a setting of verses by a minor poet, A. T. Stamatiad, entitled *Linişte*, (*Silence*); they offer a description of night falling on the Romanian landscape. Although it was commissioned for publication in a manual of songs for schoolchildren it remained, for some reason, unpublished, and the manuscript has since been lost. Only a quotation of five bars survives.[19]

[19] Printed in *Monografie*, pp. 1041–2.

The other work was altogether more ambitious: nothing less than a Fifth Symphony. Two manuscripts survive: one is of the beginning of the first movement, in 25 pages of rough orchestral score, and the other consists of 16 pages of very rough draft on two staves.[20] This appears to be the initial (and only) sketch of the complete symphony. It is in four movements, three of which bear dates at the end (all within July 1941). Once again the character of Enescu's symphonic writing seems to hark back to the Third Symphony.[21] And there is a further similarity here: the last movement was to have had a solo tenor and a chorus of women's voices. Enescu had chosen to set one of Mihai Eminescu's simplest and most beautiful poems, 'Mai am un singur dor' ('I have but one more longing'), in which the poet asks only to die in peace, close to the sea, in the quiet of the evening.

---

[20] Enescu Museum MSS 2910(b) and 2910(a) respectively.

[21] See Vancea's discussion (and examples) in *Creaţia muzicală*, pp. 271–3.

XI

1946–1955

When Enescu left Romania in September 1946 he travelled with a Romanian legation to New York, and with the blessing of the Bucharest authorities he was treated as a sort of goodwill ambassador there. (He gave several benefit concerts in aid of starving children in Romania, and sent the sum of $20,000 back to his native land.)[1] But it was in fact clear that Enescu would not return to Romania – for reasons both personal and political. He was in his mid-60s, and was now aging more rapidly in physical terms because of his progressive spinal disease. All he wanted was a simple and quiet life in order to devote his remaining years to composition.

It was already obvious that neither tranquillity nor justice would be found in Romania for a long time to come. Economically, the country was in ruins; the 'reparations' exacted by the Soviet Union, which were in reality a form of systematised looting, weakened it still further. Politically, the 'National Democratic Front' (a front for the Communists) was using all the weapons of terror and corruption to ensure an irreversible transition to Communist rule. The national elections of November 1946 were marked by the suppression of anti-Communist newspapers, the intimidation of politicians and the blatant falsification of results. In July 1947 Romania's senior statesman, the National Peasant Party leader Iuliu Maniu, was arrested, and in October he was subjected to a show-trial. In December King Michael was finally forced to abdicate and

---

[1] Drăghici, 'The Great Friend', p. 139n.

Enescu arriving at New York

leave the country. Communist power was now rapidly consolidated. At one prison camp, the notorious work-camp for the construction of the Danube–Black Sea canal, at least 100,000 prisoners are known to have perished between 1949 and 1953.[2]

Enescu's relations with the new regime in Romania were conducted in an atmosphere of frigid politeness. The government wooed him with official honours and invitations: in March 1947 he was awarded a medal, in 1948 he was nominated as a member of the Academy of the People's

---

[2] Ion Raţiu, *Contemporary Romania*, Foreign Affairs Publishing Co., Richmond, 1975, p. 11.

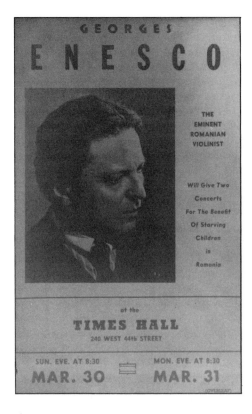

*A poster for two concerts
by Enescu in New York,
March 1947*

Republic of Romania, in 1951 he was invited to take part in
a music festival in Bucharest, and in November 1953 the
Romanian Prime Minister, a Communist stooge called
Petru Groza, sent Enescu a letter inviting him to return to
his native land.[3] Enescu's reply, written in January 1954,
displays not only diplomatic politeness – when reading that
he was too weak to travel, one should remember that he
travelled to Siena to teach at the Accademia Chigiana five
months later – but also a genuine love of his country:

> During the last two years my physical strength has declined
> considerably, and at the present moment it is altogether
> beyond my physical powers to undertake the journey home.
> My strongest desire is to return to my country, and I hope

[3] *Monografie*, p. 1059.

that with the assistance of God (and the doctors) that day will come, for which I long so much. Meanwhile I devote what little strength and energy I have left to my compositions, with which I hope to serve our Romanian people.[4]

Enescu's self-imposed exile made his true feelings quite clear enough: in his interviews with Gavoty he touched briefly on this topic, explaining that he had wished to remain true to his principles when his country became 'dominated by the Soviet Union'.[5] But on the other hand he was not a political activist by nature, and he may have felt that any open protests on his part might have endangered the safety of those friends, such as Romeo Drăghici, who had stayed behind.

Would Enescu himself have been in danger if he had stayed in Romania? It is difficult to believe that the Communist regime would have dared to imprison or openly molest someone of such international standing. Here and there in the Romanian music journals of the early 1950s one finds a few tentative attempts to denounce him on ideological grounds (alleging, for example, that his use of folk music was 'bourgeois'); but such arguments came to nothing. A more likely line of attack, had he stayed in Romania, would have been through his wife. There was no room, in the new order of things, for wealthy, eccentric and flamboyant princesses – and, in addition, Maruca could have been compromised by her old support for Maniu and her close friendship before the War with Professor Nae Ionescu, the academic theorist of the Iron Guard.[6]

Maruca's property, like that of other landowners, was expropriated. Enescu had accumulated a considerable sum from his earnings between the wars, and like a good patriot he had banked it all in Romania; this money too was denied

---

[4] *Scrisori*, Vol. 1, p. 410.

[5] *Contrepoint*, p. 58: 'On sait ce qu'il advint de mon pays, finalement dominé par l'U.R.S.S. Pour ma part, je voulus demeurer fidèle à mes principes, à mes sentiments [. . .]'.

[6] Matila Ghyka, *The World Mine Oyster*, Heinemann, London, 1985, pp. 274–5.

to him. So he began this last period of his life with the spectre of poverty looming over him. He still had his flat in Paris and, for a while, the lease of a small house in the Parisian suburb of Bellevue; but once again Enescu had to earn his living in the concert halls of Europe and America.

This meant appearing first and foremost as a violinist, since that was how Enescu was best known, and since he had for so long been out of the public eye as a conductor. (A plan to appoint him deputy conductor of the Philadelphia Orchestra fell through, apparently because Eugene Ormandy was reluctant to work in what he felt would be competition with someone of Enescu's stature.[7]) Now that Enescu was more dependent than ever before on his violin-playing, an appalling new handicap afflicted him. Shortly before he left Romania he had received treatment to his ears from a doctor, which involved having them syringed to remove wax. Soon afterwards he heard a performance by a string quartet on the radio which sounded horribly out of tune. He chided the players for this, and in suprised tones they asked him what he was talking about. Only then did he discover that he had developed a condition similar to that which afflicted Fauré (though in Enescu's case it did not involve partial deafness), a distortion of pitch in which different frequencies were differently affected, turning a simple chord into a cacophony. No doubt it was a condition which had been building up gradually (perhaps in connection with his bone disease), but the effects of which had in some way been held back until his recent syringing. The difficulty and mental pain it must have caused him as he went out onto a concert stage to play unaccompanied Bach can only be imagined. For some of his concerts he arranged with one devoted pupil that she should sit in the front row of the audience and use a discreet sign-language to tell him whether he was playing flat or sharp – this for a violinist who had once been famous for the exquisite purity of his intonation.[8] And yet he continued to earn his living in this

[7] Information from Sir Yehudi Menuhin.

[8] All these details are from the pupil in question, Helen Dowling. The facts of this additional illness were never publicly stated during Enescu's

*Enescu conducting at a BBC studio in 1949, a drawing by
Milein Cosman (courtesy of Milein Cosman)*

way for several years, despite this and despite the wasting
disease which was gradually shrinking his frame and
inexorably bending his spine into the shape of a question-
mark. The business of concert-giving was increasingly a
source of pain and exhaustion for him; and no sooner had he
earned his fees than they were frittered away on luxuries by
his wife.

There was some real pleasure, of course, in the form of
renewed contacts with other musicians. A sign of the esteem
in which he was held by the musical world was given when a
party was put on in his honour at the Waldorf-Astoria in
New York in December 1946: those welcoming him
included Kreisler, Heifetz, Toscanini, Milstein, France-
scatti, Björling, Tauber, Arrau and Damrosch.[9] Enescu
returned to America each year until 1950, and the soloists
who played under his baton included Rubinstein at Montreal, Thibaud at Indianapolis and Menahem Pressler in
Washington. There was also a memorable performance of
the Bach Double Concerto with Menuhin under the baton of
Ionel Perlea, who had himself been awarded an Enescu
Prize for composition in Bucharest more than 25 years
before.[10] Back in Europe there were other concerts
accompanying Thibaud and playing with or conducting
Menuhin – in particular in a performance of Bartók's
Second Violin Concerto at Paris in 1947. And in October
1950 there was a very special reunion on the concert
platform when Enescu and Cortot played all the Bach violin
sonatas in two concerts. A letter survives from Enescu to his
old friend, written at the end of August that year: 'Mon cher
Fred, [. . .] Need I say what happiness it gives me to think
that I shall soon be your concert-partner again? The years
may pass, but true affections only grow stronger in our
hearts [. . .]'[11] But there were also some heavy blows during

---

lifetime. He had an innate pride which made him always reluctant to
invite the sympathy of others.

[9] *Monografie*, p. 1045 and n.

[10] Oprescu and Jora, *Enescu*, p. 337.

[11] *Scrisori*, Vol. 1, p. 390.

Thibaud, Enescu and Kreisler

this period: the death of Lipatti from leukaemia in December 1950, and the death of Thibaud in a plane crash in September 1953.

The pattern of these years was, to begin with, a much-reduced version of Enescu's concert life before the war, with appearances in Paris, Liège or Strasbourg and even, in late 1947, a little tour of French provincial towns. Before America was dropped from his itineraries one new and increasingly frequent destination was added to them: England. His first post-war visit was in September 1947, when he came to conduct the London Philharmonic Orchestra. (Miron Grindea recalls that on this occasion Schnabel was staying at the same hotel and begged Enescu to look through his compositions; Enescu later said it took him a whole night to read through the first movement of Schnabel's huge and labyrinthine Fifth Symphony.[12]) Enescu returned to England each year until 1953, conducting the L.P.O., the Philharmonia Orchestra, the B.B.C. Symphony Orchestra and the Boyd Neel Orchestra. He covered a wide repertoire with these players, from Mozart concertos with Gieseking to performances of his own First Symphony; and with the Boyd Neel Orchestra he conducted for the first time Bartók's *Music for Strings, Percussion and Celesta*. But the backbone of

---

[12] *Kensington Symposium.* Schoenberg is said to have once told Schnabel: 'Rests are also permitted in twelve-tone music'.

these programmes was Bach: Brandenburg Concertos, Suites, Cantatas and a never-to-be-forgotten performance of the B minor Mass with Peter Pears and Kathleen Ferrier among the soloists.

These visits to England as a conductor were becoming Enescu's last major form of concert-giving, as his health gradually weakened and made playing the violin more and more difficult. The deformation of his spine was also aggravating his old heart trouble and beginning to cause difficulties with his breathing. A friend describes his appearance after a concert at Montreal in 1949: 'we found him in an extraordinary state of exhaustion: pale, his forehead damp with sweat, his eyes closed – he looked crushed'.[13] In his letters from 1950 onwards he was frequently obliged to mention, self-deprecatingly and often impatiently, that he was having to rest or stay in bed. In September 1950 he wrote to Harold Spivacke at Washington, referring (in English) to 'my decision to give up my American tour this fall, because too tired'; in December Maruca told Grindea that Enescu had been causing anxiety with his 'intermittences', which she attributed to fatigue. At the time she wrote, Enescu had given only two concerts during the last two months; he had spent some time earlier in the year at a sanatorium, where the doctors had forbidden him even to compose – a ban he had promptly broken by resuming work on the Second String Quartet while he was there.[14]

One form of work which imposed less strain than public concerts – though hardly requiring less stamina – was teaching, and this now began to assume a much more prominent role in Enescu's life. As well as resuming his work at Yvonne Astruc's 'Institut Instrumental' in 1947, he began to teach at several new institutions: The Mannes School of Music in New York, the music faculty at the University of Illinois, the American Academy of Music at

[13] Jean Mouton, 'Enesco dans l'intimité', *Adam*, Year 43 (1981), Nos. 434–6, pp. 33–4.

[14] *Scrisori*, Vol. 1, p. 391 (to Spivacke); Vol. 2, p. 118 (Maruca); Vol. 1, pp. 398–9 (Enescu on the Second String Quartet).

Enescu and Clara Haskil, around 1950

Fontainebleau, the Accademia Chigiana at Siena, and
summer courses at both Brighton and Bryanston.[15] (He was
also invited to teach at the Juilliard School, but abandoned
this plan when he discovered what large fees the pupils were
expected to pay for his classes.)[16] At the Mannes School
(where his colleagues included Bohuslav Martinů) he gave
in 1949 and 1950 what was officially described as a 'Special
Interpretation Course of Advanced Instrumentalists':

[15] V. Cosma, *Enescu azi*, p. 145; Constanța-Ianca Staicovici, 'George
Enesco, Professor at the Mannes School of Music, Liminary Notions',
Enesciana, Vols. 2–3, pp. 211–21 (p. 211).

[16] Staicovici, *ibid.*, p. 215; information from Helen Dowling.

Enescu at Bryanston, 1950

Enescu at Bryanston, 1950

Enescu at Bryanston, 1950

master-classes in which he coached not only violinists but
pianists and other instrumentalists as well.[17] The courses at
Bryanston, which Enescu gave from 1949 to 1952, were
part of the summer school which later moved to Dartington.
He gave master-classes in the violin, coached chamber
ensembles and also conducted the Boyd Neel Orchestra in
several concerts which were preceded by public rehearsals.
One afternoon he offered to take the young members of the
Amadeus Quartet through the complete Beethoven quartets, illustrating the tempi and the phrasing of problematic
passages. He sat hunched at the piano and, as Norbert
Brainin recalls, 'played entirely from memory, great chunks
of each movement: every part with exactly the right nuances.
His artistry was supreme [. . .]. That afternoon he went
through all seventeen quartets and we were entranced by
his magic'. Physically unable to turn round, Enescu

---

[17] Staicovici mistakenly includes details of Enescu's course for 1950–51,
which was cancelled.

remained quite unaware that the hall had silently filled with students, until he finished several hours later and was greeted with wild applause. Brainin has also written, of the handful of unaccompanied Bach recitals which Enescu gave at Bryanston, that 'he transformed everything and everybody – he transfigured us completely. After hearing Enescu we were never the same again'.[18]

Something of the majesty of Enescu's interpretation of Bach (and, sadly, also something of his inability to control precisely the intonation of his playing) can be heard in the recordings of the unaccompanied Sonatas and Partitas which he made in 1950. These were not quite his last recordings as a violinist; in 1951 and 1952 he recorded Schumann's D minor Violin Sonata, his own Second Sonata and Beethoven's *Kreutzer* Sonata with Céliny Chailley-Richez. (The last of these, recorded after his doctors had forbidden him to play the violin, is a performance of astonishing energy and power.) But the Bach Sonatas and Partitas, which he was persuaded to record in New York by Helen Dowling, are without doubt Enescu's most important interpretative legacy on record. Bach, in some symbolically appropriate way, came to dominate Enescu's programmes as violinist and conductor during the period after the Second World War, and his last major recording project was a series of eight records in which he conducted Bach concertos – mainly keyboard concertos with Chailley-Richez, but including also the Fifth Brandenburg Concerto with her, Jean-Pierre Rampal and Christian Ferras.[19] When

[18] Brainin, 'What the Amadeus Quartet owes Enescu', *Adam*, Year 43 (1981), Nos. 434–6, pp. 43–4. The summer school is also described by John Amis ('Master Classes') and John Warrack ('The Bryanston Summer School of Music', *The Musical Times*, Vol. 91, 1950, pp. 377–81), who wrote that 'of all the events of these three weeks the most moving and the most unforgettable were Georges Enesco's two concerts with the Boyd Neel Orchestra' (p. 380). I cannot leave Warrack's article without quoting his description of another unforgettable event: 'a performance of "Hora Staccato" on one violin by Norbert Brainin (violin) and Peter Schidlof (bow)' (p. 381).

[19] Christian Ferras once wrote: 'I consider myself, in principle, as his pupil, although my technical training had been with other teachers [. . .].

Chailley-Richez visited Enescu shortly before his death, he
asked her: 'What has come of our Bach concertos? Are
people at last beginning to understand? – Oh, if only they
would see that the rhythm has to be unshakable, because
the rhythm corresponds to the beating of the heart [. . .]'.[20]
One could not wish for a more perfect summary than this of
Enescu's approach to Bach: he introduced what sounded
like a new classicism in the face of the rubatos and
rallentandos of the 'romantic' style of Bach playing – but he
did so because of a feeling for the music which could only be
conveyed in such an image as that of a beating heart.

Enescu's last recordings also included a few performances
of his own works. Apart from the Second Violin Sonata
already mentioned (he had also recorded the Third with
Chailley-Richez on 78s in 1949), he conducted performances of the *Dixtuor* and the Octet in Paris for Remington
Records in 1951, and also submitted to their demand for
recordings of the *Romanian Rhapsodies*. No doubt in this last
case he was submitting also to the need to earn his living.
When a friend had written to him about plans for a concert
of his works late in 1950 he had replied: 'Thank you for
thinking of my orchestral works. But as for the two Rhapsodies, I am *absolutely fed up* with them, especially the first'.
Later in this letter he grudgingly conceded that they might
play the second, but only if it were a matter of 'une grosse
affaire commerciale'.[21] Enescu could never shake off the
incubus of these two simple pieces which had so dominated
and narrowed his reputation as a composer. But on the
other hand there were some signs of new interest in his later
works during these years, especially in America, where his

I met Enescu in 1947. I began then to work with him and continued up till
his death [. . .]' (article in *Contemporanul*, 15 August 1958, reprinted in
Crăciun and Codrea, *Gînduri închinate lui Enescu*, p. 138). Enescu also
conducted a recording by Ferras of Rodrigo's *Concierto de Estio* with the
Paris Conservatoire Orchestra (LXT 2678), which is not mentioned in
any of the published lists of Enescu's recordings.

[20] Chailley-Richez, 'Une visite parmi les dernières à Georges Enesco',
Musique et radio, No. 529, June 1955, p. 305.

[21] *Monografie*, p. 1051n.

Enescu composing

Second Piano Quartet was given its world premiere in 1947 by the Albeneri Trio with Milton Katims, and his Second String Quartet received its first performance in 1954 (played by the Stradivarius Quartet).[22] And some of the most heart-felt expressions of gratitude in Enescu's letters of this period are to be found in connection with the B.B.C.'s plan to assemble a collection of photostats of all Enescu's compositions, in order to facilitate their performance in England.[23]

---

[22] *Ibid.*, p. 1053n.

[23] Enescu, 'Letters to Adam', *Adam*, Year 43 (1981), Nos. 434–6, pp. 56–9; p. 59. The scheme, which Miron Grindea was helping to arrange, foundered on the attitude of Enescu's French publishers.

Composition remained as important as ever to Enescu.
The total output of the last eight years of his life is not a
large one, but it includes two or three of his finest works;
and the effort it involved was enormous, not only because of
his illness but also because of the immense care and
scrupulousness with which he sketched, wrote, re-wrote and
then revised and re-revised every bar and almost every note.
In a letter to the composer Mihail Andricu in late September 1953 he wrote: 'If I don't write to you more often, it's
because I have to weigh out every effort by the milli-
gram [. . .]. I am composing, but *very slowly, very carefully* –
and not exactly in accordance with the style of present-day
composers [. . .]'.[24]

Enescu's perfectionism as a composer led him to return
again and again to his compositions. In 1949 he was still
revising his First String Quartet and working further on the
Piano Quintet; in 1952 he was still planning small changes
to the score of the Third Symphony.[25] Enescu had explained
his attitude in a letter (in English) to the American critic
Lawrence Gilman in 1938: 'I like to look at them over and
over again, sometimes for years, without having them
performed. Sometimes a little improvement of nothing
changes the meening [*sic*] of the whole, or rather gives the
entire meening [*sic*] to it. I rather do little, but do it as well
as I can'.[26] One of the most striking examples of this is the
tone-poem for orchestra, choir and solo tenor, *Vox Maris*. In
his conversations with Gavoty in 1951 Enescu described this
piece as work in progress, and admitted that the progress
had lasted at least fifteen years; in fact the first complete
draft of the work was written in the summer of 1929.[27] At
the time of Enescu's death it was still thought that his
manuscript of *Vox Maris* was unfinished. Only later, with the

[24] *Scrisori*, Vol. 1, pp. 408–9.

[25] Gustave Samazeuilh, 'Le Quatuor nouveau de Georges Enesco', *La
Revue musicale*, Vol. 25, No. 209, March 1949, p. 40; *Scrisori*, Vol. 1, p. 396
and Vol. 2, p. 133.

[26] *Ibid.*, Vol. 2, p. 101.

[27] *Contrepoint*, p. 73; Oprescu and Jora, *Enescu*, p. 213.

Menuhin and Enescu, Paris, 1952

help of Marcel Mihalovici, was it realised that the incompleteness of the manuscript consisted of the absence of a few metronome timings and one or two marks of mood or dynamic. Mihalovici has also said, on the other hand, that he believes there was an even later manuscript, differing significantly from this one; but it has never been found.[28]

Enescu gave Gavoty a lengthy description of the work's programme, which he said arose from an incident he had witnessed himself. On the shore, a sailor contemplates the swelling sea; a storm rises; the signal is fired to launch the lifeboats, and anguished cries can be heard in the distance; the sailor rows into the thick of the storm, but his boat is suddenly swamped and he drowns; the sea, satisfied with its victim, is calmed, and as night falls the distant chanting of 'ancient Sirens' can be heard.[29] It must be said that if this account did not exist it would be difficult indeed to grasp all the details of what was happening from listening to the music. The same chorus is used for the cries for help and for the Sirens' song, the only difference being that tenors are added to the women's voices in the former case; it is not clear whether this is enough of a difference to remove the possibility that the cries for help are a delusive trick played by the Sirens. The only words used (apart from the interjections 'To the lifeboats!' and 'Miserere domine') are the four lines sung (in Breton) by the sailor near the beginning of the work, and these sound more like the preamble to a suicide: 'I do not want to undergo the shadowy tortures of your death, O earth-dwellers! I want, when my blood freezes in my veins, to drink a powerful draught of bitter gall from the supreme chalice of the sea'.[30]

---

[28] *Monografie*, p. 1076.

[29] *Contrepoint*, p. 73.

[30] These lines are attributed to Mlle Renée Willy. I have not been able to discover their source, nor any information about the authoress, whose surname might suggest a connection with the author and music critic Henry Gauthier-Villars (who, like his wife Colette, often used his nom-de-plume, 'Willy', as a surname). Enescu's special attachment to Brittany can be traced to his frequent visits to Rennes as violinist and conductor (see Marie-Claire Lemoigne-Mussat, 'Georges Enesco dans

This element of melodrama is, however, quite lightly applied. Most of the piece consists of orchestral music without voices, and it is possible to listen to the work simply as a sea-piece with the overall pattern of moods which is familiar from several of Enescu's other 'programme' works: calm–storm–calm. But the construction of the music is far from simple. Two analyses of it have agreed that it is in some kind of sonata-form, but have differed over the number of subjects involved; another, more convincingly, has divided it into episodes which fall into two main sections followed by a third which involves combining the material of the earlier two in an altered guise.[31] Writers about Enescu have in any case found this work difficult to 'place'. In some ways it seems very advanced – in the balance of timbres in the orchestration, for example (and especially in the final section, which ends with a quiet but astonishing coda for the percussion section alone – Ex. 25, p. 248). But in other ways (in its harmonic language, for instance) it belongs with the Third Symphony and the storm in Act Two, Scene Two of *Oedipe*. Given that it was fully drafted in 1929, it seems reasonable to think of it as essentially a work halfway between *Oedipe* and the Third Orchestral Suite, and to suspect that Enescu's revisions were most far-reaching in the final pages. As descriptive music the work is very powerful, with Enescu's techniques of heterophony and rhythmical fluidity put to good use in conjuring up the swirling and surge of the sea. It is certainly 'dramatic' in the loose sense of the word ('exciting'), but it

---

l'ouest de la France: l'accueil du public et de la critique à Rennes', *Simpozion George Enescu*, pp. 422–34), his friendships with the composers Guy Ropartz and Jean Huré, and above all to an early friendship with André Bénac, who took him to Brittany for a week's holiday in 1905 and introduced him to the great Breton poet Anatole Le Braz (*Scrisori*, Vol. 1, pp. 127 and 130).

[31] Wilhelm Berger and G. Costinescu, 'Poemul Vox Maris', *Muzica* Vol. 14, No. 9, September 1964, pp. 19–32 (sonata form, two subjects); Constantin Stihi-Boos, 'Some Analytical Specifications concerning the Symphonic Poem 'Vox Maris' in G Major Op. 31 by George Enescu', *Enesciana*, Vols. 2–3, pp. 187–92 (sonata form, three subjects); Bentoiu, *Capodopere*, pp. 350–63 (episodes).

Ex. 25

The percussion coda at the end of Vox Maris

103

is also, in a stricter sense, dramatic as opposed to pictorial: the dramatic 'plot' is reflected in the cumulative structure of the whole work and in the constant linear development of the themes themselves. In this way, as Constantin Stihi-Boos has pointed out, *Vox Maris* differs in spirit from what is usually described as the quasi-spatial conception of 'Impressionist' music, with its techniques of juxtaposition and vertical harmonic thinking.[32] Enescu had certainly benefited directly from his knowledge of *La Mer*; but *Vox Maris* could not be called a Debussian piece.

Another work which preoccupied Enescu at the same time as his revision of *Vox Maris* has an even more complicated history: the Second String Quartet, Op. 22, No. 2. In August 1951 Enescu told Andricu that he had just finished this Quartet, and that he had begun it a year before.[33] The final manuscript is indeed dated 30 May 1951; but behind this version there lies a sequence of no fewer than six other drafts, stretching back certainly into the 1920s, and perhaps even to before the First World War. Evidently Enescu took up the work again in 1950 after a long break. The fifth version is a score dated 'June 1950 – 30 January 1951'; the sixth arose as Enescu copied out separate parts from this, making further changes as he did so; and the seventh is a score incorporating yet more revisions, sent by Enescu to Harold Spivacke at the Library of Congress in December 1952.[34] The most substantial divergence between the last two versions consists of the complete

---

[32] 'A Few Specifications about the One-Movement Poem, Taken both as a Genre and as a Form, with Reference to Alfonso Castaldi and George Enescu', *Enesciana*, Vols. 2–3, pp. 173–7.

[33] *Scrisori*, Vol. 1, pp. 398–9.

[34] For a full account see Titus Moisescu, 'George Enescu's Quartet in G Major Op. 22 No. 2', *Enesciana*, Vols. 2–3, pp. 133–60; also *Scrisori*, Vol. 1, p. 405. Version 6 was published by Editura Muzicală, Bucharest, 1967 (parts only), and has been recorded by the Voces Quartet (Electrecord ST-ECE 01854); version 7 was published by Salabert in 1956 (parts only) and by Editura Muzicală in 1985 (photo-reproduction of the manuscript score), and has been recorded by the Romanian Radio Quartet (Electrecord ECD 15; Monitor MC 2049) and the Academica Quartet (Dynamic DS 4007).

reworking of four bars at the climax of the first movement; but otherwise the differences amount to little more than the occasional transposition of a note or the stretching of the intervals in a phrase to render it more sinuously chromatic.

This sort of revision is in keeping with the whole spirit of the work, which displays more finely than any other of Enescu's compositions his gift for endless motivic development. Looking back through the score, one finds that almost every phrase can be derived from previous phrases by procedures of inversion, rhythmical or harmonic alteration, melodic reduction or amplification (paring a phrase down to a skeletal form or filling it out), developing a new melody from a small section of a previous one, or stretching or squeezing the intervals in a phrase while retaining the same overall shape. All these methods (except the first) are also associated with heterophony, which is present on many of these pages.

But to concentrate on Enescu's procedural skills risks giving a false impression of this work, which is certainly not an exercise in procedures. The slow movement, which follows without a break from the first movement and is a sort of quiet meditation on the opening theme of the work, contains some of Enescu's most intimately expressive music. (It is followed by a quick, nervous *Allegretto* and a rondo-like last movement, beginning as a carefree dance.) What fascinates Enescu is the way in which new and different worlds of feeling can be conjured up and given life through new developments of the same musical substance. As he brings these worlds together in a characteristic cyclical recombination in the last movement, the listener experiences both the sense of difference between those emotional worlds and the sense of sameness in their underlying substance: this can give an extraordinary sensation of seeing into the heart of things, a feeling of inter-relation and self-enclosed completeness.

Enescu finished only two other works during his last years. One was an *Ouverture de Concert sur des Thèmes dans le Caractère Populaire Roumain* (*Concert Overture on Themes in the Character of Romanian Folk Music*), which he completed in

September 1948.[35] This is close in style and spirit to the last movement of the Third Orchestral Suite: the main subject is a brisk, spiky but exuberantly playful dance, which is first introduced against the sound of two folk fiddlers sawing away on their open strings. The tune is thickened and embroidered in following sections; it is also contrasted, in a rondo-like alternation of episodes, with a nostalgically voluptuous slow dance and a flute doina which is developed in one of Enescu's magical passages of scoring for flutes, muted trumpets, suspended cymbal, celesta, piano and string harmonics. The whole Overture lasts just less than ten minutes, but in that brief space of time it conveys much of the depth and vividness of Enescu's feelings for the country he had left.

With the *Chamber Symphony*, completed in 1954, Enescu returns to the elusive musical language of the late chamber works. As with the Second String Quartet, the prehistory of this work stretches back into his earliest period as a composer – in this case, to sketches for a wind septet which seem to date from the turn of the century. That project was abandoned, probably because it was superseded by the *Dixtuor* in 1906, but the opening theme of the septet remained in Enescu's head and became, with astonishingly little alteration, the first part of the first subject of the *Chamber Symphony*.[36] Enescu told Chailley-Richez that the *Chamber Symphony* itself was first conceived as a work for strings; perhaps the original wind-instrument associations of some of its themes helped to bring about his change of mind.[37] But without this remark by Enescu it would be impossible to guess that he had ever thought of writing it for a string orchestra. The contrast of timbres among the wind instruments is an essential feature of this work, and the string parts (together with the piano) seem to play a

---

[35] *Monografie* p. 1062. Further revisions may have followed: Enescu told Mihalovici on 29 May 1949 that he had just completed the work (*Scrisori*, Vol. 1, p. 383).

[36] See Valentin Timaru, 'Analiza Simfoniei de Camera, a lui George Enescu', *Centenarul George Enescu 1881–1981*, pp. 227–44, esp. pp. 240–1.

[37] Chailley-Richez, 'Une visite'.

secondary role. There are twelve instruments in all: flute, oboe, cor anglais, clarinet, bassoon, horn, trumpet, violin, viola, cello, double bass and piano.

Enescu's skill in transmuting familiar classical forms is displayed in this work in a typically unostentatious way. At first sight it falls simply enough into its traditional four-movement pattern: *Molto moderato, un poco maestoso*; *Allegretto molto moderato*; *Adagio*; and *Allegro molto moderato* (the last two movements following without a break). The slow movement uses the same thematic material as the scherzo-like second movement. On closer inspection one sees that the scherzo is a sequence of variations, and that the third movement (Ex. 26, pp.254–7) is simply a further variation in the series, capped by a final restatement of the theme at the beginnin of the last movement. The whole work is something like a strange adaptation of sonata form, in which the subjects (three instead of two) are stated in the first movement, the sequence of variations takes the place of a development section, and the last movement combines recapitulation with further development and cyclical recombination.[38] But no cut-and-dried analysis can do justice to the *Chamber Symphony's* perpetually shifting atmosphere of melodic expansion, compression and development. The same material is endowed, in different contexts, with yielding tenderness and fierce angularity; the *Chamber Symphony* as a whole seems a very private work, both intimate and impassive. When Constantin Silvestri conducted the Romanian premiere of the work in 1958 he told the audience that this, Enescu's greatest composition, was harder to understand than any of his other works because its musical language was so modern, and he therefore played it for a second time in the same concert.[39] Present-day audiences will find its language less unfamiliar – one critic has compared it to Schoenberg – but there remains something oblique and distant about the *Chamber Symphony* which makes it one of

[38] See Timaru, 'Analiza Simfoniei', and Bentoiu, *Capodopere*, pp. 527–41.

[39] Bentoiu, *ibid.*, p. 527.

Enescu's strangest and most personal creations.[40]

Enescu was still completing the *Chamber Symphony* when he suffered a severe stroke in July 1954, which left him semi-paralysed; the final touches to the score were dictated to Marcel Mihalovici. This was not the first attack he had suffered. On his last visit to England he had collapsed one evening in his hotel room. Helen Dowling, who was helping to look after him, was in the next room. Hearing a strange noise, she entered his room and found him slumped across his bed, unable to move. He could not even speak; but to show that he was still alive and conscious he whistled under his breath the theme of the Brandenburg Concerto which he was due to conduct the next day. When the power of speech did return to him he refused to be seen by a doctor; he hated being fussed over and would not tolerate the usual medical advice to stop working on his compositions. Finally he was flown back to Paris on a stretcher.[41]

Enescu's last years were clouded by poverty as well as ill health. He remained at his old Paris address, 26 Rue de Clichy, but had to give up his spacious third-floor apartment and retreat to two tiny, ill-lit rooms in the *basse-cour*. Lady Menuhin has written a touching account of the impression he made on her in April 1953:

> There, uncomplaining as ever, he sat in a miserable little dark room just large enough to contain his cot, his grand piano, a chair and a piano stool. 'Eh bien, chers enfants', he said with a heart-rending mixture of defensive pride and hidden shame. 'Me voilà!' Yehudi talked to him of music and at one point Enesco turned to the piano and ran his sadly twisted hands over it as though it were an extension of his own being [. . .]. I noticed the frayed tie, the shabby jacket, the waxen face with its clean, beautiful bones and serene eyes [. . .].[42]

---

[40] For the (hesitant) comparison to Schoenberg see Waterhouse and Cosma, 'Enescu', p. 166.

[41] Information from Helen Dowling.

[42] Diana Menuhin, *Fiddler's Moll. Life with Yehudi*, Weidenfeld and Nicolson, London, 1984, p. 105.

Ex. 26

Chamber Symphony, *third movement (opening bars)*

The Menuhins got in touch with Queen Elizabeth of the Belgians, who was herself a fine amateur violinist and a pupil of Enescu. Together they tried to find some way to help him financially.

But they were up against two formidable obstacles. On the one hand there was Enescu's unconquerable pride, which would make him refuse to accept charity so long as he was still capable of supporting himself; a scheme concocted by Menuhin which involved paying Salabert to reprint Enescu's music (and give him royalties on the new edition) eventually foundered, apparently because Enescu saw through it. And on the other hand there was the Princess Cantacuzino-Enescu, who not only frittered away what money there was but also surrounded herself with a fantastic web of Balkan intrigue in which ulterior motives were read into every action. When Enescu entrusted his Guarnerius violin to Menuhin for safe-keeping, the Princess managed to convince herself that Menuhin had stolen it; Enescu's reason for putting it into his hands was in fact that he feared it would be taken from him and sold by the Princess.[43] During his final illness, while he lay half-paralysed in bed, his wife began to sell off his manuscripts, many of which thus found their way to Bucharest.[44] Those who visited Enescu at this time all recall the Princess's grotesque, excessively made-up appearance and her strident voice, screeching away about Bucharestian gossip and other trivialities; she seemed almost oblivious of her husband's sufferings. Lady Menuhin has described her as 'imperious, totally self-absorbed and not a little mad'.[45] Enescu bore it all with serene patience. John Amis, who visited him once in Paris during these final years, writes that 'He never asked for anything, never wanted anything [. . .].

---

[43] See the document drawn up by Enescu in April 1954 (Enescu, 'Letters to Menuhin', p. 55), in which he says: 'I apologise to Yehudi for laying this burden upon him, but *he is the only person* whom I completely trust'. Enescu later reclaimed the violin, apparently at his wife's insistence; it was sold by her, and passed to Romania.

[44] Information from Helen Dowling.

[45] *Fiddler's Moll*, p. 106.

Enescu in his basement flat, Paris, around 1953

No, that's not true, I can now recall just one thing he asked for – a spoonful of jam'.[46]

With all his visitors Enescu's first concern was to ask about their own musical lives, their compositions or performances, and to enquire after mutual friends. When a

[46] 'Master classes', p. 42.

deputation of Romanian composers visited him in early
1955 he asked for news of Jora and Constantinescu; when
Robert Simpson spoke to him shortly before his death he
asked after musicians he had met in London, and wanted to
know if any interesting new works were being written.[47]
This was not mere small-talk. Despite the tragic isolation
and neglect of his last years, Enescu remained receptive and
alive to any new writing that struck him as a true expression
of musical feelings; on his previous visits to London he had
read through the manuscript of Robert Simpson's First
String Quartet, and had made a special effort to attend the
recording of Tippett's Second String Quartet at a B.B.C.
studio.[48]

Enescu had no patience, however, with music which he
felt was modernistic for modernism's sake, nor with the
subjection of music to cerebral compositional techniques.
Once when Mihalovici asked him why he did not compose
any serial music he replied, 'I have so much to write in my
own technique that I don't have time to write in the
technique of others'; but this was a classic piece of Enescian
politeness. He spoke more directly when, on his death-bed,
he told Sergiu Comissiona: 'All this twelve-tone music . . .
tell them, tell them, this is not *music*! Music should go from
heart to heart'.[49] In the late 1940s he had told Louis
Lochner: 'When a thing is good, it should be written no
matter what the present generation thinks of it. At present
there is too much emphasis on mechanical perfection. But
that will pass, just as the striving of atonalists now is back to
tonality – witness Schoenberg and Hindemith'.[50] And on
another occasion he had explained: 'Although my musical
language may resemble that of my contemporaries, it does

---

[47] *Monografie*, p. 1062n; Simpson, 'He was Made of Music', p. 36.

[48] Simpson, *ibid.*; Amis, *Kensington Symposium*.

[49] For the remark to Mihalovici see Ingebord Allihn, 'Consideraţii
comparatie, la 'Simfonia de Camera Op. 33' de George Enescu şi
'Simfonia de Camera Op. 9' de Arnold Schoenberg', *Simpozion George
Enescu*, pp. 397–400 (p. 399); Comissiona, 'The God-given', p. 32.

[50] Lochner, *Fritz Kreisler*, p. 359.

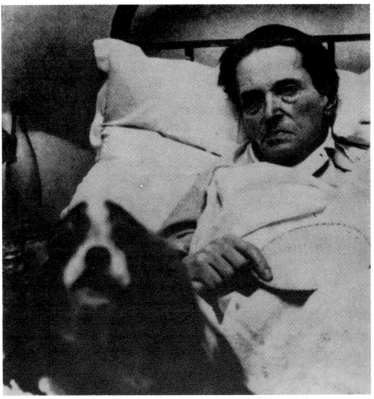

Enescu during his final illness, 1954–5

in fact differ radically from theirs. At a profound level it bears the mark of the past from which it has grown; it does not share their attitude of repudiation'.[51] Enescu was not a modernist, but nor was he a 'conservative'. Both terms are inappropriate, because they would imply that his music was in some way governed by the concepts he held about his relation to the past. Quite simply, he accepted the past; he felt an underlying unity of expressive purpose between his own writing and that of all the earlier composers whose works he had known, remembered and loved. And at the

---

[51] From a quotation (source not recorded) in Vancea, 'George Enescu, muzician umanist', *Studii de muzicologie*, Vol. 4 (1968), pp. 23–8; p. 26.

The tomb of Enescu (and Maruca, who died in 1968) at the Père Lachaise cemetery in Paris (courtesy of Christelle Levasseur)

same time this did not hinder him from developing new and strange resources of expression for his own music. That is a lesson which can still be learned from his music, more than thirty years after his death.

He died on the night of 3–4 May 1955. For the last ten months of his life he had borne uncomplainingly the crushing frustration of being unable to compose. He told Mihalovici that 'if I could put down on paper everything that I have in my head, it would take hundreds of years . . .'.[52] Those who knew him well would not doubt the essential truth of this last

[52] *Monografie*, p. 1076n.

despairing remark. They would know that he was incapable of boastfulness, and they would agree with Casals' claim that Enescu was, in the depth and range of his gifts, the greatest musical phenomenon since Mozart. Seen in this light, Enescu's entire œuvre may seem pitifully small. I believe that it contains, nevertheless, some of the finest and most extraordinary music of this century.

LIST OF WORKS

A. Juvenilia

(Unpublished works and works without opus number, up to 1900)

1886

'Opera' for violin and piano

1887

Waltz for piano

1889

Pièce d'Église for piano

1891–4

Three overtures for orchestra

1893

Rondo and Variations for piano

Piano quartet (fragment)

1894

Ballade for piano

Introduction, Adagio and Allegro for piano

Piano sonata (performed by Enescu, Cracalia, 1894)

'Sonata for orchestra' (MS unknown; piano version performed by Enescu, Cracalia, 1894)

String quartet, C major (fragment)

String quartet, D minor (fragment)

Quartet for four violins

Suite of variations for two violins

1894–5

Polka for piano

Sonatina for piano, four hands

Romance for piano, four hands

1895

First 'School' Symphony, D minor (performed Bucharest, 1934, cond. Enescu)

Vision de Saül, cantata

Tarantelle for violin and piano

Ahasvérus, cantata (prologue only)

Violin sonata (performed by Eva Rolland (violin) and E. Bernard, Paris, 1897)

Ballade for violin and piano (or orchestra)

Tragic Overture

Second 'School' Symphony, F major

1896

Violin concerto, A minor (two movements only; first movement performed by Enescu, Paris, 1896)

Andantino from an orchestral suite

Third 'School' Symphony, F major

String quartet (unfinished)

Triumphal Overture

Piano Quintet (dedicated to Martin-Pierre-Joseph Marsick; performed by Eva Rolland, Mlle Murer (piano) and others, Paris, 1897)

Fantaisie for piano and orchestra

Four *Divertissements* for orchestra

1896–7

Two Romanian Suites for orchestra (unfinished)

1897

Nocturne et Saltarello for cello (performed Paris, 1897)

String quartet (first movement, unfinished)

Barcarolle for piano (unfinished)

La Fileuse, for piano

1898

L'Aurore, cantata

Regrets for piano

Fourth 'School' Symphony, E flat major (dedicated to André
    Gédalge; first performance conducted by Ion Baciu, Bucharest,
    1970)

Pensée Perdue for voice and piano, verses by Sully Prudhomme

Prélude for two pianos, violin and cello

Wüstenbild for voice and piano, verses by A. Roderich

Sphinx for voice and piano, verses by Carmen Sylva

Impromptu for piano

Suite for piano, four hands

Octet for strings, D major (fragment)

c. 1898 (date uncertain)

Moderato for violin and piano, F minor (fragment)

Piano concerto, D minor (draft of one movement only)

Piano concerto, E minor (draft of one movement only)

Modérément for piano

Chant Indou for voice and piano, verses by Mlle Géraldine Rolland

1899

Pastorale-Fantaisie for orchestra (performed Paris, 1899)

Dédicace for voice and piano

Quarantaine for voice and piano, verses by Enescu

c. 1899 (date uncertain)

Allemande for piano

Sérénade en Sourdine for violin and cello

Trio for two violins and cello

1895–9

Many other undated student works, including drafts of five other string quartets, eight other cantatas (among them *La Fille de Jephthé, Antigone, Daphne*) and Act I of a 'drame lyrique', *Le Lotus Bleu*

1900

Andante Religioso for two cellos and organ (performed Bucharest, 1900)

Pastorale, Menuet Triste et Nocturne for violin and piano, four hands

De Ziua ta for voice and piano

c. 1900 (date uncertain)

Suite Orientale for orchestra (fragment)

Septet for flute, oboe, french horn, clarinet, bassoon, horn and piano

B. Published Works, Works with Opus Numbers and All Known Works after 1900

The dates are those of completion, where known; precise dates (in brackets) are those given on the manuscripts

Abbreviations:
B.M.R. – *Biblioteca muzicală romînă*
E.M. – Editura muzicală
E.S.P.L.A. – Editura de stat pentru literatură şi artă

1895–6

Four-part fugue on an original subject, publ. André Gédalge, *Traité de la Fugue*, Part I, Paris, 1900, Appendix

1896

Prelude for piano, ded. Mme Aronovici (17 August); 1st pf. Theodor Fuchs, Bucharest, 1900; publ. B.M.R., Vol. 1, 1898, No. 9

Scherzo for piano, ded. Mme Aronovici (18 August); 1st pf. Madeleine Cocorăscu, Bucharest, 1925; publ. B.M.R., Vol. I, 1898, No. 23

1897

Poème Roumain, Op. 1, symphonic suite for orchestra, ded. in memory of Elena Bibescu; 1st pf. Edouard Colonne and Colonne Orchestra, Paris, 1898; publ. Enoch, 1899

First Piano Suite ('*Dans le style ancien*'), Op. 3, G minor, ded. Mlle Murer (6 May); 1st pf. Mlle Murer, Paris, 1897; publ. Enoch, 1898

First Violin Sonata, Op. 2, D major, ded. Joseph Hellmesberger junior (2 June); 1st pf. Enescu and Cortot, Paris, 1898; publ. Enoch, 1898, and E.S.P.L.A., 1957

c. 1897–8

Si j'étais Dieu, for voice and piano, verses by Sully Prudhomme; publ. Hachette, n.d. (now by Salabert)

1898

Der Bläser, for voice and piano, verses by Carmen Sylva (21 March); 1st pf. Edgar dall'Orso and Enescu (piano), Bucharest, 1900; publ. *Literatură şi artă romînă*, Vol. 2, 1898, pp. 635–7

Variations for Two Pianos on an Original Theme, Op. 5, A flat major, ded. Edouard Risler and Alfred Cortot (2 June); 1st pf. Risler and Cortot, Paris, 1899; publ. Enoch, 1899, E.S.P.L.A., 1957

Three Songs, Op. 4: No. 1 'Le Désert', verses by Jules Lemaître (13 April); No. 2, 'Le Galop', verses by Sully Prudhomme (14 April); No. 3, 'Soupir', verses by Sully Prudhomme 5 June); ded. Mathilde Colonne; 1st pf. (Nos. 1 and 2) Mathilde Colonne (pianist unknown), Paris, 1898; publ. Enoch, 1899

Zaghaft, for voice and piano, verses by Carmen Sylva (21 August); publ. B.M.R., Vol. 2, 1899, No. 43, and Salabert

Armes Mägdlein for voice and piano, verses by Carmen Sylva (21 August); 1st pf. Onoria Popovici (soprano) and Ernesto Narice, Bucharest, 1900; publ. B.M.R., Vol. 2, 1899, No. 29, and Salabert

Junge Schmerzen, for mezzo-soprano, bass and piano, verses by Carmen Sylva (22 August); publ. Salabert

Der Schmetterlingskuss, for voice and piano, verses by Carmen Sylva (24 August); 1st pf. Edgar dall'Orso and Enescu (piano), Bucharest, 1900; publ. B.M.R., Vol. 2, 1899, No. 32, and Salabert

Reue, for voice and piano, verses by Carmen Sylva (24 August); publ. Salabert

Schlaflos, for voice and piano, verses by Carmen Sylva (27 August); publ. Salabert

Frauenberuf, for voice and piano, verses by Carmen Sylva (30 August); publ. Salabert

First Cello Sonata, Op. 26, No. 1, F minor, ded. Dimitrie Dinicu (8 November); 1st pf. Joseph Salmon and Enescu (piano), Paris, 1899

Waldegesang, for mixed choir *a cappella*, verses by Carmen Sylva (13 November); publ. Salabert

1899

Second Violin Sonata, Op. 6, F minor, ded. Jacques and Joseph Thibaud (20 April); 1st pf. Jacques Thibaud and Enescu (piano), Paris, 1900; publ. Enoch, 1901 and E.S.P.L.A., 1956

Maurerlied, for voice and piano, verses by Carmen Sylva (13 September); publ. Salabert

Königshusarenlied, for voice and piano, verses by Carmen Sylva (14 September); publ. Salabert

Aubade, Trio for violin, viola and cello, (November); 1st pf. Enescu (violin), Loebel (viola) and Dinicu (cello), Bucharest, 1899; publ. Enoch, 1903.

Souhait, for voice and piano, verses by Enescu, ded. Ella Bengescu (27 November); publ. *Muzica*, 1956, Supplement No. 5

1900

Die Nächtliche Herschau, for baritone, choir and orchestra, verses by Joseph Christian Zedlitz; publ. *Literatură şi artă romîna*, Vol. 4, 1900, Nos. 5–7, pp. 350–54

Mittagsläuten, for voice and piano, verses by Carmen Sylva (January–April); 1st pf. Onoria Popovici (soprano) and Ernesto Narice, Bucharest, 1900; publ. B.M.R., Vol. 2, 1900, No. 41

Impromptu, for piano (26 April); publ. *Literatură şi artă romînă*, Vol. 4, 1900, Nos. 5–7, p. 354

Plugar, for mixed four-part choir *a cappella*, verses by Rădulescu-Niger (first written for four-part choir, June 1899; re-written for six-part or three-part choirs, 14 May 1900; re-written for four-part choir, 15 May 1900 and revised 25 May); final version publ. *Albina*, Vol. 4, 26 October 1903, pp. 111–12

Octet for Strings, Op. 7, (four violins, two violas, two cellos), ded. André Gédalge (5 December); 1st pf. Geloso and Chailley Quartets, Paris, 1909; publ. Enoch, 1905 and E.S.P.L.A., 1957

1901

Romanian Rhapsodies, Op. 11, No. 1, A major, ded. B. Crocé-Spinelli (14 August); No. 2, D major, ded. J. Pennequin (26 October); both 1st pf. Enescu and Orchestra Filarmonica, Bucharest, 1903; publ. Enoch, 1909, E.S.P.L.A., 1957

Symphonie Concertante, Op. 8, for cello and orchestra, B minor, ded. Joseph Salmon (2 November); 1st pf. Salmon, Enescu and Colonne Orchestra, Paris, 1909; publ. Enoch, 1938 and E.S.P.L.A., 1957

Prinz Waldvogelsgesang, for voice, cello and piano (November); 1st pf. Bucharest, 1901

Ein Sonnenblick, for voice and piano (25 November)

1902

First *Intermède* for Strings, Op. 12, No. 1, ded. in memory of Elena Bibescu (20 September); 1st pf. Enescu and Orchestra Filarmonica, Bucharest, 1903

De la Flûte au Cor, for voice and piano, verses by Fernand Gregh, ded. Edgar dall'Orso (15 October); publ. Salabert, 1965 and E.M., 1967

1903

Second *Intermède* for Strings, Op. 12, No. 2, ded. in memory of Elena Bibescu (20 January); 1st pf. Enescu and Orchestra Filarmonica, Bucharest, 1903

First Orchestral Suite, Op. 9, ded. Saint-Saëns (January–February); 1st pf. Enescu and Orchestra Filarmonica, Bucharest, 1903; publ. Enoch, 1909 and E.S.P.L.A., 1957

Second Piano Suite, Op. 10, D major, ded. Louis Diémer (25 August); 1st pf. Enescu, Paris, 1903(?); publ. Enoch, 1904, E.S.P.L.A., 1956

Prelude and Fugue, for piano (11 September)

Regen, for voice and piano, verses by Carmen Sylva (15 September), revised 1936; publ. Salabert

Impromptu Concertant, for violin and piano, G flat major (23 October); publ. *Muzica*, 1958, Supplement No. 7

1904

Cantabile and Presto, for flute and piano, ded. Paul Taffanel; 1st pf. in Conservatoire competitions, Paris, 1904; publ. Enoch, 1904 and E.S.P.L.A., 1956

Allegro de Concert, for chromatic harp, ded. Gustave Lyon; 1st pf. in Conservatoire competitions, Paris, 1904; publ. Enoch, 1904 and E.S.P.L.A., 1956

Oda, for choir and piano or organ, verses by I. Soricu, ded. Iosif Vulcan (25 May); publ. *La Roumanie d'aujourd'hui*, 1963, No. 3, p. 44

Die Kirschen, for soprano, baritone, cello and piano, verses by Carmen Sylva (9 November); publ. Salabert

1905

Silence, for voice and piano, verses by Albert Samain, ded. Mlle Victoire Peridé; publ. *Muzica*, 1958, Supplement No. 7

First Symphony, Op. 13, E flat major, ded. Alfredo Casella; 1st pf. Colonne and Colonne Orchestra, Paris, 1906; publ. Enoch, 1908, E.S.P.L.A., 1957

Doina for baritone, viola and cello, on folk verses from a collection by Vasile Alecsandri (9 November); 1st pf. Bucharest, 1956; publ. *Muzica*, 1956, Supplement No. 5, and Salabert, 1965

1906

Dixtuor, Op. 14, for two flutes, oboe, cor anglais, two clarinets, two bassoons and two horns, D major, ded. in memory of Elena Bibescu; 1st pf. Société moderne d'instruments à vent, Paris, 1906; publ. Salabert, 1965

Légende, for trumpet and piano, ded. Merri Franquin; 1st pf in Conservatoire competitions, Paris, 1906; publ. Enoch, 1906 and E.S.P.L.A., 1956

Concertstück (or *Pièce de Concert*), for viola and piano, ded. Théodore Laforge; 1st pf. in Conservatoire competitions, Paris, 1906; publ. Enoch, 1906 and E.S.P.L.A., 1957

Au Soir, 'poème' for four trumpets; 1st pf. Société Mozart, Paris, 1910

String Quartet, C major, one movement only (11 September); publ. (photo-reproduction of the MS) E.M., 1985

Hymn Jubiliar, for choir, military band and harp (October); 1st pf. Bucharest, 1906

1907

Entsagen, for voice and piano, verses by Carmen Sylva (21 August); publ. Salabert

Nocturne, for piano, D flat major (16 October)

1908

Cantate pour la Pose de la Première Pierre du Pont à Transbordeur de Bordeaux, for military band, two harps, string orchestra, solo cello, choir, baritone solo and cannons, verses by Albert Bureau (27 May 1908)

Sept Chansons de Clement Marot, Op. 15, for tenor (or soprano) and piano, ded. as follows: No. 1: Renée Criticos; No. 2: Jean Ythier; No. 3: Ninette Duca; No. 4: Marie Crane; No. 5: Maggie Teyte; No. 6: André Bénac; No. 7: Jean Altchewski (7 July–10 October); 1st pf. Jean Altchewski and Enescu (piano), Paris, 1908, publ. Enoch, 1909 and E.S.P.L.A., 1957

Morgengebet, for voice and piano, verses by Carmen Sylva (10 November); publ. Salabert

1909

Aria and *Scherzino* for violin, viola, cello, double bass and piano;

MS unknown; *Scherzino* publ. *Le Monde musical*, 30 August 1909, Supplement

First Piano Quartet, Op. 16, D major, ded. Mme Ephrussi (10 December); 1st pf. Paris, 1909; publ. Salabert, 1965 and E.M. 1967

1911

Suite Châtelaine, for orchestra, unfinished: first movement, 'Entrée' (dated 13 May) and fragment of scherzo, 'Chasse'

Violin Sonata, A minor, fragment (5 October); publ. E.M., 1983

1912

Piano sonata, first movement (July); MS unknown[1]

1914

Second Symphony, Op. 17, A major, ded. in memory of Colonne (18 November); 1st pf. Enescu and Orchestra of the Ministry of Education, Bucharest, 1915; publ. Salabert, 1965 and E.M., 1968

1915

Second Orchestral Suite, Op. 20, C major, ded. Orchestra of the Ministry of Education and its conductor, Dimitrie Dinicu (14 December); 1st pf. Enescu and that orchestra, Bucharest, 1916; publ. Salabert, 1954 and E.M., 1965

1916

Trois Mélodies sur Poèmes de Fernand Gregh, Op. 19: No. 1, 'Pluie' (27 June 1915); No. 2, 'Le Silence Musicien' (2 July 1915); No. 3, 'L'Ombre est Bleue' (3 March 1916, revised 30 May 1936); No. 2 publ. *L'Indépendance roumaine*, December 1915, Supplement; Nos. 1–3 publ. (with *De la Flûte au Cor*, listed above, 1902) as *Quatre Mélodies sur Poèmes de Fernand Gregh*, Salabert, 1965, and E.M., 1967

Piano Trio, A minor (22 March)

Third Piano Suite, *'Pièces Impromptues'*: seven pieces (1 June 1913–2 July 1916); 1st pf. Ion Filionescu, Bucharest, 1959; publ. *Muzica*, 1958, Supplement No. 8, and Salabert

(11 November) *Strigoii*, for soprano, tenor, baritone, chorus and orchestra, verses by Eminescu; rough draft

---

[1] See above, p. 110, note 45.

1917

(4 January) *Hora Unirei*, for violin and piano, based on motifs from Flechtenmacher's *Hora Unirii* (1856); publ. *Muzica*, 1975, No. 6, p. 2

c. 1917

Eu mă Duc, Codrul Rămîne ('I depart, the forest remains'), for voice and piano

Symphony, for baritone, choir and orchestra, on the words of Psalm 86, F minor; fragments

1918

Third Symphony, Op. 21, last movement with four-part choir, C major, ded. in memory of Elena Bibescu (20 August); 1st pf. Enescu and Orchestra of the Ministry of Education, Bucharest, 1919; publ. Salabert, 1965 and E.M., 1968

1920

First String Quartet, Op. 22, No. 1, E flat major, ded. Flonzaley Quartet (1 December); 1st pf. Enescu, Nottara, Popovici and Ochialbi, Bucharest, 1921; publ. Salabert, n.d.

1922

Pièce sur le Nom de Fauré (11 April); 1st pf. Henri Gil-Marchex, Paris, 1922; publ. *La Revue musicale*, October 1922 (special number)

Complete draft for piano of *Oedipe* (19 November): see **1931** for full entry

1924

First Piano Sonata, Op. 24, No. 1, F sharp minor, ded. Émile Frey (27 August); 1st pf. Enescu, Bucharest, 1925; publ. Enoch, 1926 and E.S.P.L.A., 1957

1926

Third Violin Sonata, Op. 25, 'dans le caractère populaire roumain', A minor, ded. in memory of Franz Kneisel (18 November); 1st pf. Enescu and Niculae Caravia (piano), Oradea, 1927; publ. Enoch, 1933 and E.S.P.L.A., 1957

c. 1928

Caprice Roumain, for violin and orchestra; draft, unfinished

1929

First complete draft of *Vox Maris*: see **c. 1954** for full entry

1931

Oedipe, Op. 23, 'tragédie lyrique' in four acts, libretto by Edmond Fleg, ded. Marie Rosetti-Tescani (Maruca Cantacuzino) (27 April); 1st pf. cond. Philippe Gaubert (with André Pernet as Oedipe), Grand Opera, Paris, 1936; publ. Salabert 1934 (piano reduction by Henri Lauth), 1952 (photo-reproduction of full score), the latter also by E.M., 1964

1932

Symphonie Concertante, for violin and orchestra, C major (10 October); draft, unfinished

1934

Fourth Symphony, draft of first movement and fragment of second movement (20 December)

1935

Third Piano Sonata, Op. 24, No. 3, D major, ded. Marcel Ciampi (11 May); 1st pf. by him, Paris, 1938; publ. Salabert, 1939

Second Cello Sonata, Op. 26, No. 2, C major, ded. Pablo Casals (30 November); 1st pf. Diran Alexanian and Enescu (piano), Paris, 1936; publ. Salabert, 1952 and E.M., 1964

1938

Third Orchestral Suite, Op. 27, 'Suite Villageoise', D major, ded. in memory of Elena Bibescu (4 November); 1st pf. Enescu and New York Philharmonic Orchestra, New York, 1939; publ. Salabert, 1965 and E.M., 1967

1940

Impressions d'Enfance, Op. 28, suite for violin and piano, D major, ded. in memory of Caudella (10 April); 1st pf. Enescu and Lipatti, Bucharest, 1942; publ. Salabert, 1952

Piano Quintet, Op. 29, A minor (first movement dated 24 September, second movement undated), ded. in memory of Elena Bibescu; 1st pf. Valentin Gheorghiu (piano), Stefan Gheorghiu (first violin) and others, Bucharest, 1964; publ. Salabert, 1965 and E.M., 1968

1941

Fifth Symphony, for tenor, female choir and orchestra, D major, last movement on verses by Eminescu (July); draft, unfinished

1942

Piano Trio (fragment)

1944

Second Piano Quartet, Op. 30, D minor, ded. in memory of Fauré (4 May); 1st pf. Albeneri Trio and Milton Katims, Washington, 1947; publ. Salabert and E.M., 1968

1946

Linişte ('Silence'), for choir of three equal voices *a cappella*, verses by A.T. Stamatiad (July); brief extracts (all that seems to have survived) publ. in *Monografie*, pp. 1041–2

1948

Ouverture de Concert sur des Thèmes dans le Caractère Populaire Roumain, Op. 32, A major, ded. in memory of Elena Bibescu (11 September); 1st pf. Enescu and National Symphony Orchestra, Washington, 1949; publ. Salabert, 1965 and E.M., 1967

1951–2

Second String Quartet, Op. 22, No. 2, G major (sixth version dated 30 May 1951; seventh version bears same date, but was completed in late 1952[2]), ded. in memory of Elizabeth Coolidge; 1st pf. Stradivarius Quartet, Boston, 1953; publ.: sixth version, E.M., 1967; seventh version, Salabert, 1956 (parts) and E.M., 1985 (score)

c. 1954

Vox Maris, Op. 31, symphonic poem for tenor, three-part choir and

[2] See p. 249.

orchestra, G major (first full draft: 1929), ded. in memory of Elena Bibescu; 1st pf. Iosif Conta and the Romanian Radio-Television Symphony Orchestra, Bucharest, 1964; publ. Salabert, 1965 and E.M., 1967

1954

Chamber Symphony, Op. 33, for flute, oboe, cor anglais, clarinet, bassoon, horn, trumpet, violin, viola, cello, double-bass and piano, E major, ded. Fernand Oubradous and the Association des Concerts de Chambre de Paris (28 May); 1st pf. by them, Paris, 1955; publ. Salabert, 1959 and E.M., 1965

C. Undated Works

Allegro for chamber orchestra (draft, unfinished)

Nocturne 'Ville d'Avrayen' for piano quartet (draft, unfinished)

Voix de la Nature, symphonic suite (?): fragment of one movement entitled 'Nuages d'automne sur les forêts'[3]

D. Transcriptions and Cadenzas

Enescu, *Poème Roumain*: transcr. for piano, four hands; publ. Enoch, 1900

Enescu, *Romanian Rhapsody* No. 1: transcr. for piano, two hands; publ. Enoch, 1951 and E.S.P.L.A., 1956

Brahms, Violin Concerto: cadenza; publ. Enoch, 1903

Mozart, Violin Concerto No. 7: cadenzas

Albéniz, *Rapsodie Espagnole*: transcr. for piano and orchestra; 1st pf. A. Ribo (piano), cond. Gabriel Pierné, Paris, 1911; publ. Salabert

Bach, Invention in B flat major, transcr. for orchestra; 1st pf. cond. Pierre Monteux, Paris, 1911

Schubert, Piano Trio No. 2, E flat major, second movement: transcr. for orchestra; 1st pf. Bucharest, 1916

Paganini, *Caprices* Nos. 6, 16 and 24: piano accompaniments

Sarasate, *Zigeunerweisen* (*Gypsy Airs*), transcr. for piano

[3] See above, p. 208, note 37.

Appendix 2

RECORDINGS BY GEORGE ENESCU

This is a checklist rather than a technical discography. I have not seen copies of all these recordings, and I have not attempted to supply matrix numbers. Nor can I be certain that the listing here of recordings in the Romanian radio archives is complete; my requests for further information have been unsuccessful. Nevertheless, this checklist is more comprehensive than any previously published list.

The original issue is given first, with the date of recording when know, followed by subsequent re-issues. All recordings are 12-inch long-playing records, unless otherwise described. All 78 rpm records are 12-inch.

Abbreviations
CRAA: copies of these recordings are available (on tape or cassette) from Classical Recording Archive of America, PO Box 1112, El Cerrito, California 94530, USA
HMV: His Master's Voice
ORTF: Office de Radiodiffusion Télévision Française

1. Enescu as Violinist

ALFREDO D'AMBROSIO
Serenade for violin and piano, Op. 4 (pianist: Edward Harris): Columbia 7006 (78 rpm); Columbia 20023D (78 rpm); Columbia 2008M (78 rpm); Discopaedia MB 1017; Electrecord ELE 02715

JOHANN SEBASTIAN BACH
Sonatas Nos. 1–3 for solo violin (BWV1001, 1003, 1005) and Partitas Nos. 1–3 for solo violin (BWV1002, 1004, 1006): Continental Records CLP 104/6 (three-disc set, 1950); Olympic Records 8117/3 (three-disc set); Loga 1001 (three-disc set); Philips 422

298–2 (two-CD set). The *Adagio* from Sonata No. 1 has been re-issued on Melodiya M10 42633 004; Partita No. 1 was re-issued on Remington PL1-149 (10-inch LP); the Prelude from Partita No. 3 and the Fugue from Sonata No. 3 were re-issued on Electrecord ECE 0166.

Concerto for two violins and orchestra in D minor (BWV 1043), with Yehudi Menuhin and the Orchestre Symphonique de Paris, conducted by Pierre Monteux: HMV (Great Britain) DB 1718/9 (78 rpm, two discs; 1932); Victor (HMV America) 7732/3 (78 rpm, two discs); Victor 11–18601/2 (78 rpm, two discs); Victor 11–8603/4 (78 rpm, two discs; also issued as Victor Album M 932); Victor LCT 1120; Victor LVT 1006; Les Gravures Illustres (EMI France) COLH 77; EMI France FJLP 5018; EMI (Great Britain) HLM 7078 (in three-disc set, RLS 718); Studio (EMI Italy) 53 1430701; Références (EMI France) C 051–43070; Melodiya M10 42633 004; Références (EMI France) CDH 7 61018 2 (CD)

LUDWIG VAN BEETHOVEN[1]
Sonata for No. 9 for violin and piano, in A major, Op. 47, 'Kreutzer' (pianist: Céliny Chailley-Richez): Columbia FC 1058 (10-inch LP; 1952); Angel (EMI Japan) GR 2212

'Chorus of the Dervishes' from Incidental Music to *The Ruins of Athens*, Op. 113, arranged for violin and piano by Leopold Auer (pianist: Edward Harris): Columbia (America) 7007 (78 rpm); Columbia 20029D (78 rpm); Columbia 2026M (78 rpm); Discopaedia MB 1017; Electrecord ELE 02715

ERNEST CHAUSSON
Poème for violin and piano, Op. 25 (pianist: Sanford Schlüssel): Columbia (America) 50273/4D (78 rpm, two discs); Columbia (America) 5118/9m (78 rpm, two discs); Columbia (Austria and Hungary) DVX 5/6 (78 rpm, two discs); Columbia (France and Belgium) LFX 125/6 (78 rpm, two discs); Veritas VM 111; Angel (EMI Japan) GR 2212; Melodiya M10 42633 004; Discopaedia MB 1017; Electrecord ELE 02715

---

[1] A recording of Enescu playing the Beethoven Violin Concerto has been rumoured to exist in the archives of Radio France; M. Maïc Chomel, the director of the recordings library there, assures me that no trace of such a recording can be found. I am very grateful to him for the trouble he has taken to check this claim.

ARCHANGELO CORELLI
Sonata for violin and continuo, in D minor, Op. 5, No. 12 ('La
Follia'), arranged by Ferdinand David, revised by Henri Petri
(pianist: Sanford Schlüssel): Columbia (America) 51061D (78
rpm); Columbia (America) 5109M (78 rpm); Columbia (British
export) D 41013 (78 rpm); Veritas VM 111; Discopaedia MB 1017;
Electrecord ECE 0166; Electrecord ELE 02715

GEORGE ENESCU
Sonata No. 2 for violin and piano, in F minor, Op. 6 (pianist: Dinu
Lipatti): Romanian Radio recording (1943) issued on 'Discoteca'
label (78 rpm, three discs); Electrecord ECD 61 (10-inch LP);
Monitor MC 2049; Electrecord ECD 0766/7 (two-disc set); Ever-
est 3413; Disques Déesse DDLX 40/1 (two-disc set)

Sonata No. 2 for violin and piano, in F minor, Op. 6 (pianist:
Céliny Chailley-Richez): Remington R–149–42 (10-inch LP;
1951); Varèse Sarabande VC 81048.[2]

Sonata No. 3 for violin and piano, in A minor, Op. 25, 'Dans le
caractère populaire roumain' (pianist: Dinu Lipatti): Romanian
Radio recording (1943) issued on 'Discoteca' label (78 rpm, three
discs); Electrecord ECD 95 (10-inch LP); Electrecord ECD 0766/7
(two-disc set); Everest 3413; Disques Déesse DDLX 40/1 (two-
disc set)

Sonata No. 3 for violin and piano, in F minor, Op. 25, 'Dans le
caractère populaire roumain' (pianist: Céliny Chailley-Richez):
Columbia GFX 121/3 (78 rpm, three discs; 1949); Angel (EMI
Japan) GR 2212

Impressions d'Enfance, suite for violin and piano, Op. 28 (pianist:
Dinu Lipatti): Romanian Radio recording on 78 rpm masters
(1943), now apparently lost

GEORG FRIEDRICH HÄNDEL
Sonata for violin and continuo, in D major, Op. 1, No. 13 (pianist:
Sanford Schlüssel): Columbia (America) 50187/8D (78 rpm, two
discs; 1928); Columbia (America) 5110/1M (78 rpm, two discs);
Columbia (Japan) 7632/3 (78 rpm, two discs); Veritas VM 111;
Discopaedia MB 1017; Electrecord ELE 02715

---

[2] Remington R–149–42 is incorrectly listed in Francis Clough and
G. J. Cuming, *The World's Encyclopaedia of Recorded Music*, three vols.,
Sidgwick and Jackson, London, 1952–5, Supplement II, p. 72, as the
Sonata No. 3 for violin and piano.

FRITZ KREISLER
Aubade Provençale in the style of Couperin, for violin and piano (pianist: Edward Harris): Columbia 7006 (78 rpm); Columbia 20023D (78 rpm); Columbia 2008M (78 rpm); Discopaedia MB 1017; Electrecord ELE 02715

Tempo di minuetto in the style of Pugnani, for violin and piano (pianist unidentified, but very probably Sanford Schlüssel): Columbia (America) 50235D (78 rpm); Columbia (Austria and Hungary) DVX 7 (78 rpm); Columbia (France and Belgium) DFX 145 (78 rpm); Discopaedia MB 1017; Electrecord ELE 02715; Melodiya M10 42633 004

WOLFGANG AMADEUS MOZART
Concerto for violin and orchestra, 'No. 7' (attribution disputed), in D major, K271i, conducted by Léon Barzin: unauthorised recording on 78 rpm discs of performance on 7 March 1933;[3] no copy of this recording has yet been found

GAETANO PUGNANI
Largo espressivo from Sonata for violin and continuo in D major, Op. 8, No. 3, arranged by Alfred Moffat (pianist unidentified, but very probably Sanford Schlüssel): Columbia (America) 50235D (78 rpm); Columbia (Austria and Hungary) DVX 7 (78 rpm); Columbia (France and Belgium) DFX 145 (78 rpm); Veritas VM 111; Discopaedia MB 1017; Electrecord ELE 02715; Melodiya M10 42633 004

MAURICE RAVEL
Tzigane, for violin and orchestra, conducted by Léon Barzin: unauthorised recording on 78 rpm discs of performance on 7 March 1933;[4] no copy of this recording has yet been found

ROBERT SCHUMANN
Sonata for violin and piano No. 2, in D minor, Op. 121 (pianist: Céliny Chailley-Richez): Remington 149–50 (1952)

RICHARD WAGNER
Albumblatt, in C major, arranged for violin and piano by August Wilhelmj (pianist: Edward Harris): Columbia (America) 7007 (78

[3] See p. 197–8, above.

[4] See p. 197–8 above.

rpm); Columbia 20029D (78 rpm); Columbia 2026M (78 rpm); Discopaedia MB 1017; Electrecord ELE 02715; Melodiya M10 42633 004

2. Enescu as Conductor

JOHANN SEBASTIAN BACH
Mass in B minor, BWV232, with Suzanne Danco (soprano), Kathleen Ferrier (contralto), Peter Pears (tenor), Bruce Boyce (baritone), Norman Walker (bass), BBC Chorus and Boyd Neel Orchestra: BBC Radio recording 1951.

Concerto for violin and orchestra No. 1, in A minor, BWV1041, with Yehudi Menuhin (violin) and L'Orchestre Symphonique de Paris: HMV (Great Britain) DB 2911/2 (78 rpm, two discs; 1936); Victor (HMV America) 14370/1 (78 rpm, two discs); Les Gravures Illustres (EMI France) COLH 77; EMI (Great Britain) 7078 (in three-disc set RLS 718); Studio (EMI Italy) 53 1430701 M; Références (EMI France) C 051–43070; Références CDH 7 61018 2 (CD)

Concerto for violin and orchestra No. 2, in E major, BWV1042, with Yehudi Menuhin (violin) and L'Orchestre Symphonique de Paris: HMV (Great Britain) DB 2003/5 (78 rpm, three discs; 1934); HMV (Australia) ED 684/6 (78 rpm, three discs); Victor (HMV America) 8367/9 (78 rpm, three discs; also issued as Victor Album M 221); Les Gravures Illustres (EMI France) COLH 77; Studio (EMI Italy) 53 1420701 M; Références (EMI France) C 051–43070; Références (EMI France) CDH 7 61018 2 (CD)

Concerto for clavier, flute violin and orchestra, in A minor, BWV1044, with Céliny Chailley-Richez (piano), Jean-Pierre Rampal (flute) and Christian Ferras (violin) and L'Association des Concerts de Chambre de Paris: Decca (France) FAT 133530

'Brandenburg' Concerto No. 2, in F major, BWV1047, with the Bucharest Philharmonic Orchestra: Romanian Radio recording on 78 rpm masters

'Brandenburg Concerto No. 5, in D major, BWV1050, with Céliny Chailley-Richez (piano), Jean-Pierre Rampal (flute), Christian Ferras (violin) and L'Association des Concerts de Chambre de Paris: Decca (France) FAT 133530

Concerto for clavier and orchestra, No. 1, in D minor, BWV1052, with Céliny Chailley-Richez (piano) and L'Association des Concerts de Chambre de Paris: Decca (France) FAT 133053

Concerto for clavier and orchestra, No. 2, in E major, BWV1053, with Céliny Chailley-Richez (piano) and L'Association des Concerts de Chambre de Paris: Decca (France) FAT 133050

Concerto for clavier and orchestra, No. 3, in D major, BWV1054, with Céliny Chailley-Richez (piano) and L'Association des Concerts de Chambre de Paris: Decca (France) FAT 133119

Concerto for clavier and orchestra, No. 4, in A major, BWV1055, with Céliny Chailley-Richez (piano) and L'Association des Concerts de Chambre de Paris: Decca (France) FAT 133068

Concerto for clavier and orchestra, No. 5, in F minor, BWV1056, with Céliny Chailley-Richez (piano) and L'Association des Concerts de Chambre de Paris: Decca (France) FAT 133053

Concerto for clavier and orchestra, No. 6, in F major, BWV1057, with Céliny Chailley-Richez (piano) and L'Association des Concerts de Chambre de Paris: Decca (France) FAT 133068

Concerto for clavier and orchestra, No. 7, in G minor, BWV1058, with Céliny Chailley-Richez (piano) and L'Association des Concerts de Chambre de Paris: Decca (France) FAT 133050

Concerto for two claviers and orchestra, No. 1, in C minor, BWV1060, with Céliny Chailley-Richez and F. le Gonidec (pianos) and L'Association des Concerts de Chambre de Paris: Decca (France) FAT 133094

Concerto for two claviers and orchestra, No. 2, in C major, BWV1061, with Céliny Chailley-Richez and F. le Gonidec (pianos) and L'Association des Concerts de Chambre de Paris: Decca (France) FAT 133094

Concerto for two claviers and orchestra, No. 3, in C minor, BWV1062 (originally for two violins and orchestra, in D minor, BWV1043), with Céliny Chailley-Richez and F. le Gonidec (pianos), and L'Association des Concerts de Chambre de Paris: Decca (France) FAT 133119

Concerto for three claviers and orchestra, No. 1, in D minor, BWV1063, with Céliny Chailley-Richez, F. le Gonidec and J. J. Painchaud (pianos), and L'Association des Concerts de Chambre de Paris: Decca (France) FAT 133097

Concerto for three claviers and orchestra, No. 2, in C major BWV1064, with Céliny Chailley-Richez, F. le Gonidec and J. J. Painchaud (pianos), and L'Association des Concerts de Chambre de Paris: Decca (France) FAT 133097

Appendix 2

Concerto for four claviers and orchestra, in A minor, BWV1065 (arranged from Vivaldi's Concerto for four violins and string orchestra, Op. 3, No. 10), with Céliny Chailley-Richez, F. le Gonidec, J. J. Painchaud and M. Grimaud (pianos), and L'Association des Concerts de Chambre de Paris: Decca (France) FAT 133538

BÉLA BARTÓK
Music for Strings, Percussion and Celesta, with the ORTF Orchestra: French Radio recording of a performance at the Besançon Festival (1951), CRAA.

LUDWIG VAN BEETHOVEN
Symphony No. 3, in E flat major, Op. 55, *Eroica*, with the Bucharest Philharmonic Orchestra: Romanian Radio recording on 78 rpm masters (1936)

Overture to the incidental music to Goethe's *Egmont*, Op. 84, with the 'Magic Key' Orchestra: RCA radio recording (1938)

JOHANNES BRAHMS
Symphony No. 4, in E minor, Op. 98, with the Bucharest Philharmonic Orchestra: Romanian Radio recording on 78 rpm masters

ERNEST CHAUSSON
Poème for violin and orchestra, Op. 25, with Yehudi Menuhin (violin) and L'Orchestre Symphonique de Paris: HMV (Great Britain) DB 1961/2 (78 rpm, two discs; 1933); Victor (HMV America) 7913/4 (78 rpm, two discs); EMI (Great Britain) HLM 7079 (in three-disc set RLS 718); Références (EMI France) 2908431

CLAUDE DEBUSSY
Prélude à L'Après-midi d'un Faune, with the 'Silvertone Symphony Orchestra': Silvertone 35 (78 rpm); Mercury MG 10021[5]

[5] Enescu made three recordings – see also the entries under Fauré and Ravel, pp. 286 and 288 below – for Silvertone. John Holmes writes that these recordings were made in Paris in the 1930s for HMV (*Conductors on Record*, Victor Gollancz, London, 1982, p. 173), but I believe this is an error. Silvertone records were sold exclusively by Sears Roebuck, the American mail-order firm. These three recordings are not listed in Robert Reid (ed.), *The Gramophone Shop Encyclopaedia of Recorded Music*, 3rd edn., Crown Publishers, New York, 1948, but they are listed in Clough and Cuming, *op. cit.* They must therefore have been issued between January 1948 and April 1950.

SABIN DRĂGOI
'Colind' ('Carol') and 'Cîntec de Nuntă' ('Wedding Song') from *Divertisment Rustic*, with the New York Philharmonic Orchestra: CBS radio recording (1939)

ANTONÍN DVOŘÁK
Concerto for violin and orchestra, in A minor, Op. 53, with Yehudi Menuhin and L'Orchestre du Conservatoire de Paris: HMV (Great Britain) DB 2838/41 (78 rpm, four discs; 1936); Victor (HMV America) 14518/21 (78 rpm, four discs; also issued as Victor Album M 387); HMV Treasury (EMI Great Britain) EH 7 49395 1

GEORGE ENESCU
Octet for Strings, in C major, Op. 7, with L'Ensemble Louis de Froment: Remington 199-52 (1951)

First Orchestral Suite, in C major, Op. 9, with the Bucharest Philharmonic Orchestra: Romanian Radio recording (1943) issued on 'Discoteca' label (78 rpm, three discs); Electrecord ECD 91 (10-inch LP); Electrecord ECD 01388

Romanian Rhapsody No. 1, in A major, Op. 11, with the Bucharest Radio Orchestra: Romanian Radio recording on 78 rpm masters (1936; incomplete)

Romanian Rhapsody No. 1, in A major Op. 11, with the USSR State Orchestra: USSR 013661/3 (78 rpm, two discs; 1946; Supraphon 40063/4 (78 rpm, two discs)

Romanian Rhapsody No. 1, in A major, Op. 11, with L'Orchestre des Concerts Colonne: Remington 149–47 (1952); Remington REP 116 (45 rpm); Concerteum ECR 83 (45 rpm); Festival (Australia) 10–100; Remington 199–207; Varèse Sarabande VC 81042; Colosseum V 81042[6]

Romanian Rhapsody No. 2, in D major, Op. 11, with the Bucharest Radio Orchestra: Romanian Radio recording on 78 rpm masters (1936)

Romanian Rhapsody No. 2, in D major, Op. 11, with the ORTF Orchestra: French Radio broadcast of a performance at the Besançon Festival (1951), CRAA

[6] The orchestra has been incorrectly identified on this re-issue as the 'Gürzenich Orchester, Köln'; this arises presumably from a misreading of 'Colonne'.

Romanian Rhapsody No. 2, in D major, Op. 11, with L'Orchestre des Concerts Colonne: Remington 149–52 (1952); Concerteum TCR 269; Remington 199–207; Varèse Sarabande VC 81042; Colosseum V 81042.[7]

Symphony No. 1, in E flat major, Op. 13, with the Bucharest Philharmonic Orchestra: Romanian Radio recording issued on Discoteca DP 628–32 (78 rpm, five discs; 1943)

Symphony No. 1, in E flat major, Op. 13, with the Cleveland Orchestra: 'Mutual Eastern Network' broadcast (1946), CRAA

Dixtuor in D major, Op. 14, with wind soloists of the ORTF Orchestra: Remington 199–107 (1951); Varèse Sarabande VC 81042; Colosseum V 81042

Gigue from the Second Orchestral Suite, in C major, Op. 20, with the USSR State Orchestra: USSR 013664 (78 rpm; 1946); Supraphon 40064 (78 rpm).[8]

Second Orchestral Suite, in C major, Op. 20, with L'Orchestre Nationale, French Radio recording (1952)

GABRIEL FAURÉ
Les Fileuses, the second movement (*Andantino quasi allegretto*) of the orchestral suite from Fauré's incidental music to Maeterlinck's *Pelléas et Mélisande*, orchestrated by Charles Koechlin, with the 'Silvertone Symphony Orchestra': Silvertone 47 (78 rpm); Mercury MG 10021[9]

CÉSAR FRANCK
Symphony in D minor, third movement (*Allegretto non troppo*), with the 'Magic Key' Orchestra: RCA radio recording (1938)

ÉDOUARD LALO
Symphonie Espagnole for violin and orchestra, Op. 21, with Yehudi Menuhin (violin) and L'Orchestre Symphonique de Paris: HMV (Great Britain) DB 1999/2002 (78 rpm, four discs, also issued as HMV Album 195; 1933); Victor (HMV America) 7943/6 (78 rpm,

---

[7] See note 6.

[8] This recording has been mis-identified in all previous listings as an orchestral arrangement of a – non-existent – *Gigue* from the Second Suite for Piano.

[9] *See* entry for Debussy, *Prélude à L'Après-midi d'un Faune*, p. 284, above.

four discs, also issued as Victor Album M 136); HMV (Great Britain) DB 7582/5 (78 rpm, four discs); Références (EMI France) 2908431

DINU LIPATTI

Şătrării (*The Gypsies*), Symphonic Suite, Op. 2: third movement only (*Allegro*) entitled 'Ivresse' ('Drunkenness'), with the ORTF Orchestra: French Radio broadcast of a performance at the Besançon Festival (1951), CRAA

Symphonie Concertante for two pianos and string orchestra, Op. 5, with Béla Siki and Madeleine Lipatti (pianos), and the ORTF Orchestra: French Radio broadcast of a performance at the Besançon Festival (1951), CRAA

FELIX MENDELSSOHN-BARTHOLDY

Concerto for violin and orchestra, in E minor, Op. 64, with Yehudi Menuhin (violin) and L'Orchestre des Concerts Colonne: HMV (Great Britain) DB 3555/8 (78 rpm, four discs; 1936); Victor (HMV America) 15320/3 (78 rpm, four discs, also issued as Victor Album M 531); HMV (Great Britain) DB 5012/5 (78 rpm, four discs); HMV (Great Britain) DB 8586/9 (78 rpm, four discs); EMI (Great Britain) HLM 7080 (in three-disc set RLS 718); HMV Treasury (EMI Great Britain) EH 7 49395 1; the slow movement (*Andante*) was also re-issued on Electrecord ECE 0166

WOLFGANG AMADEUS MOZART

Concerto for violin and orchestra, No. 3, K216, cadenzas by Sam Franko, with Yehudi Menuhin (violin) and L'Orchestre Symphonique de Paris: HMV (Great Britain) DB 2729/31 (78 rpm, three discs; 1935); Victor (HMV America) 15078/80 (78 rpm, three discs; also issued as Victor Album M 485); HMV (Great Britain) DB 8184/6 (78 rpm, three discs); EMI (Great Britain) HLM 7079 (in three-disc set RLS 718); Biddulph LAB 004 (CD)

Concerto for violin and orchestra, No. 3, in G major, K216, cadenzas by Eugène Ysaÿe, with Jacques Thibaud (violin) and the ORTF Orchestra: French Radio broadcast (1951), CRAA

Concerto for violin and orchestra, No. 4, in D major, K218, with Jacques Thibaud (violin) and the ORTF Orchestra: French Radio broadcast (1951), CRAA

Concerto for violin and orchestra, No. 5, in A major, K219, cadenzas by Joseph Joachim, with Jacques Thibaud (violin) and the ORTF Orchestra: French Radio broadcast (1951), CRAA

Concerto for violin and orchestra, 'No. 7' (attribution disputed) in D major, K271i, cadenzas by Enescu, with Yehudi Menuhin and L'Orchestre Symphonique de Paris: HMV (Great Britain) DB 1735/8 (78 rpm, four discs; 1932); Victor (HMV America) 7734/7 (78 rpm, four discs, also issued as Victor Album M 231); HMV (Great Britain) DB 7157/60 (78 rpm, four discs); Biddulph LAB 004 (CD); the slow movement (*Andante*) was also re-issued on Electrecord ECE 0166

Overture to *The Marriage of Figaro*, K492, with the New York Philharmonic Orchestra: 'Columbia Network' broadcast (1937), CRAA

Symphony No. 40, in G minor, K550, with the New York Philharmonic Orchestra: 'Columbia Network' broadcast, (1937), CRAA

ION NONNA OTESCU
Two excerpts, 'Symphony of the Lake' and Prelude to Act II, from the opera *De la Matei Citire* (*A Reading from St Matthew*), with the New York Philharmonic Orchestra: 'Columbia Network' broadcast, (1937), CRAA

IONEL PERLEA
Symphonic Variations on an Original Theme, with the New York Philharmonic Orchestra: CBS radio recording (1939)

MAURICE RAVEL
Pavane pour une Infante Défunte, with the 'Silvertone Symphony Orchestra': Silvertone 47 (78 rpm); Mercury MG 10021[10]

JOAQUIN RODRIGO
Concierto de Estio (*Summer Concerto*) for violin and orchestra, with Christian Ferras (violin) and L'Orchestre de la Societe des Concerts du Conservatoire de Paris: Decca (Great Britain) LXT 2678; London (Decca America) LL 546

THEODOR ROGALSKI
'Înmormîntare la Pătrunjel' ('Burial at Pătrunjel'), from *Two Symphonic Sketches*, with the New York Philharmonic Orchestra: CBS radio recording (1939)

ROBERT SCHUMANN
Symphony No. 2, in C major, Op. 61, with the New York

[10] *See* entry for Debussy, *Prélude à L'Après-midi d'un Faune*, p. 284, above.

Philharmonic Orchestra: 'Columbia Network' broadcast, (1937), CRAA

Symphony No. 2, in C major, Op. 61, with the London Philharmonic Orchestra: Decca (Great Britain) AK 1748/52 (78 rpm, five discs; 1949)

RICHARD WAGNER
Overture to *Tannhäuser* (Paris version), with the Bucharest Philharmonic Orchestra: Romanian Radio recording on 78 rpm masters (1939)

'Venusberg Music' (or 'Bacchanale') from *Tannhäuser*, Act I, with the Cleveland Orchestra: 'Mutual Eastern Network' broadcast, (1946), CRAA

HENRYK WIENIAWSKI
Légende, for violin and orchestra, Op. 17, with Yehudi Menuhin (violin) and L'Orchestre des Concerts Colonne: HMV (Great Britain) DB 3653 (78 rpm, 1938); Victor (HMV America) 15243 (78 rpm); EMI (Great Britain) HLM 7079 (in three-disc set RLS 718)

3: Enescu as Pianist

GEORGE ENESCU
First Piano Suite (*Dans le style ancien*); in G minor, Op. 3, *Prélude*, *Fugue* and *Adagio* only: Romanian Radio recording (1943) issued on 'Discoteca' label (78 rpm, two discs); Electrecord ECD 1151 (10-inch LP); Electrecord ECE 01388

First Piano Suite (*Dans le style ancien*), in G minor, Op. 3, *Adagio*: Duo-Art piano roll No. 6728 (issued 1924), recorded on Fone 90 F 15 (CD)

Second Piano Suite, in D major, Op. 10, *Sarabande* and *Pavane* only: Romanian Radio recording on 78 rpm masters (1943); Electrecord ECD 1151 (10-inch LP); Electrecord ECE 01388

Cantabile and Presto for flute and piano, with Vasile Jianu (flute): Romanian Radio recording issued on 'Discoteca' label (78 rpm)

Concertstück for viola and piano, with Alexandru Rădulescu (viola): Romanian Radio recording (1943) issued on 'Discoteca' label; Electrecord ECD 95 (10-inch LP); Electrecord ECE 01311

Sept Chansons de Clément Marot, Op. 15, all except 'Présent de Couleur Blanche', with Constantin Stroescu (tenor): Romanian Radio recording on 78 rpm acetates (1943); Electrecord ECE 01976

Sept Chansons de Clément Marot, Op. 15, with Sophie Wyss (soprano): recording of unknown origin, made in London in 1951. I am very grateful to Eugen Pricope for letting me hear a copy of this recording

Second Cello Sonata, in C major, Op. 26, No. 2, with Theodor Lupu (cello): Romanian Radio recording, issued on Discoteca DP 11–644 (78 rpm, four discs; 1943)

Accompaniment to Niccolò Paganini, *Caprice* for solo violin, in G minor, No. 6: HMV (Great Britain) DB 2841 (78 rpm; 1936); Victor (HMV America) 14228 (78 rpm); Références (EMI France) 2 C 051–43322

PABLO DE SARASATE
Zigeunerweisen (Gypsy Airs), in C minor, Op. 20, transcr. by Enescu: Duo-Art piano roll No. 7237 (issued 1928), recorded on Fone 90 F 15 (CD)

Accompaniments improvised by Enescu to thirteen Romanian folk songs, with Stella Roman (soprano): this recording, on the 'Folio' label, is listed with no further details in Oprescu and Jora, *Enescu*, p. 375. I am very grateful to Eugen Pricope for letting me hear a copy of this recording. Miss Roman, whose original name was Florica Blasu, sang at the Metropolitan Opera, New York, from 1941 to 1950. A photograph (possibly taken in connection with this recording) of Enescu accompanying her at the piano is reproduced in Enescu, *Contrepoint*, p. 70, over the caption 'Avec Stella Roman, New York, 1948'.

Appendix 3

BIBLIOGRAPHY

This bibliography is confined to listing works cited or referred to in the text. The alphabetical order is English rather than Romanian: 'Î' is treated as 'I', 'Ş' as 'S' and so on. Anonymous interviews with Enescu are listed under Enescu.

ALDRICH, RICHARD, *Concert Life in New York, 1902–1923*, Putnam, New York, 2nd edn., 1941

ALESSANDRESCU, ALFRED, *Scrieri alesi* (ed. I. Raţiu), Editura Muzicală, Bucharest, 1977.

ALEXANDRU, TIBERIU, *Béla Bartók despre folclorul romînesc*, Editura Muzicală, Bucharest, 1958

——, *Romanian Folk Music* (tr. Constantin Stihi-Boos and A.L. Lloyd), Musical Publishing House, Bucharest, 1980.

ALLIHN, INGEBORD, 'Consideraţii comparatie, la "Simfonia de Camera Op. 33" de George Enescu şi "Simfonia de Camera Op. 9" de Arnold Schoenberg', in M. Roşu (ed.), *Simpozion George Enescu*, Bucharest, 1984, pp. 397–400.

AMIS, JOHN, 'Master Classes at Bryanston', *Adam*, Year 43 (1981), Nos. 434–6, pp. 39–42.

——, see *Kensington Symposium*

ANON, *Georges Enesco. Notes biographiques*, Bucharest, 1928.

AXELROD, HERBERT, (ed.), *Heifetz*, Paganiniana Publications, Neptune City (New Jersey), rev. edn. 1981.

BĂLAN, GEORGE, *George Enescu. Mesajul – estetica*, Editura Muzicală, Bucharest, 1962.

BARTÓK, BÉLA, *Rumanian Folk Music* (ed. Benjamin Suchoff), five vols., Nijhoff, The Hague, 1967–75.

BENTOIU, PASCAL, *Capodopere enesciene*, Bucharest, 1984.

BERGER, WILHELM, *Muzica simfonică modernă-contemporană 1930–1950*, Editura Muzicală, Bucharest, 1976.

——, and COSTINESCU, G., 'Poemul Vox Maris', *Muzica*, Vol. 14, No. 9, September 1964, pp. 19–32.

BOCU, M., 'De vorbă cu George Enescu', *Vestul*, Vol. 7, No. 1828, 25 December 1936.

BOSCHOT, A., Concert Review in *L'Écho de Paris*, 5 December 1910.

BRĂILOIU, CONSTANTIN, 'La Musique populaire roumaine', *La Revue Musicale*, special no., February–March 1940, pp. 146–53.

——, 'Enescu', *Die Musik in Geschichte und Gegenwart* (ed. F. Blume), seventeen vols., Bärenreiter, Kassel/Basel, 1949–68, Vol. 3, p. 1343.

——, *Opere* (ed. E. Comişel), five vols., Bucharest, 1967–81.

BRAININ, NORBERT, 'What the Amadeus Quartet owes Enescu', *Adam*, Year 43 (1981), Nos. 434–6, pp. 434.

BRÂNCUŞI, PETRE, *Muzica românească şi marile ei primeniri*, Vol. 2, Editura Muzicală, Bucharest, 1980.

BROŞTEANU, AUREL, 'De vorbă cu George Enescu despre muzica românească', *Propăşirea*, Vol. 2, No. 75, 17 December 1928.

BRUNSCHWIG, DANIEL, Concert Review in *Le Monde musical*, 31 May 1928, p. 190.

——, 'Cours d'interprétation de Georges Enesco', *Le Monde musical*, 30 September and 30 November 1928, pp. 295–6 and 367–8.

BRUYR, JOSÉ, *Honegger et son œuvre*, Corrêa, Paris, 1947.

BUGHICI, DUMITRU, *Repere arhitectonice în creaţia muzicală românească contemporană*, Bucharest, 1982.

BUSH, ALAN, see *Kensington Symposium*.

BUSONI, FERRUCCIO, *Letters to his Wife* (tr. Rosamund Ley), Edward Arnold, London, 1938.

CAMPBELL, MARGARET, *The Great Violinists*, Granada Publishing, London, 1980.

CANTACUZINO-ENESCU, MARIE, 'Pynx – le créateur', in *Adam*, Year 43 (1981), Nos. 434–6, pp. 60–2.

CARAVIA, NICULAE, 'A Collaboration of more than 40 Years', *Romanian Review*, Vol. 35, 1981, No. 8, pp. 127–8.

——, 'Fifty Years of Friendship', *Adam*, Year 43 (1981), Nos. 434–6, pp. 25–8.

CARDINE-PETIT, 'Oedipe de George Enescu la Opera din Paris' (anon. tr. of interview by Cardine-Petit in *Paris Midi*), *Adevěrul*, Vol. 50, No. 15994, 12 March 1936.

CASELLA, ALFREDO, *Music in my Time* (transl. Spencer Norton), Oklahoma University Press, Norman, 1955.

CEILLIER, LAURENT, *Roger-Ducasse. Le Musicien – l'œuvre*, Paris, 1920.

CHAILLEY-RICHEZ, CÉLINY, 'Une visite parmi les dernières à Georges Enesco', *Musique et radio*, No. 529, June 1955, p. 305.

CHASINS, ABRAHAM, *Leopold Stokowski. A Profile*, Hawthorn, New York, 1979.

CHIRIAC, MIRCEA, 'Rapsodiile Romîne de George Enescu', *Muzica*, Vol. 8 (1958), Nos. 7, pp. 19–28.

'CLEANTE', 'Psihologia creaţiunei artistice. Cum o defineşte Maestrul George Enescu', *Rampa nouă ilustrată*, Vol. 1, No. 279, 19 June 1916, pp. 1–2.

CLOUGH, FRANCIS, and CUMING, G. J., *The World's Encyclopaedia of Recorded Music*, Sidgwick and Jackson, London, 1952–55.

COMISSIONA, SERGIU, 'The God-given', *Adam*, Year 43 (1981), Nos. 434–6, pp. 31–2.

CONRAD, DODA, 'Maître', *Adam*, Year 43 (1981), Nos. 434–6, pp. 37–9.

Contrepoint: see ENESCU

CORREDOR, J. M., *Conversations with Casals* (transl. André Mangeot), Hutchinson, London, 1956.

COSMA, OCTAVIAN, *Oedip-ul Enescian*, Editura Muzicală, Bucharest, 1967.

——, 'Istoricul unui cîntec patriotic: "Mama lui Ştefan cel Mare"', *Studii de muzicologie*, Vol. 8, 1972, pp. 71–95.

——, *Hronicul muzicii româneşti*, Vol. 4, Editura Muzicală a Uniunii Compozitorilor din R.P.R., Bucharest, 1976.

COSMA, VIOREL, 'Date noi cu privire la familia lui George Enescu', *Studii muzicologice*, Vol. 5, 1957, pp. 19–48.

——, *Compozitori şi muzicologi români. Mic lexicon*, Editura Muzicală a Uniunii Compozitorilor din R.P.R., Bucharest, 1965.

——, *Enescu azi. Premise la ridimensionarea personalităţii şi operei*, Facla, Timişoara, 1981.

COSTIN, M., (?),: see ANON

CRĂCIUN, VICTOR, and CODREA, PETRE, (eds.), *Gînduri închinate lui Enescu*, Comitetul pentru cultură şi artă al judeţului Botoşani, Botoşani, 1970.

CREIGHTON, JAMES, *Discopaedia of the Violin 1889–1971*, Toronto University Press, Toronto, 1974.

CRISTIAN, VASILE, 'Un geniu autentic artei romîneşti, George Enescu', *Femeia şi caminul*, Vol. 2, No. 22, 6 May 1945, p. 7.

DANIELS, ROBIN, *Conversations with Menuhin*, Futura, London, 1980.

DIANU, ROMULUS, 'Cu d. George Enescu despre el şi despre alţii', *Rampa*, Vol. 13, No. 3148, 23 July 1928.

DRĂGHICI, ROMEO, *George Enescu, biografie documentară. Copilărie şi anii de studii (1881–1900)*, Muzeul de istorie se artă al judeţului Bacău, Bacău, 1973.

——, 'Cînd şi cum l'am cunoscut pe Enescu', in Victor Crăciun and Petre Codrea (eds.), *Gînduri închinate lui Enescu*, Comitetul pentru cultură şi artă al judeţului Botoşani, Botoşani, 1970, pp. 219–22.

——, 'The Great Friend in my Life', *Romanian Review*, Vol. 35 (1981), No. 8, pp. 130–40.

ENESCU GEORGE, 'À propos de l'opéra chez nous', *L'Indépendance Roumaine*, Vol. 38, No. 12229, 26 October/8 November 1915, p. 1.

——, 'Despre muzica românească', *Muzica. Revista pentru cultura muzicală*, Vol. 3, Nos. 5–6, May–June 1921, p. 115.

——, 'Ce ne-a spus Maestrul Enescu', *Revista Muzicală*, Vol. 1, No. 1, November 1928, pp. 9–10.

——, 'De la musique roumaine', *La Revue musicale*, July–August 1931, p. 158.

——, *Despre Iacob Negruzzi şi despre intrarea muzicei la Academia Română*, Discursuri de recepţiune, No. 64, Academia Română, Bucharest, 1933.

——, 'Hommage à Paul Dukas', *La Revue Musicale*, No. 166 (special number), May–June 1936, p. 119.

——, *Contrepoint dans le miroir* (ed. Bernard Gavoty), Editrice Nagard, Paris and Rome, 1982 (first published as *Les Souvenirs de Georges Enesco*, Flammarion, Paris, 1955).

——, *Scrisori*, (ed. Viorel Cosma), two vols., Editura Muzicală, Bucharest, 1974–81.

——, 'Letters to Yehudi Menuhin. Master to Disciple', *Adam*, Year 43 (1981), Nos. 434–6, pp. 52–5.

——, 'Letters to Adam', *Adam*, Year 43 (1981), Nos. 434– 6, pp. 56–9.

Entretiens: 20 tapes of conversations between Enescu and Bernard Gavoty, recorded in 1951–2, in the collection of the Institut National de l'Audiovisuel, Maison de la Radio, Paris: ref: MC 8655–8674.

FAURÉ, GABRIEL, Concert Review in *Figaro*, Series 3, No. 347, 12 December 1904.

FERRAS, CHRISTIAN, 'Mă consider elevul lui' in Crăciun, Victor, and Codrea, Petre, (eds.), *Gînduri închinate lui Enescu*, Comitetul pentru cultură şi artă al judeţului Botoşani, Botoşani, 1970, p. 138.

FIRCA, CLEMANSA, *Direcţii în muzica românesca 1900–1930*, Editura Academiei Republicii Socialista România, Bucharest, 1974.

——, 'From Manuscript to Finished Composition', *Romanian Review*, Vol. 35 (1981), No. 8, pp. 64–71.

FIRCA, GHEORGHE, (ed.), *George Enescu. Omagiu cu prilejul aniversării a 100 ani de la naştere*, Bucharest, 1981.

FLEG, EDMOND, *Why I am a Jew* (tr. L.W. Wise), New York, 1929.

FLESCH, CARL, *The Art of Violin Playing* (transl. F. H. Martens), two vols., Vol. 1, Carl Fischer, New York, 1924, rev. edn. 1939; Vol. 2, Carl Fischer, New York, 1930.

——, *Memoirs* (tr. and ed. Hans Keller), Rockliff, London, 1957.

FOTINO, MARIA, 'The Mentor', *Romanian Review*, Vol. 35 (1981), No. 8, pp. 141–3.

GAVOTY, BERNARD, *Alfred Cortot*, Buchet/Chastel, Paris, 1977.

——, *Yehudi Menuhin – Georges Enesco*, Kister, Geneva, 1955.

——, and DANIEL-LESUR, *Pour ou contre la musique moderne?*, Flammarion, Paris, 1957.

GÉDALGE, ANDRÉ, *Traité de la fugue*, Part 1, Enoch, Paris, 1900.

GHYKA, MATILA, *The World Mine Oyster*, Heinemann, London, 1985.

GINISTY-BRISSON, A. M., 'Floraison musicale roumaine', *La Revue musicale*, special no., February–March 1940, pp. 154–60.

GITLIS, IVRY, *L'Âme et la Corde*, Éditions Robert Laffont, Paris, 1980.

GREGH, FERNAND, *L'Age d'or*, Paris, 1947.

GRINDEA, MIRON, 'Notes on a Genius', *Adam*, Year 43 (1981), Nos. 434–6, pp. 2–12.

——, see *Kensington Symposium*.

HAENDEL, IDA, *Woman with Violin, An Autobiography*, Gollancz, London, 1970.

HODOROABA, N., *George Enescu. Contribuţiuni la cunoaşterea vieţii sale*, Iaşi, 1928.

HOFFMANN, ALFRED, 'Lettres de Georges Enesco adressées à des musiciens français', in M. Voicana (ed.) *Enesciana*, Vol. 1, Editura Academiei Republicii Socialiste România, Bucharest, 1976, pp. 63–70.

HOLMES, JOHN, *Conductors on Record*, Gollancz, London, 1982.

Hommage à Proust, special number of *La Nouvelle Revue française*, Vol. 10, No. 112, 1 January 1923.

HYATT-KING, ALEC, *Mozart Wind and String Concertos*, BBC, London, 1978.

IAMPOLSKI, I., *George Enescu* (pamphlet tr. into Romanian from Russian), n.p. (Moscow?), 1947.

IENEI, AURORA, 'Nocturna în Re bemol major de George Enescu', in S. Rădulescu (ed.), *Centenarul George Enescu 1881–1981*, Editura Muzicală, Bucharest, 1981, pp. 247–61.

KENNEDY, MICHAEL, *Barbirolli, Conductor Laureate*, Macgibbon and Kee, London, 1971.

Kensington Symposium: recording of a symposium held at the Central Library, Kensington, 21 May 1982 (speakers: Alan Bush, Miron Grindea, John Amis, John Ogdon). National Sound Archive (British Institute of Recorded Sound), T 5107 BW.

KOECHLIN, CHARLES, 'Souvenirs de la classe Massenet (1894–5)', in: (i) *Le Ménestrel*, Vol. 97, No. 10, 8 March 1935, pp. 81–2; (ii) *ibid.*, Vol. 97, No. 11, 15 March 1935, pp. 89–90; (iii) *ibid.*, Vol. 97, No. 12, 22 March 1935, pp. 97–8.

KOLNEDER, WALTER, *Das Buch der Violine*, Atlantis, Zurich, 1972.

LA GRANGE, HENRY-LOUIS DE, *Mahler*, Vol. 1., Gollancz, London, 1974.

LAZAROVICI, B., 'Una din primele cronici aparute la noi despre George Enescu', *Studii muzicologice*, Vol. 3, (1957), No. 5, pp. 57–63.

LEMOIGNE-MUSSAT, MARIE-CLAIRE, 'Georges Enesco dans l'ouest de la France: l'accueil du public et de la critique à Rennes', in M. Roşu (ed.), *Simpozion George Enescu*, Bucharest, 1984, pp. 422–34.

LIPATTI, MADELEINE, (*et al.*), *In Memoriam Dinu Lipatti 1917–1950*, Geneva, 2nd edn., 1970.

LOCHNER, L. P., *Fritz Kreisler*, Rockliff, London, 1951.

LOCKSPEISER, EDWARD, *Debussy. His Life and Mind*, two vols., Cambridge University Press, Cambridge and London, rev. edn., 1978.

MAGHERU, ALICE, 'Being near the Maestro, *Romanian Review*, Vol. 35 (1981), No. 8, pp. 143–9.

MAGIDOFF, ROBERT, *Yehudi Menuhin*, Robert Hale, London, 1956

MAHLING, C. H., 'Bemerkungen zum Violinkonzert B-dur KV 271 i', *Mozart-Jahrbuch 1978/79*, Basel, 1979, pp. 252–68.

MANOLIU, GEORGE, 'Bach în concepţia interpretativă Enesciană', S. Rădulescu (ed.), *Centenarul George Enescu 1881–1981*, pp. 45–55.

——, 'Enescu's Violin-Playing', *Romanian Review*, Vol. 35, (1981), No. 8, pp. 71–81.

MARIE, QUEEN OF ROMANIA, *The Story of My Life*, three vols., London, 1934–5.

MASSOFF, IOAN, 'George Enescu vorbeşte 'Rampei' ', *Rampa*, Vol. 8, No. 2111, 7 November 1924.

——, 'George Enescu intim', *Rampa*, Vol. 14, No. 4131, 26 October 1931.

——, 'George Enescu – omul', *Adevěrul*, Vol. 50, No. 15995, 13 March 1936.

MENUHIN, DIANA, *Fiddler's Moll. Life with Yehudi*, Weidenfeld and Nicolson, London, 1984.

MENUHIN, MOSHE, *The Menuhin Saga*, Sidgwick and Jackson, London, 1984.

MENUHIN, YEHUDI, 'Georges Enesco', *The Score and I.M.A. Magazine*, No. 13, 1955, p. 39–42.

——, *Unfinished Journey*, Macdonald and Jane's, London, 1976.
——, 'My Great Master', *Adam*, Year 43 (1981), Nos. 434–6, pp. 19–22.
MILHAUD, DARIUS, *Études*, Aveline, Paris, 1927.
MOISESCU, TITUS, Lucrari inedite de George Enescu', *Muzica*, Vol. 25, No. 3, March 1975, pp. 11–15.
——, 'Cvartetul de coarde în creaţia lui George Enescu', in (i) *Muzica*, Vol. 25, No. 6, June 1975, pp. 5–11; (ii) *ibid.*, Vol. 25, No. 9, September 1975, pp. 7–14.
——, 'George Enescu's String Quartet in G Major Op. 22 No. 2' in M. Voicana (ed.), *Enesciana*, Vol. 2–3, Bucharest, 1981, pp. 133–60.
——, 'Manuscrisele lui George Enescu. Doua cvartete de coarde', editorial note in Enescu, *Cvartete de coarde, manuscriptum* (Op. 22, No. 2 and C major quartet), Editura Muzicală, Bucharest, 1985, pp. 109–13.
Monografie,: see VOICANA, M.,
MONSAINGEON, BRUNO, *Mademoiselle, Conversations with Nadia Boulanger* (tr. R. Marsack), Carcanet Press, London, 1985.
MOORE, GERALD, *Am I Too Loud? Memoirs of an Accompanist*, Hamish Hamilton, London, 1962.
MOUTON, JEAN, 'Enesco dans l'intimité', *Adam*, Year 43 (1981), Nos. 434–6, pp. 33–4.
NICULESCU, ŞTEFAN, 'Aspecte ale folclorului în opera lui George Enescu', *Studii şi cercetări de istoria artei*, Vol. 8, 1961, pp. 417–30.
——, *Reflecţii despre muzica*, Editura Muzicală, Bucharest, 1980.
O'CONNOR, G., *The Pursuit of Perfection. A Life of Maggie Teyte*, London, 1979.
OISTRAKH, DAVID, 'A Great Love of Art', *Romanian Review*, Vol. 35 1981, No. 8, pp. 123–4.
ONICESCU, OCTAV, 'A Founder of Romanian Culture', *Romanian Review*, Vol. 35 (1981), No. 8, pp. 149–51.
OPRESCU, GEORGE, and JORA, MIHAIL, (eds.), *George Enescu*, Bucharest, 1964.
PASCALL, R. J., 'Robert Fuchs', *The New Grove Dictionary of Music and Musicians*, 20 vols., Macmillan, London, 1980, Vol. 7, pp. 4–5.
PASCU, GEORGE, 'Enescu and Caudella', in M. Voicana, (ed.), *Enesciana*, Vol. 2–3, Bucharest, 1981, pp. 17–22.
PASS, W., 'Zemlinskys Wiener Presse bis zum Jahre 1911', in Otto Kolleritsch (ed.), *Alexander Zemlinsky. Tradition im Umkreis der Wiener Schule*, Institut für Wertungsforschung/Universal Edition, Graz, 1976, pp. 80–92.
PETROVICI, ALEXANDRU, 'Maestrul Enescu are aproape terminata opera Oedip', *Rampa*, Vol. 14, No. 3493, 14 September 1929.

PEYSER, HERBERT, 'Enesco, Composer and Violinist, Analyses Himself', *The Musical Standard*, illustrated series, Vol. 38, 28 September 1912, pp. 194–5.

PINCHERLE, MARC, *The World of the Virtuoso*, Gollancz, London, 1964.

PINTEAN, T., 'Enescu în apărarea demnității umane', *Magazin istoric*, Vol. 8, No. 3, March 1974, p. 43.

PINTÉR, LAJOS, *Mărturii despre George Enescu* (transl. Tereza and George Sbârcea), Editura Muzicală, Bucharest, 1980.

——, 'Enescu în presa budapestiana, in S. Radulescu (ed.), *Centenarul George Enescu 1881–1981*, Editura Muzicală, Bucharest, 1981, pp. 77–117.

PIROUÉ, GEORGES, *Proust et la musique du devenir*, Denoël, Paris, 1960.

PIRU, ELENA, 'A propos de quelques lettres de Georges Enesco', *Revue roumaine d'histoire de l'art*, Vol. 5, 1969, pp. 177–82.

PRICOPE, EUGEN, 'George Enescu – interpret al suitei Op. 9: "Preludiu la unison"', *Muzica*, Vol. 31, No. 7, July 1981, pp. 3–9.

——, 'George Enescu şef de orchestra', in S. Rădulescu (ed.), *Centenarul George Enescu 1881–1981*, Editura Muzicala, Bucharest, 1981; pp. 58–74.

——, 'Momente din arta dirijorală a lui George Enescu', in M. Roşu (ed.), *Simpozion George Enescu*, Bucharest, 1984, pp. 508–11.

PRUNIÈRES, HENRI, Review of *Oedipe* in *La Revue musicale*, Vol. 17, No. 164, March 1936, pp. 202–4.

RĂDULESCU, MIHAI, *Violinistica Enesciană*, Bucharest, 1971.

RANTA, ADRIAN, 'Sub vraja lui George Enescu', *Lupta*, Vol. 15, No. 4501, 18 October 1936, p. 5.

RAŢIU, ION, *Contemporary Romania*, Foreign Affairs Publishing Co., Richmond, 1975.

RĂSVAN, C., Interview with Alexandru Rădulescu in *Muzica*, Vol. 25, No. 6, June 1975, pp. 12–13.

RIEGLER-DINU, EMIL, 'George Enescu. În al cincizecilea an de viaţa', *Facla*, Vol. 10, No. 422, 7 September 1931, p. 2.

ROSTAND, CLAUDE, *Brahms*, two vols., Plon, Paris, 1954.

ROŞU, M., (ed.) *Simpozion George Enescu*, Bucharest, 1984.

SAMAZEUILH, GUSTAVE, 'Le Quatuor nouveau de Georges Enesco', *Le Revue musicale*, Vol. 25, No. 209, March 1949, p. 40.

SCHENK, ERICH, 'Zu Enescus Wiener Lehrjarhen', *Studii de muzicologie*, Vol. 4 (1968), pp. 61–66.

SCHMITT, FLORENT, Concert Review in *Le Temps*, Vol. 77, No. 27678, 19 June 1937.

SCHNABEL, ARTUR, *My Life and Music*, Longman, London, 1961.

SCHORSKE, CARL, *Fin-de-Siècle Vienna. Politics and Culture*, Weidenfeld and Nicolson, London, 1980.

SCHWARZ, BORIS, *Great Masters of the Violin*, Robert Hale, London, 1984.

Scrisori: see ENESCU

SIMPSON, ROBERT, 'He was Made of Music', *Adam*, Year 43 (1981), Nos. 434–6, pp. 34–6.

SOFRONIA, T., 'George Enescu a dieci anni dalla morte, la vita e l'opera il suo capolavoro: l' "Edipo"', off-print from *Iniziative*, Vol. 14 (1965), Nos. 3–4.

STAICOVICI, CONSTANŢA-IANCA, 'George Enesco, Professor at the Mannes School of Music, Liminary Notions', in M. Voicana (ed.), *Enesciana*, Vol. 2–3, Bucharest, 1981, pp. 211–21.

ŞTEFĂNESCU, IOANA, 'Brahms – Enescu', in S. Rădulescu (ed.), *Centenarul George Enescu 1881–1981*, Editura Muzicală, Bucharest, 1981, pp. 347–65.

STIHI-BOOS, CONSTANTIN, 'A Few Specifications about the One-Movement Poem, Taken both as a Genre and as a Form, with Reference to Alfonso Castaldi and George Enescu', in M. Voicana, (ed.), *Enesciana*, Vol. 2–3, Bucharest, 1981, pp. 173–7.

——, 'Some Analytical Specifications concerning the Symphonic Poem "Vox Maris" in G Major Op. 31 by George Enescu', in M. Voicana (ed.), *Enesciana*, Vol. 2–3, Bucharest, 1981, pp. 187–92.

SZIGETI, JOSEPH, *With Strings Attached. Reminiscences and Reflections*, Knopf, New York, 1947.

——, 'One of the Least "Promoted"', *Adam*, Year 43 (1981), Nos. 434–6, pp. 13–14.

ŢĂRANU, CORNEL, *Enescu în constiinţa prezentului*, Editura pentru literatură, Bucharest, 1969.

——, 'Enescu în lumina unor lucrări inedite' in M. Roşu (ed.), *Simpozion George Enescu*, Bucharest, 1984, pp. 231–4.

TIMARU, VALENTIN, 'Analiza Simfoniei de Camera a lui George Enescu', in S. Rădulescu (ed.), *Centenarul George Enescu 1881–1981*, Editura Muzicală, Bucharest, 1981, pp. 227–44.

TODUŢA, SIGMUND, 'Un aspect înnoitor al structurii vocale în tragedia lirică "Oedip"', in M. Roşu (ed.), *Simpozion George Enescu*, Bucharest, 1984, pp. 94–110.

TOMAZIU, GIGI, '"Mosh" Georges', *Adam*, Year 43 (1981), Nos. 434–6, pp. 28–30.

VANCEA, ZENO, *Creaţia muzicală romanească sec. XIX–XX*, Vol. 1, Bucharest, 1968.

——, 'George Enescu, muzician umanist', *Studii de muzicologie*, Vol. 4, 1968, pp. 23–8.

—— (ed.), *George Enescu. Omagiu cu prilejul aniversarii a 100 de ani de la naştere*, Meridiane, Bucharest, 1981.

VAN DIEREN, BERNARD, *Down among the Dead Men*, Oxford University Press, Oxford and London, 1935.

VLAD, ROMAN, 'Enescu şi Italia', in M. Roşu (ed.), *Simpozion George Enescu*, Bucharest, 1984, pp. 313–20.

VOICANA, MIRCEA, 'Un coleg vienez al lui Enescu – Zemlinsky', *Studii şi cercetari de istoria artei*, Vol. 15, 1968, pp. 214–20 (tr. in *Revue roumaine d'histoire de l'art*, Vol. 5, 1968, pp. 155–62).

——, (ed.), *George Enescu. Monografie*, two vols., Editura Academiei Republicii Socialiste România, Bucharest, 1971.

VOICULESCU, LUCIAN, *George Enescu şi opera sa Oedip*, Editura de stat pentru literatură şi arta, Bucharest, 1956.

VUILLERMOZ, ÉMILE, 'Oedipe a l'Opéra', *Candide*, 19 March 1936.

VYSLOUŽIL, J., 'L'Origine, l'apparition et la fonction du quart de ton dans l'œuvre de Georges Enesco', *Studii de muzicologie*, Vol. 4, 1968, pp. 253–9.

WARRACK, JOHN, 'The Bryanston Summer School of Music', *The Musical Times*, Vol. 91, 1950, pp. 377–81.

WATERHOUSE, JOHN and COSMA, VIOREL, 'Enescu', in Stanley Sadie (ed.), *The New Grove Dictionary of Music and Musicians*, 20 vols., Macmillan, London, 1980, Vol. 6, pp. 163–6.

WEBER, HORST, *Alexander Zemlinsky*, (Österreichischer Komponisten des XX. Jahrhunderts, Vol. 23), Verlag Elisabeth Lafite/ Österreichischer Bundesverlag, Vienna, 1977.

Index of Works

* indicates unfinished or fragmentary works

301

General Index